THE PSYCHOLOGY OF WANTS, INTERESTS AND ATTITUDES

THE CENTURY
PSYCHOLOGY SERIES

EDITED BY

RICHARD M. ELLIOTT, PH.D., *University of Minnesota*

---

*EXPERIMENTAL CHILD STUDY, by Florence L. Goodenough and John E. Anderson

*HUMAN LEARNING, by Edward L. Thorndike

*HISTORY OF EXPERIMENTAL PSYCHOLOGY, by Edwin G. Boring

*EFFECTIVE STUDY HABITS, by Charles Bird

*GREAT EXPERIMENTS IN PSYCHOLOGY, by Henry E. Garrett

*PHYSIQUE AND INTELLECT, by Donald G. Paterson

*PURPOSIVE BEHAVIOR IN ANIMALS AND MEN, by Edward C. Tolman

*ASSOCIATION THEORY TO-DAY, by Edward S. Robinson

*DIAGNOSING PERSONALITY AND CONDUCT, by P. M. Symonds

*THE WILD BOY OF AVEYRON, by Jean-Marc-Gaspard Itard, translated by George and Muriel Humphrey

*THE PHYSICAL DIMENSIONS OF CONSCIOUSNESS, by Edwin G. Boring

*SEVEN PSYCHOLOGIES, by Edna Heidbreder

*HYPNOSIS AND SUGGESTIBILITY, by Clark L. Hull

*DEVELOPMENTAL PSYCHOLOGY, by Florence L. Goodenough

*BEAUTY AND HUMAN NATURE, by Albert R. Chandler

*THE PSYCHOLOGY OF WANTS, INTERESTS, AND ATTITUDES, by Edward L. Thorndike

SOCIAL PSYCHOLOGY, by Charles Bird

HUMAN MOTIVES AND INCENTIVES, by H. A. Toops

CHILD PSYCHOLOGY, by John E. Anderson

THE PSYCHOLOGY OF EMOTIONS, by Florence L. Goodenough

ABNORMAL PSYCHOLOGY, by W. S. Taylor and Milton H. Erickson

A STUDY OF THE CONDITIONED RESPONSE, by Ernest R. Hilgard and Donald G. Marquis

THE PSYCHOLOGY OF THINKING, by Edna Heidbreder

OTHER VOLUMES TO BE ARRANGED

* Published

January, 1935.

The Century Psychology Series
Richard M. Elliott, Editor

THE PSYCHOLOGY OF WANTS, INTERESTS AND ATTITUDES

BY EDWARD L. THORNDIKE

and the

STAFF OF THE DIVISION OF PSYCHOLOGY OF THE
INSTITUTE OF EDUCATIONAL RESEARCH
TEACHERS COLLEGE, COLUMBIA UNIVERSITY

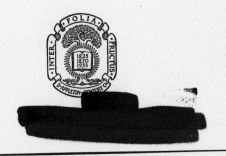

D. APPLETON–CENTURY COMPANY
INCORPORATED
NEW YORK   LONDON

*The work reported in this volume was made possible
by a grant from the Carnegie Corporation.*

PREFACE

(This book reports work done to discover how wants, interests, and attitudes influence learning, and how they themselves are learned.) It is limited to dynamic problems and adds nothing to previous descriptions of the appetitive and emotional life of man nor to observations of the maturation of such tendencies—their sequences and dates of appearance and course of strengthening by the forces of inner growth.

I have been responsible for planning the experiments in general, but the detailed arrangements for experiments 35 and 36 are entirely due to Dr. Woodyard; those for experiments 2, 3, 39, 40, 62, 64, and 72 to 75 are due to Dr. Lorge; and those for experiment 68, to Dr. Bregman. The execution of experiments 5 and 6 was in charge of Mr. Rock; that of experiments 62 and 63 was in charge of Miss Wilcox; that of experiment 68 was in charge of Dr. Bregman; the others were carried out by Dr. Woodyard, Dr. Lorge, and myself. Except as noted in the text, the organization and writing of the book have been my responsibility.

I take this occasion to acknowledge generous financial support from the Carnegie Corporation and courteous coöperation from the departments of education at the College of the City of New York, Hunter College, and Brooklyn College of the City of New York.

EDWARD L. THORNDIKE.

Teachers College, Columbia University
December, 1934

CONTENTS

Contents

Appendices

TABLES

THE
PSYCHOLOGY OF WANTS,
INTERESTS, AND ATTITUDES

Chapter 1

INTRODUCTION

COMMON sense separates wants, interests, attitudes, and emotions roughly from sensations, ~~percepts~~, images, and ideas, and ~~from movements or acts, and psychologists often find~~ it ~~convenient to do so~~. The term *drive* is often used by ~~them~~ to refer to wants, interests, attitudes, and emotions when these are considered as active forces. There are obvious differences between the facts stated in ~~A and those stated in~~ B or C.

"A. John wanted to go to sleep, but he wanted still more to hear the news. ~~So he attended to Mr. H. with interest.~~ He felt happy at some items, sad at others, surprised and bored occasionally." These facts report the occurrence of wants, interests, attitudes, and emotions.

"B. John hears a sound, sees a man, thinks of his father, remembers that he is 67 years old, thinks of old age, and judges that the variation among individuals in the loss of intellectual ability with old age must be very great." These facts report the occurrence of sensations, ~~percepts~~, images, and ideas.

"C. John shivers, lowers his hand, writes his name, and then rises abruptly and puts on his hat and coat." These facts report the occurrence of certain movements.

In present-day psychology, little effort is made to divide a man's mind up into intellectual, emotional, and volitional functions. There are all sorts of combinations. A want often has imbedded in it an idea of what is wanted. An attitude of attentiveness consists partly of certain acts (movements and restraints from movements). The feelings of excitement and depression which are observable as components of certain emotions may be sensations arising from internal stimuli, as hunger does. It is, however, convenient to distinguish a want from a movement or act, an attitude toward a thing from a percept or image of it, an emotional state of enjoyment from a mere sensation of red or sour. And it is reasonable to do so provided nothing unreal is assumed.

In this volume we distinguish wants, interests, attitudes, and emotions from other facts in mental life, not in order to define them rigidly or to infer anything from the contrast but simply because we are to study them rather than sensations, images, ideas, inferences and their like, as bodily movements. The facts to be reported in this volume will be just as true if all the wants, interests, attitudes, and emotions with which we experiment are alloyed by sensory or ideational elements.

Our study is of the dynamics of wants, interests, attitudes, and emotions. It is concerned with what they do and what is done to them, that is, with the changes which they produce and the changes which are produced in them. They obviously have great potency in directing the course of ideas and acts. Thought and action occur largely in the service of wants, interests, and attitudes and are stimulated and guided by them.

The chief business of Part I of our discussion is to study the ways in which their potency operates—the ways in which they do stimulate and guide thought and action. If a certain want (including its physiological basis) could be removed from an animal which had had it, what difference would be made in that animal's nature and behavior? If a certain want (including its physiological basis) could be inserted in an animal which had lacked it, what would be the result?

A want, attitude, or interest may conveniently be considered as quiescent, latent or potential, and as active or kinetic. So infants potentially want food, bodily exercise, and sensory experience even when they are asleep; but these cravings are active only under special conditions. Our concern is naturally with their active forms. The active want, interest, or attitude may be considered as a force by itself or as a fraction more or less of the total dynamic system of the person at the time. The former line of thought is commonly the more useful for science, though certain combinations and coöperations of these forces require study. In the ordinary flow of life, however, animals, especially civilized men, are often moved by a complex of active wants.

The influence of an acting want, interest, or attitude is twofold. It works forward to evoke, then and there, behavior which the animal would not have displayed except for the presence of the acting want. It also works backward, so to speak, to alter the nature of the animal so that the animal is, from then on, different from what he was before and will behave differently. It works forward by virtue of the special potencies or tendencies with which nature or nurture has endowed it to evoke this, that, or the other consequence. So active hunger makes an infant suck under certain conditions; active interest in exploration or food-getting makes the rat sniff at and enter an alley new to him. It works backward in little-known ways which we must investigate with care, but with the general result that the animal is changed so as to favor increasingly the connections which satisfied the want or interest. The child comes to suck the nipple, and with movements which secure food better. The rat exploring for food comes to enter the food-box or alleys that lead thereto rather than go past the food-box entrance or into blind alleys.

Wants, attitudes, and interests not only influence behavior and modify the behavior of organisms; they also are themselves changed. They are strengthened and weakened by the course of inner development and by the experiences of life. They may be shifted in respect of their attachments so that different situations call them forth.

The chief business of Part II of our discussion is to study the ways in which wants, interests, and attitudes are strengthened, weakened, and shifted in their attachments.

PART I

THE INFLUENCE OF WANTS, INTERESTS, AND ATTITUDES

Chapter 2

THE INFLUENCE OF WANTS, INTERESTS, AND ATTITUDES IN DETERMINING WHAT RESPONSE A SITUATION SHALL EVOKE

General Principles

WHAT response any stimulus or situation will evoke depends upon the general nature of the animal and its particular condition at the time. Its wants, interests, and attitudes are important features of its general nature and temporary status. Each of them has, by the original inherent constitution of the animal in question, by the circumstances of its training, or by both, an influence on the course of behavior. Situation A may evoke response 1 in men and response 2 in dogs partly because men and dogs have different wants. Situation B may evoke response 10 in John Smith and response 11 in Henry Jones partly because Smith and Jones have different wants. Situation C may evoke response 101 in Smith to-day and response 102 in Smith to-morrow for the same reason.

The force in all such cases is natural and biological, operating in and by the animal's connection system or neurones. There need be nothing logical or teleological about it; and never is anything mystical or capricious. An animal's wants and interests are features of his nature like his muscles, blood cells, or glands, and would illustrate the uniformity of nature as truly if we knew the truth about them.

The fact that an animal wants a certain result in itself gives no warrant for supposing that this want will evoke behavior producing this result, and certainly none for supposing that it will perform neurological miracles to evoke it. The provisions of nature for the preservation of individuals and species do not follow the one simple pattern that animals want what is good for them and that each want leads to an appropriate response to the situation in which the want is felt. Nature provides neurones of certain sorts arranged in certain ways, such as have been on the whole consistent with survival and in certain respects admirably adaptive. But the genes are far from omniscient, omnipotent, and infallible. A want or interest does not evoke the responses which either a benevolent deity of the species or the foresight of one of its more prudent members would choose in the premises. It evokes what the structure and functioning of the animal's neurones dictate.

The usages of language, dating from periods when man observed behavior crudely and animistically, often hinder effective thought concerning the nature of wants and their mode of action in the determination of responses. In particular they led to the use in science of such terms as *the instinct of self-preservation* and *the instinct of reproduction,* which implied that some forces acted to favor behavior which would keep the animal alive and produce its kind, and to such terms as *the constructive interest* or *the play interest,* which suggested that the animal possessing them favored activities in proportion to the amount of construction or playfulness which characterized them. Such terms may have been useful in default of better, but they seem to deny, and surely neglect, the important fact that an animal's equipment consists largely of a multitude of specific tendencies to do thus and so in response to real things and events and features thereof, not of logical adaptations in advance to eventual outcomes, or of general adjustments to abstract qualities. A description of the attitudes, interests, and wants active in getting food, eating, drinking, or sleeping which reported that the animal felt a desire to live and acted so as to gratify it would be useless and misleading. An explanation of a child's proclivities in handling objects by a law of gravitation toward the maximum of construction would mislead again and again. There are no such royal roads to an easy inventory of an animal's wants under a few logical, teleological, or verbal principles. Actual observation of what happens is required.

What happens in the neurones cannot in the present state of science be observed. The series of physiological events from the situation to the response is inaccessible. We can consequently do no better than such records as that "animal I when deprived of food for time X responds to situation A by responses 1, 2, 3, and 4," or that "animal II when deprived of sex indulgence for time Y responds to situation B by responses 5, 6, 7, and 8," or the like.

An objective and detailed record of just what A, B, 1, 2, 3, 4, 5, 6, 7, 8, etc., are is got only by much labor and skill. A superficial record of certain main features and consequences of wants is easy to make. Anybody, for example, can see and say that, in a male rat craving sex indulgence, the situation *a female in heat* will tend to evoke behavior resulting in copulation, but such studies as those of Calvin Stone involved hundreds of hours and many ingenious arrangements.

Convenience coöperated with the habit of considering wants teleologically to breed the crop of facts or pseudo-facts such as "the human infant is interested in moving objects," "sex craving produces courting behavior," "the sight of a desired object within reach produces the response of grasping it," "maternal affection makes a mother fondle her child," "a baby craves something to cling to," "an attitude of fear favors responses of withdrawal," "an attitude of curiosity facilitates approach movements," "the gregarious instinct makes man seek the presence of his fellowmen," "the sight of other members of his species engaged in a certain activity stimulates man to engage in it," "anger directed toward an object makes man attack that object." Statements such as these may be useful if used discreetly, so long as none more accurate and adequate are available. In so far as they are true, they inform us that a certain want or interest or attitude tends to evoke responses which in due time, directly or indirectly, attain a certain result. They are comparable to such statements as "nature abhors a vacuum," "the sun draws water from the ground," "cod-liver oil benefits children," "oxygen has an affinity for metals." They do not, as a rule, tell us the analytic facts which we need to know, namely, what differences wants make in the detailed responses evoked directly by situations. They do suggest three important facts about behavior.

I. The behavior is sometimes determined much more by the inner attitude or want than by any ordinary variations in the external situation. Cases could indeed be quoted where the efficacy of the latter approaches zero. So a fit of rage may vent itself almost equally on anything. So the sight of an object may be followed by various reaching movements until it is clasped.

II. The immediate effect is often to evoke a response which alters the situation or the animal or both in such ways as to increase the probability that sequent events will satisfy the want.

Restlessness and locomotion, for example, may be the first response to sex craving.

III. The immediate effect of an active want or interest or attitude plus a situation is often to evoke one response after another until the animal hits upon one that does satisfy it.

What positive knowledge is there concerning general characteristics of the "forward" action of wants, interests, and attitudes?

First, a want or interest may be extremely sensitive. For example, whether an animal will eat a bit of a given food in a given place depends not only on how hungry it is but also upon whether some other animal is taking bits of it. After it has ceased eating when alone, it will begin again if it sees another animal approach and eat. The baby in the experiment of Watson and Rayner who avoided the rat and wailed at the sight of it would not do so if it was sucking its thumb.

Second, there may be action of parts or features or distortions of wants, interests, and attitudes. There may be predominance now of one and now of another feature. So a pugnacious attitude may express itself in blows or screams or negativism.

Third, they often act together, with summations, alternations, inhibitions, and reinforcements. Curiosity and fear is the classic illustration. When wants coöperate or compete, what their combined action will be is not a problem in mathematics but in physiology. The solution is not necessarily given by adding and subtracting the influences which each would have alone but depends upon the facts of facilitation and inhibition in the neurones. It is conceivable that in some cases the combined similar influences of two might be no greater than the single influence of one. When two having opposite influences compete, the result will rarely be a steady maintaining of the balance of influence but more often an alternation from one to the other, and possibly a new condition including perplexity or irritation.

Fourth, the responses evoked by a want at first or early occurrences of a situation are often "imperfect," that is, much less well fitted to satisfy the animal than they could be or than they often become after many occurrences. The eventual behavior is due largely to the "backward" action of the want or interest or attitude, which strengthens the connections which satisfy the animal. If the want at the beginning evokes something which is thus perfectible, that something may itself be very far from perfect.

Fifth, the responses evoked are often multiple and varied. The same situation, according to changes in the animal (the change may be due to nothing more than the continuance of the want and the occurrences of the responses so far made with their results on the animal), evokes one after another of whatever responses are in the animal's repertory in connection with the want, the situation, and the aforesaid changes. The range of these is sometimes fairly wide.

The fact of multiple response or varied reaction in the case of wants which are themselves wide and varied (such as those which motivate many of the movements of early infancy) has led to the error of assuming that man at least had a tendency to make responses that were random, truly fortuitous, any one being as likely as any other to occur in response to any situation, and that he acquired many of his motor habits by selection from this chance assortment. This is highly improbable for general reasons; and the more competent and careful observers of infants are, the more inclined they are to disbelieve it. There doubtless is a residuum of behavior that may be called random in the sense that it is caused by neural changes unrelated to the animal's equipment of specific tendencies with predictable consequences. But any such residuum is in my opinion very small and productive of very little in learning. The great bulk of a child's motor behavior and learning is determined by definite abilities, wants, and interests and the circumstances of his life.

Sixth, the existence of an active want in a creature need not involve any consciousness of what it wants—any ideas or expectations that such and such will satisfy it. At their first occurrences all instinctive wants are typically barren of ideas, and in the lower animals many of them may remain so. Hens probably go to roost and tuck their heads under their wings with never a thought of wanting sleep. Even in man there are, if we may trust the psychiatrists, many cases of wants in the form of annoying lacks with no awareness by the person of what he lacks. Ideas or expectations about what one wants, what may happen, and whether it will be satisfying or annoying come to have enormous importance in the life of man, but they are secondary. All the essential activities of wants in working forward to cause behavior (and also backward to select certain features of behavior for survival) can operate without them.

Seventh, there are obvious differences in the strength or intensity of wants, but our measurements of these are as yet extremely crude. One want may be stated as stronger or more intense than another by observations of how they feel or by observations of how they make the person behave. The former sort of observation is specially useful for cravings (as for food, drink, rest, and sleep) which have sensory symptoms. It is ordinarily limited to comparisons of more or less of the same sort of want, though a person could perhaps reasonably report, "I want a drink now more than I want anything else," or "I want sleep more now than I wanted a drink yesterday noon" from observations of his feelings alone. The latter sort of observation of behavior has, of course, far wider scope and is what is commonly relied on in scientific studies of wants and practical utilization and management of them.

The latter sort of comparison or measurement of the strength or intensity or degree or magnitude of a want may be in terms of relative position only or in relative position plus some crude or vague specification in units of some scale. Common illustrations of the first are a person's answers to the questions "Which would you rather do?" "Which would you rather have?" His answers may, of course, be in actions rather than words, words being trustworthy measures in so far as they predict and parallel acts.

Common illustrations of the second are such answers as "I would much rather do this" or "I would cut off my right hand to avoid that." The only common illustrations of the third are in terms of units on the scale of money.* But the methods used by Moss ['24], Warden ['31], and others to compare the magnitudes of animal wants could be adapted to give measures such as: "Animal A will endure one shock to gratify want alpha, two

* The measurement of wants by the scale of money or value in exchange would, of course, not be measurement by ordinary market prices. These are related to wants only remotely and to any single individual's wants only with a wide margin of variation. The fact that a person will use one dollar of his purchasing power to gratify want A, two dollars of it to gratify want B, three dollars of it to gratify want C, etc., is significant in measuring the person's wants only in a very artificial market in which the person bidding expresses honestly how much general purchasing power he would give up to gratify A, B, and C respectively.

similar shocks to gratify want beta, three similar shocks to gratify want gamma," etc.

Up to the present, no human wants have been conveniently and precisely measured. Some are perhaps incommensurable, and some come into competition one with another so seldom (for example, the craving of the infant for a romp and of the octogenarian for a nap) that it is an academic question whether or not they are commensurable. Scientific work at the measurement of wants has just barely begun in the experiments of Moss, Warden, and others, mentioned above. Until it has progressed further, the treatment of the magnitude of any want or satisfaction has to be extremely crude.

Eighth, the individual differences within the human species in the strength of various wants are very great. The differences in original, unlearned wants are probably of the order of magnitude of the differences in original capacities of intellect or skill. The differences in acquired wants are probably even greater than the differences in acquired abilities. The variations in craving to solve arithmetical problems are, for example, probably wider than variations in ability to solve them.

Particular Facts

It would be useful to present an inventory of the wants, interests, and attitudes which belong to the human species as products of its genes and of the "forward" influence of each of them, of each feature of them that may operate separately, and of each group of them (or of features of them) which may operate together. Even so inaccurate and inadequate an inventory as could be drawn up in the present state of knowledge would be valuable. From these original propensities all wants that any individual ever acquires somehow develop. In spite of the selections, repressions, and transmutations caused by modern physical and social environments, they may persist and crop out with important consequences. Especially when the task is to deny or reverse them, we need knowledge of what they are. Experts in sociology, economics, and government are constantly making assumptions, often tacit, about what they are. We hope to make such an inventory later and elsewhere. For the present, we shall note only one fact about such an inventory of original, unlearned wants, interests, and motives and their "forward" influence upon responses to various situations. It would differ enormously from inventories of similar facts for living adults in the present world. For example, the responses which their wants evoke to heat, cold, darkness, pains of various sorts, plants, clothes, furniture, money, words, numbers, tools, machines, laws, religions, and customs would differ enormously from man's unlearned responses to these —more, probably much more, than the latter differ from those of a dog or cat. The seed of appetitive behavior is the action of original wants working "forward" to influence the responses to situations, but the nature of the tree which grows from this seed is determined largely by other forces.

The forward influence of wants (and this is true of abilities as well) can explain only a small fraction of the life of civilized man. What happens the first time a situation plus a certain want occurs usually bears little resemblance to what happens at its tenth or hundredth occurrence. What our wants lead us to do and be in the long run is not what they lead us to do at the start. The differences are due, first, to the "backward" influence of wants, second, to changes in the wants themselves.

Chapter 3

THE INFLUENCE OF WANTS, INTERESTS, AND ATTITUDES IN DETERMINING WHICH RESPONSES TO A SITUATION SHALL BE SELECTED FOR SURVIVAL

AMONG the varied reactions or multiple responses which follow and are connected with a situation there is usually selection for survival. Some become more likely to appear than they were at the first occurrence. By and large these are such as satisfy the wants prevailing at the time. Wants work "backward" to alter the person's neurones or connection system for the future as well as forward to determine his response at the time.

Selective modifiability by after-effects of connections reigns where modifiability of behavior occurs at all. The mere repetition of situations does little or nothing. The repetition of a connection may strengthen it relatively to other connections leading from the same situation but has its main efficacy by permitting the after-effects of the connection to operate.

We have investigated the action of after-effects in relation to wants, etc., as fully as our abilities and facilities have permitted and shall report the results in chapters 3 to 10.

We ask the reader to adopt for the purposes of the inquiry the vocabulary of what may be called a situation-response or connectionist psychology, in which the word *situation* or the symbol S is used to mean any state of affairs outside or inside an organism; the word *response* or the symbol R is used to mean any state of affairs in some organism which is, or seems to be, related to some S by sequence at least and perhaps in more dynamic ways; and the word *connection* or the symbol → is used to mean the fact that S is followed by R or the probability that S will be followed by R, other things being equal. A situation may be as minute and definite as a pin-prick on a certain spot, or as large and vague as a thunderstorm. It may be short, e.g., a flash of light, or long, e.g., a sermon. It may literally be, as stated, any state of affairs in nature. A response may be any real event in an organism—a movement, an idea, a mood, a liking, a craving, or any part or feature of any such real event. It may be as little and short and unitary as the knee-jerk or as big and long and elaborate as writing an encyclopedia. A connection may be as direct as that between the tap on the knee and the jerk of the muscle, or as mediated as that between the receipt of a bill and the writing of a check. It may be as single as that between thinking *a, b, c, d* and thinking *e* or as multiple as that between the impression of tennis-court, opponent, and balls and the position, timing, force, and direction of one's return stroke. *Situation, response,* and *connection* are terms used here to help describe and prophesy what an animal does, not to make any assumptions concerning how or why the animal does it. I use them rather than *state of affairs* or *event* or *related state of affairs* or *related event and probability that, other things being equal, the related event will follow the event* partly for brevity and partly because they are terms favored by scientific workers.

I use S → R instead of *process* or *tendency* to represent a segment of an animal's life. The former is much more convenient for expressing changes in segments beginning with the same external state of affairs. The separation of the rest of the tendency or process into what the organism will probably do and how great the probability is that it will do it is advantageous because it fits the variability of living (and especially of mental) processes. It also encourages the use of quantitative methods. Anybody may restate the facts in any terms that he prefers if these do not involve unjustified assumptions.

It will be helpful for the reader to have in mind the facts we reported in *The Fundamentals of Learning* concerning the repetition of a situation, the repetition of a connection, the difference between two events which "belong" one with the other and two which are merely in temporal sequence in the same organism, identifiability, availability, mental set, and the strengthening of a connection by a satisfying state of affairs which "belongs" to it as its after-effect.

From now on I shall occasionally use the single word *wants* to include interests, attitudes, and any other propensities which can play a part in determining whether a state of affairs is acceptable or intolerable, satisfying or annoying, sought or avoided, welcomed or rejected, liked or disliked, desired or eschewed.

The want most used in our experiments with the lower animals has been the want for food. Those most used in our experiments with man have been the want for money and what it can purchase, the want for self-respect, the desire for the esteem of the experimenter, and the general desire to succeed rather than fail. There is no reason to suppose that the results (all of which concern very general facts and principles) would be any different if more violent wants such as those related to sex, fear, or conquest had been used, or if very mild and tame wants had been used.

There are, of course, two main sorts of possible influence to be studied. The first is the case of an after-effect which satisfies some want. It may cause the animal to repeat then and there the connection to which it is attached. If the situation vanishes or changes so that this is not possible, the satisfying after-effect may cause the animal to be more likely to repeat that connection when the situation plus the want recur. It may cause the animal to do both. It may cause other events, as we shall see. The second is the case of an after-effect which is positively annoying or which leaves the want unsatisfied. Such an after-effect might be expected to make the animal less likely to repeat the connection to which it is attached then and there, either by directly weakening it or by strengthening other connections than it. We shall present strong evidence that a direct weakening does not occur or occurs only in very special cases. It might be expected also to make the animal (supposing the situation to vanish or change so that this is impossible) less likely to repeat the connection (or more likely to repeat other connections than it) if the situation recurs. We shall present evidence that the status here is very different from the opposite of that in the case of a satisfying after-effect.

Since we find the psychology and physiology of after-effects that satisfy wants to be very different from that of after-effects which fail to satisfy them, which thwart them, or which produce new annoyances, we shall keep the two lines of study separate in the main. Since our studies of the former are much more extensive and penetrating than our studies of the latter, much more space will be devoted to the former.

We have facts concerning the influence of the magnitude or intensity of the satisfaction, its relevance to the active want, its intimacy of belonging with the connection which it follows, the spread or scatter of its influence to other connections in close proximity to it, its mode of operation, its operation to strengthen tendencies of whose very existence the person is unaware (unconscious learning), and its possible physiological explanation. In many cases we are specially concerned to keep separate the influence which an after-effect has by causing the person to repeat the connection or some inner equivalent of it from the direct influence which it has apart from any such repetition.

We have also facts concerning the influence of irrelevant discomfort, the influence of frequency of satisfaction in the case of a long series of tasks, the influence of opposed wants, and what may seem superficially to be learning in opposition to wants.

Let us consider first the ordinary sort of satisfying after-effect working upon the ordinary sort of mental connection, as when a pupil gives answers which his teacher calls right or makes shots which hit the target or makes movements that let him escape from pain or confinement. In such cases the situation connects with a response which is followed by a state of affairs which (1) belongs to that $S \rightarrow R$ process as its after-effect and (2) is relevant to the set of mind or purpose or drive which possesses the animal. The satisfying after-effect or reward (call it E)—the teacher's "Right" or the shot in the bull's-eye or the freedom—belongs to the $S \rightarrow R$ in question in the sense that the neural equivalent of $S \rightarrow R$ leads to the neural equivalent of E in a more direct and intimate way than it leads to some other contemporaneous events and in the sense that if the person is aware of that $S \rightarrow R$ and E at all, he regards that E as an outcome of the $S \rightarrow R$ more than he so regards some other events contemporaneous with E. The E is relevant to the person's mental set or purpose in the sense that it is satisfying to *it*, that it is successful from that point of view, that it fits into the general course of activity and expectation without notable shock or discord. An irrelevant but belonging after-effect would be such as the teacher's giving the boy, without warning, a dollar at the correct answer. An irrelevant, and also probably a non-belonging, after-effect would be the sudden appearance of the marksman's best and long-absent friend beside him just after he made his shot. The influence of various degrees of belonging and relevance will be studied in due time, but for the present we consider the influence of a satisfying after-effect that does belong to the S → R which it follows or accompanies and is relevant to the purpose and activity then prevailing in the person.

In *The Fundamentals of Learning* evidence was presented to show that such a satisfier could strengthen the connection whose after-effect it was. Much more evidence to the same effect has accumulated since that volume was published, and an independent proof has been derived from evidence of a different sort. Some of this later evidence has been reported in *An Experimental Study of Rewards* [Thorndike, '33], and in various papers by Lorge and Thorndike. Some of it will be reviewed briefly later in this chapter. Some of it will be reported in later chapters, since investigations of the influence of belongingness, relevance, the amount or intensity of the rewards, delayed rewards, and other facts about after-effects incidentally provide evidence that a belonging and relevant satisfying after-effect does strengthen the connection which it follows and to which it belongs.

Accepting then the fact that such a satisfying after-effect does work back upon the connection to which it is attached, we now inquire concerning what it does and how it does it. In order to furnish the general abstract account with illustrative material, a typical experiment (Experiment 1) is reported.

Experiment 1

The experimenter instructs the subject as follows:

"I shall say a word; you will say any number from 1 to 6 as soon as you hear the word. You will also say any letter. Then I will say another word and you will say 1, or 2, or 3, or 4, or 5, or 6 as before and any letter, but you must not use the same letter twice in succession and you must not use any device or sequence of letters like *a* for the first word, *b* for the second word, *c* for the third word, *d* for the fourth word, etc. You can always choose any number from 1 to 6 as you please, but the letters that you choose must not be chosen by any system. After you have said a number and letter, I shall say 'Right' or 'Wrong.' This announcement of 'Right' or 'Wrong' refers to the numbers only. You will not have to be told whether any letter is right or wrong because, as a matter of fact, none of the letters is right and none of them is wrong. They are not to be learned as the numbers are, but are for an entirely different purpose. You understand that the best that you can possibly expect to do in the first trial is to get one right out of every six. Moreover, going as fast as we do with rather difficult material to remember, you must not expect to get anywhere near perfection in the small number of trials that we make. The money payment made to you as a bonus after each division of the experiment will show you how rapidly you are learning. We shall also tell you the total number of rights made by you in each division of the experiment. The number you would get by chance is thirty-three. Consequently anything over that means learning.

"We will do a practice series to make sure that you have the procedure in mind and to show you about the rate at which the words and numbers will be said."

The subjects were twenty-four adult students, to whom the money was an important matter. The materials used were twenty-four sets, each consisting of forty words, for each of which some number from 1 to 6 was called "Right," the other five numbers being called "Wrong" as responses to that word. A subject was put through a series of forty five times without stop. He then had a rest of about two minutes during which he was told his score and given his money bonus. This was repeated set after set for an hour. On later days, usually in three more sessions, the rest of the twenty-four sets were used in the same way.

The experimenter said a word, recorded the number and letter said by the subject, and announced "Right" or "Wrong," the total time for such a unit averaging from 3.1 to 4.0 sec. according to the quickness of response of the subject.

The word-letter connections do not now concern us. Those word-number connections which are rewarded are strengthened in the case of every subject. The facts for one rewarded first occurrence of a connection in comparison with one punished (by the announcement of "Wrong" and no money reward) first occurrence appear in Table 1. For all subjects together the percentage of repetitions in the following trial is 43.6 for connections which were rewarded. A single rewarded occurrence thus raises the probability of reoccurrence far above chance. The percentage of repetition in the following trial for connections which were punished at their first occurrence is 22.5. The facts for rewarded connections occurring twice consecutively (i.e., in Trial 1 and Trial 2 or in Trial 2 and Trial 3) and for punished connections occurring twice consecutively appear in Table 2. For all subjects together the percentage of repetitions in the following trial is 81.1 for these twice-rewarded and 33.4 for these twice-punished connections. The facts for non-consecutive doubles also appear in Table 2. The percentages of repetition in the following trial is 74.1 for these twice-rewarded, and 29.0 for these twice-punished connections.

TABLE 1

The frequency with which a connection, which at its first occurrence was rewarded, was repeated (S) or replaced by a different connection (D) in the next trial; and the same facts for a connection which, at its first occurrence, was punished (Experiment 1, word → number connections, trials 1 to 4)

SUBJECT	REWARDED CONNECTIONS			PUNISHED CONNECTIONS		
	S	D	$\frac{100\,S}{S+D}$	S	D	$\frac{100\,S}{S+D}$
1	138	205	39.1	547	1222	30.9
2	133	273	32.8	393	1504	20.7
3	145	242	37.5	374	1525	19.7
4	170	230	42.5	349	1526	18.6
5	111	261	29.8	381	1571	19.5
6	228	164	58.2	371	1454	20.3
7	164	210	43.9	437	1383	24.0
8	188	200	48.5	409	1371	23.0
9	195	217	47.3	418	1331	23.9
10	155	237	39.5	462	1342	25.6
11	182	212	46.2	359	1496	19.4
12	191	190	50.1	430	1338	24.3
13	257	159	61.8	384	1367	21.9
14	175	207	45.8	385	1493	20.5
15	105	300	25.9	435	1456	23.0
16	141	244	36.6	413	1469	21.9
17	244	148	62.2	340	1540	18.1
18	130	262	33.2	409	1413	22.4
19	123	274	31.0	411	1465	21.9
20	161	189	46.0	510	1192	30.0
21	166	235	41.4	418	1391	23.1
22	217	141	60.6	427	1341	24.2
23	113	244	31.7	457	1346	25.3
24	197	178	52.5	349	1511	18.8
All	4029	5222	43.6	9868	34047	22.5

The percentage of repetition which mere chance would give is of course 16.7. If we could be sure that each person was, except for the occurrences of the experiment and their after-effects, equally likely to choose 1, 2, 3, 4, 5, or 6, we could simply subtract

TABLE 2

The frequency with which a connection, which at both its first and second occurrences was rewarded, was repeated (S) or replaced by a different connection (D) in the next trial; and the same facts for a connection which was punished at its first two occurrences (Experiment I, word → number connections, trials I to 4)

| | OCCURRENCES IN TRIALS I AND 2 OR 2 AND 3 | | | | | | OCCURRENCES IN TRIALS I AND 3 | | | | | |
| | Rewarded Connections | | | Punished Connections | | | Rewarded Connections | | | Punished Connections | | |
SUBJECT	S	D	$\frac{100\,S}{S+D}$	S	D	$\frac{100\,S}{S+D}$	S	D	$\frac{100\,S}{S+D}$	S	D	$\frac{100\,S}{S+D}$
1	16	14	53.3	46	54	46.0	7	3	70.0	11	21	34.4
2	37	19	66.1	29	67	30.2	5	4	55.6	7	24	22.6
3	53	22	70.7	35	90	28.0	6	3	66.7	5	28	15.2
4	39	7	84.8	14	45	23.8	9	2	81.8	2	11	15.4
5	24	11	68.6	35	71	33.0	2	3	40.0	6	15	28.6
6	25	4	86.3	7	27	20.6	5	2	71.4	2	8	20.0
7	85	15	85.0	61	101	37.6	4	2	66.7	15	33	31.2
8	85	17	83.3	52	110	32.1	8	1	88.9	9	32	22.0
9	44	4	91.7	23	59	28.1	11	2	84.6	6	17	26.1
10	23	7	76.7	50	80	38.4	7	1	87.5	16	17	48.5
11	28	8	77.8	21	51	29.2	9	2	81.8	4	16	40.0
12	80	17	82.5	67	117	36.4	15	4	78.9	21	37	36.2
13	65	5	92.9	29	56	34.1	7	0	100.0	8	16	33.3
14	43	3	93.5	34	53	39.1	5	2	71.4	1	15	6.3
15	22	14	61.2	30	80	27.3	3	3	50.0	5	26	16.1
16	31	5	86.2	34	79	30.1	5	6	45.5	8	19	29.6

17	41.7	7	5	90.0	1	9	28.2	46	18	95.8	3	68
18	30.0	21	9	70.6	5	12	37.0	51	30	79.2	5	19
19	25.0	18	6	37.5	5	3	18.1	50	11	70.4	8	19
20	29.2	17	7	87.5	1	7	42.0	69	50	87.4	6	42
21	14.3	12	2	72.7	3	8	35.4	42	23	89.3	3	25
22	50.0	16	16	90.0	1	9	32.4	48	23	70.9	14	34
23	38.9	11	7	60.0	2	3	36.4	68	39	71.5	10	25
24	30.0	14	6	100.0	0	7	32.0	34	16	90.4	3	28
All	29.0	451	184	74.1	58	166	33.4	1548	777	81.1	224	460

16.7 and obtain the following as the influences of the various histories:

One rewarded first occurrence, a strengthening of...... 26.9
One punished first occurrence, a strengthening of...... 5.8
Two consecutive occurrences (rewarded), a strengthening of 64.4
Two consecutive occurrences (punished), a strengthening of 16.7
Two non-consecutive occurrences (rewarded), a strengthening of 57.4
Two non-consecutive occurrences (punished), a strengthening of 12.3

We cannot be sure, however, that each person at each stage of the experiment would have been, apart from the occurrences and the rewards or punishments, equally likely to choose 1, 2, 3, 4, 5, or 6. Some may have had favoritisms for certain numbers. Favoritism for certain numbers in consecutive trials would raise the probability above 0.167. A favoritism for certain numbers in one trial changing to a favoritism for different numbers in the next trial would lower the probability below 0.167.* So we investigate the frequency of choice of each number by each person at each stage of the learning. The results appear in Appendix I. The percentage of repetitions that would result from the influence of chance and number-favoritism is 18.8. The excess over this for a first occurrence that was rewarded is about 24 percent (median, 23.0; average, 24.8). For a first occurrence that was punished, the excess is about 4 percent (median, 3.3; average 3.8). Even a punished occurrence thus adds some strength to the connection, but a rewarded occurrence adds over six times as much. These facts and those for two occurrences of the same connection appear in Table 3. These results are typical of what we find in all such multiple-choice learning when the situations change rapidly and only one choice is allowed at each occurrence of a situation. A punished connection gains more strength by occurring than it

---

* The probability of a repetition of the same number for the same word in two successive trials is $a_1a_2 + b_1b_2 + c_1c_2 + d_1d_2 + e_1e_2 + f_1f_2$, in which a_1, b_1, c_1, d_1, e_1, and f_1 are the probabilities of occurrence of 1, 2, 3, 4, 5, and 6 respectively as responses in any trial, and a_2, b_2, c_2, d_2, e_2, and f_2 are the probabilities of occurrence of 1, 2, 3, 4, 5, and 6 respectively as responses in the following trial. If the probabilities are the same in the two trials, it is $a^2 + b^2 + c^2 + d^2 + e^2 + f^2$. If a, b, c, d, e, and f are taken as frequencies instead of probabilities, we have, of course, $(a^2 + b^2 + c^2 + d^2 + e^2 + f^2)/n^2$.

loses by being punished. A rewarded connection gains very much more.

TABLE 3

The strengthening due to one or two rewarded or punished occurrences of a connection in Experiment 1; excesses over the expectation from chance plus number-favoritism

Occurrences	Median	Average
One first occurrence, rewarded	23.0	24.8
One first occurrence, punished	3.3	3.8
Two consecutive occurrences, rewarded	62.5	61.0
Two consecutive occurrences, punished	14.2	13.5
Two non-consecutive occurrences, rewarded	56.2	54.1
Two non-consecutive occurrences, punished	10.3	9.8

The strengthening is not the same for all the punished occurrences but varies in accordance with their proximity to a rewarded connection. This is the phenomenon of the "spread" or "scatter" of the influence of a reward, reported briefly in *Science* (Feb. 10, 1933, vol. 77, p. 173 f.) and in detail in *An Experimental Study of Rewards*.

In Experiment 1 the strengthenings for punished connections (first occurrences) (1) between two rewarded connections, (2) next to a rewarded connection but not between two, (3) two steps removed from each of two rewarded connections, (4) two steps removed from one rewarded connection and more than two steps removed from any other, and so on through greater and greater remoteness to connections five or more steps away from any rewarded connection are as shown in Table 4. The strengthening from one occurrence of a punished connection is about seventy-seven permilles (median 72; average 82) when it occurs between two rewarded connections and about twenty permilles (median 16; average 23) when it is five or more steps away from any rewarded connection. One occurrence plus a reward in this experiment had thus about twelve times as much strengthening influence as one occurrence plus a punishment, if the latter was five or more steps away from any reward. A punished connection occurring between two rewarded connections was strengthened about four times as much as a punished connection remote from any reward. The reward or satisfying after-effect in such experiments could conceivably produce this strengthening in two ways.

TABLE 4

The excesses of repetition in the next round or trial over the amount of repetition expected from chance plus number-favoritism; first occurrences only

	Median	Average
REWARDED CONNECTIONS	230	247
PUNISHED CONNECTIONS:		
Next to a rewarded connection:		
Between two rewarded connections	72	82
Before a rewarded connection	39	36
After a rewarded connection	51	62
Two steps removed from a rewarded connection:		
Between two	72	73
Before	27	22
After	36	42
Three steps removed from a rewarded connection:		
Between two	19	40
Before	25	33
After	10	20
Four steps removed from a rewarded connection:		
Between two	−18	5
Before	34	45
After	26	35
Five or more steps removed from a rewarded connection	16	23

It could act directly upon the neural fact (whatever it is) which corresponds to the connection (that is, the probability that S will evoke R), producing some change in it which heightens that probability; or it could act upon it indirectly by establishing the connection "The number . . . is right for the word . . . ," or more probably "word—number—Right." We may call the former the direct confirming influence of a reward or the pressure exerted by a reward and the latter the indirect validating influence of a reward or the information given by a reward.

In the case of the latter, the increased probability that S will evoke R comes about as follows: When the word recurs in the next trial of the series, and the subject considers what number he shall say for that word, the thought of the number which was rewarded will be more likely to make him think of "Right" and less likely to make him think of "Wrong" than the thought of one of the other numbers; and the thought of "Right" along with the thought of that number for that word will more or less validate that choice, and incline him toward it. In the case of the former, the learner simply is more impelled to choose the right number, without having any memory of its having been right or any idea of right associated with it as a precursor of his impulsion. He may think that it is right as a consequence of his impulsion to say it. Or he may think nothing about it.

The direct confirming influence exerted by a satisfying after-effect is responsible for all save a small fraction of the strengthening by rewards in the experimental results which will be reported in this book. We have tried to keep the informative influence at or near zero.

This has been accomplished by using the influence of only the first occurrences, or only the first two occurrences, of a rewarded connection and by requiring very prompt choice of the responses. The evidence that it has been substantially accomplished is, first, that the subjects are very rarely aware of any such precursory and guiding images or ideas of "Right" associated with the responses they give. They rarely take time to consider the possible merits of two or more responses on any basis. Second, in experiments which are prolonged for enough trials to give quadruple or quintuple consecutive rewarded occurrences, the subject as a rule establishes the connection at a strength of 1.00 before he has confidence in its correctness. Third, the strengthening by reward occurs when the subject does not even know what the tendency is which is being rewarded.* Fourth, the informative influence of a punishment by the announcement of "Wrong" should cause the guiding association "word—number—Wrong" somewhat nearly or quite as often and emphatically as the reward causes the parallel one. If a reward informatively made the subject repeat response X, that called up the idea of "Right" when it came to mind, a punishment should informatively make the subject avoid repeating response Y, that called up the idea of "Wrong" when it came to mind. In our experiments, the informative influence of the punishments is not sufficient to reduce the repetition of punished connections below what they would be by chance and response favoritism alone.

Fifth, the informative influence of a reward would not be expected to spread or scatter to strengthen neighboring wrong

* See Chapter V and Thorndike and Rock ['34], *Journal of Experimental Psychology*, vol. 17, pp. 1-19.

connections. For a direct neural influence strengthening whatever connection it impinges upon, an occasional missing the connection which immediately precedes it, and hitting some connection that is, so to speak, in the vicinity, is not only possible but to be expected with some frequency in experiments such as ours. But a secondary image or idea of "Right" derived from the informative influence of a reward would have not only to get loose from the "word—number—Right" sequence to which it was attached, but also to knock out the third member of some "word—number— Wrong" sequence and take its place. This is possible, but would surely be an extremely rare event in such experiments.

It is then certain that in these experiments the strengthening influence of the reward upon the rewarded connection and neighboring connections is chiefly and probably almost exclusively a direct confirming of it and upon them at or near the time when the reward occurs, not an indirect influence from information acquired at the time of the reward but used minutes or hours later to validate a choice among responses when the situation recurs. Unless otherwise specified, the influence of a satisfying after-effect will mean in our discussion its direct and immediate confirming or strengthening influence, not its indirect action by the association of ideas at the recurrence of the situation.

The remainder of this chapter will present some of the facts which have been so far discovered concerning its action. The reader should bear in mind that we are still considering the ordinary relevant satisfying after-effects working upon ordinary sorts of mental connections to which they "belong." The order of topics will be: The "spread" or "scatter" phenomenon; the amount of strengthening of the rewarded connection and of neighboring connections; the combination of influences from two or more satisfiers; the spread to connections intimately associated with the rewarded connection, but irrelevant to the learner's purposes; the restriction of a satisfier's influence by time.

The Spread or Scatter of the Influence of a Reward

A relevant satisfying after-effect strengthens very greatly the connection which it immediately follows and to which it belongs, but it also strengthens to a much less extent punished connections which are in close enough proximity to it. This is demonstrated by

Table 5

The influence of proximity to a reward upon connections which themselves were punished. The frequency with which a punished connection which at its first occurrence was distant from a rewarded connection as stated was repeated (S) or replaced by a different connection (D) in the next trial

EXPERIMENT	ONE STEP REMOVED			MORE REMOTE THAN ONE STEP			DIFFERENCE IN STRENGTHENING
	S	D	$\frac{100\,S}{S+D}$	S	D	$\frac{100\,S}{S+D}$	
A	783	1628	32.5	623	1790	25.8	6.7
B	462	1401	24.8	540	1720	23.9	0.9
C	342	940	26.7	444	1377	24.4	2.3
D	366	1114	24.7	550	1617	25.4	—0.7
E	91	220	29.3	64	245	20.7	8.6
F	550	2503	18.0	589	3111	15.9	2.1
G	90	375	19.3	150	521	17.7	1.6
Ha+Hl	1092	3044	26.4	1186	4225	21.9	4.5
Hb	179	845	17.4	266	1331	16.7	0.7
Hc	215	932	18.7	252	1304	16.2	2.5
I	1700	6374	21.1	2785	11807	19.1	2.0
J	559	1526	26.8	1962	6547	23.1	3.7
K	509	1754	22.5	774	2792	21.7	0.8
L	163	646	20.1	578	2439	19.2	0.9
M	312	776	28.7	477	1511	24.0	4.7

EXPERIMENT	ONE OR TWO STEPS REMOVED			THREE OR MORE STEPS REMOVED			DIFFERENCE IN STRENGTHENING
	S	D	$\frac{100\,S}{S+D}$	S	D	$\frac{100\,S}{S+D}$	
A	1131	2527	30.9	275	891	23.6	7.3
B	674	2092	24.4	328	1029	24.2	0.2
C	528	1460	26.6	258	857	23.1	3.5
D	583	1721	25.3	333	1010	24.8	0.5
E	133	323	29.2	22	142	13.4	15.8
F	822	3822	17.7	317	1792	15.0	2.7
G	144	609	19.1	56	287	16.3	2.8
Ha+Hl	1623	4763	25.4	655	2506	20.7	4.7
Hb	293	1303	18.4	152	873	14.8	3.6
Hc	314	1409	18.2	153	827	15.6	2.6
I	2678	10121	20.9	1777	8060	18.1	2.8
J	945	2773	25.4	1573	5300	22.9	2.5
K	825	2867	22.3	458	1679	21.4	0.9
L	283	1182	19.3	458	1903	19.4	—0.1
M	489	1273	27.7	300	1014	22.8	4.9

the facts of Table 5.§ In fifteen experiments with different sorts of learning, punished connections otherwise alike differed in the amount of strength they gain from occurring. Those which came just before or just after a rewarded connection were strengthened more than those farther removed from a rewarded connection. Those which came within one or two steps of a rewarded connection were strengthened more than those three or more steps removed from a rewarded connection.

The Amount of Strengthening of the Rewarded Connection and of Neighboring Connections

Using as a base the percentage of repetitions in the following trial for a punished connection five or more steps removed from

TABLE 6

The frequency of repetition in the following trial or round of the series of (1) a punished connection five or more steps removed from any rewarded connection, (2) a punished connection one step before a rewarded connection (but not between two rewarded connections), (3) a punished connection between two rewarded connections (and next to each), and (4) a rewarded connection

EXPERIMENT	1	2	3	4	2 − 1	3 − 1	4 − 1	$\dfrac{4-1}{2-1}$
A	20.0	32.1	30.3	58.1	12.1	10.3	38.1	3.15
B	23.3	22.4	32.8	45.6*	−0.9	9.5	22.3*	high
C	23.1	23.3	35.6	39.7*	0.2	12.5	16.6	high
D	26.3	23.4	28.9	43.5†	−2.9	2.6	17.2†	high
E	7.5	30.6	34.2	45.0	23.1	26.7	37.5	1.62
F	12.2	16.3	20.6	23.9	4.1	8.4	11.7	2.85
G	16.4	16.4	13.8	23.4	0.0	−2.6	7.0	high
Ha+Hl	20.8	24.5	29.4	47.8*	3.7	8.6	27.0*	7.30 or >
Hb	16.2	17.7	24.3	54.1*	1.5	8.1	37.9*	high
Hc	16.5	18.4	21.3	58.2*	1.9	4.8	41.7*	high
I	17.0	20.7	24.4	38.0*	3.7	6.7	21.0*	5.68 or >
J	23.0	29.0	28.5	31.4	6.0	5.5	8.4	1.40
K	21.0	22.4	28.4	32.3*	1.4	7.4	11.3*	8.07 or >
L	20.0	22.6	20.5	39.7‡	2.6	0.5	19.7‡	7.58 or >
M	23.5	26.8	30.3	41.2	3.3	6.8	17.7	5.36

* Minimal estimates, obtained after omitting all cases of connections rewarded in Trial 1 and repeated in Trial 2.

† A minimal estimate, obtained from a sampling of 329 first occurrences, none of which were in Trial 1.

‡ This percentage may be too high because Experiment L continued Experiment J after an interval of four weeks. As a minimal estimate the 31.4 of Experiment J may be used, giving 11.4 as a minimal estimate for 4 − 1.

§ A description of Experiments A to M will be found in *An Experimental Study of Rewards*.

any rewarded connection, the rewarded connection gains about eight times as much from one occurrence and one reward as the next preceding punished connection gains from its proximity to the reward. The facts appear in the column of Table 6 headed $(4 - 1)/(2 - 1)$. Using as a base the percentage of repetitions in the following trial that would be expected from chance plus favoritism for certain responses, we have the facts of Table 7 for the experiments for which we have been able to compute the favoritism for responses.

TABLE 7

The approximate frequency of repetition in the following trial or round of the series due to chance plus favoritism for certain responses; the excess repetition over this due to one occurrence of (a) a punished connection five or more steps removed from any rewarded connection, (b) a punished connection one step before a rewarded connection (but not between two), (c) a punished connection one step after a rewarded connection (but not between two), (d) a punished connection between two rewarded connections and next to each, and (e) a rewarded connection

EXPERIMENT	CHANCE PLUS FAVOR- ITISM	EXCESS OVER CHANCE PLUS FAVORITISM					RATIOS	
		a	b	c	d	e	e/a	$e/\frac{1}{2}(b+c)$
F	13.0	—0.8	3.3	6.7	7.6	10.9	high	2.2
Ha+Hl	11.4	9.4	13.1	16.9	18.0	36.4*	3.9	2.4
M	22.1	1.4	4.7	8.6	8.2	19.1	13.6	2.8
Pb †	27.0	9.5	12.4	8.8	12.2	16.8	1.8	1.6
I	18.8	2.3	3.6	6.2	8.2	24.7	10.7	5.0

* Minimal estimate.

† Experiment P is described in Lorge and Thorndike ['33].

The varying results for these different experiments are probably due to differences in what is learned and to other differences in the procedures. We are here concerned with the general trends. These are clearly to great concentration of the confirming influence of the reward upon the one connection that is rewarded, with some spread or scatter in rough accord with proximity. Roughly, one rewarded occurrence gives a strengthening ten times that of one punished occurrence remote from a reward, and two and a half times that of one punished occurrence next to a rewarded connection but not between two such.

There are differences among individual subjects in the amount of influence of the reward and in the degree to which it is concentrated. These will be investigated elsewhere.

The Direction of the Spread of Reward

The confirming influence, when it misses or goes beyond the rewarded connection itself, is about as likely to act on one side of the rewarded connection as on the other. Figure 1 is a weighted average curve from experiments F, Ha, Hl, and I, which were alike in the material learned and in which the time for a unit consisting of situation, response, and announcement of "Right"

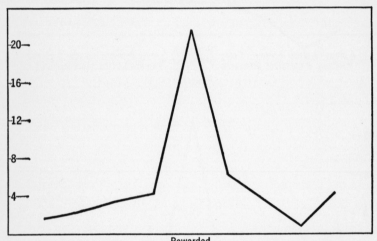

4 steps 3 steps 2 steps 1 step	Rewarded Connection	1 step 2 steps 3 steps 4 steps
Punished connections preceding		Punished connections following

FIGURE 1

or "Wrong" was about three seconds. Figure 2 is a similar curve for experiments K and M, in which the learning was to pick out the right part of a geometrical picture and the time per unit was always 1.5 sec. Figure 3 is a similar curve for experiment 1. The base-line or zero-line in these diagrams represents the probability of repetition in the following trial for a connection that occurred once, was punished, and was five or more steps removed from any rewarded connection. The height of a curve at any one of its nine points represents the excess over this for a connection that occurred once, was punished, and was one, two, three, or four steps removed from any rewarded connection, or was re-

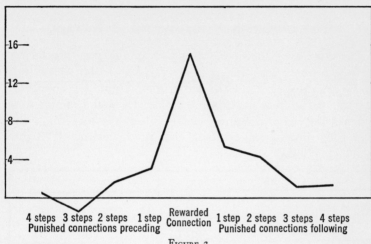

FIGURE 2

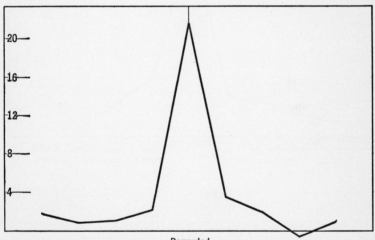

FIGURE 3

warded. The scale of height is in hundredths of probability or percents of repetition.

Including the rewarded connection, the bulk of the confirming influence works on connections prior to the reward. Excluding the rewarded connection, the influences back and forward are as 0.82 and 1.00.

The Combination of the Influences from Two or More Satisfiers

The facts of learning in ordinary life and in experimental studies prove that repetitions of a connection and of whatever satisfying after-effects it may have exert a cumulative effect. But the respective shares of the occurrences and of the rewards have not been often isolated. The latter can be measured separately by comparing the strengthening due to n rewarded occurrences with that due to n punished or ambiguous occurrences all so remote from any rewarded occurrence as to be little or not at all influenced by "spread" or "scatter," and by comparing the strengthenings within each group that are due to various values of n. The results are unanimous in all our experiments and leave no doubt that the second or third or fourth reward of a connection adds to the influence of the earlier rewards of it. We quote in Table 8 the facts for some cases where the subjects had to make their choice in the first trial blindly, the right response being so for no reason save the arbitrary plan of the experiment, and where the numbers of cases runs from about 200 to over 8,000, so that probable errors of the percentile frequencies run from 2 percent to less than one-half of one percent.

The general fact just presented could have been inferred from the general facts of learning, if a satisfying after-effect has any strengthening at all. But inferences concerning whether the strengthenings of a punished connection by spread or scatter from a near-by reward will be cumulative are more hazardous. If the spread phenomenon is a genuine natural consequence of the method of action of a satisfier, cumulative action of two or more proximities in different occurrences of the punished connection should be found. It is found.* If the spread phenomenon, though genuine and natural, loses force with repeated rewarding of a connection, giving way to greater concentration of the confirming force, the cumulative action should appear for second occurrences, but be less for third occurrences. There is some evidence that this is the case.

It is of still more interest to learn whether the spread or scatter influence cumulates in the case of two or more satisfiers

---

* The facts are presented in *An Experimental Study of Rewards*, p. 56 f.

TABLE 8

The frequency with which a connection which has occurred and been rewarded once, twice, or thrice is repeated (S) in the next trial; in permilles

EXPERIMENT	FREQUENCY BY CHANCE	ONE REWARDED OCCURRENCE	TWO REWARDED OCCURRENCES			THREE REWARDED OCCURRENCES		
			Successive	Not successive	Either successive or not successive	Successive	Not successive	Either successive or not successive
Rock I	250	511	739	...	...	859	...	...
Rock II*	250	387	635	...	...	825	...	...
Rock II-o†	250	425	622	...	...	806	...	...
Rock II-1	250	426	616	...	...	810	...	...
Rock II-2	250	409	639	...	...	811	...	...
Rock II-3	250	426	668	...	...	783	...	...
Rock II-4	250	478	666	...	...	799	...	...
Pa	250	594	...	...	826	...	...	940
Q	167	436	811	741	...	...	...	...
Tuckman 1	50	546	774	...	...	905	...	...
Tuckman 2	250	537	766	...	...	894	...	...
Tuckman 3	167	271	395	...	...	660	...	...
Tuckman 4	167	286	426	...	...	701	...	...

* In this row the permilles are for cases where the response in Trial 1 was wrong and punished.

† In these rows the permilles are for cases where the response in Trial 1 was right and rewarded. The figures 0, 1, 2, 3, and 4 refer to amounts of money reward.

acting upon the same punished connection at the same occurrence thereof. If a punished connection occurs just before a sequence of two rewarded connections, will it be strengthened more than if it occurred before only one? If it occurs between two rewarded connections, will it be strengthened more than if it occurred only before or after one such? Will the spread or scatter from the different rewarded connections (C) in C C X, X C C, and C X C combine, or will the action of one C block the action of others? *

* We use C as an abbreviation for a rewarded connection (situation → correct response with a satisfying after-effect). We use X as an abbreviation for a punished connection (situation → wrong response with an annoying after-effect). C X C X X X C C X X C C C X X X X then represents a rewarded

For the case of C X C, we have proof that the two proximities do combine and that the strengthening due to the two is about 1.6 times that of one alone. The median Between/ (Before + After) is 0.8 ± a probable error of 0.05.

For differences like C C X versus C X, X C C versus X C, C C C X versus C C X, X C C C versus X C C, C C X C or C X C C versus C X C, C C C X C versus C C X C, and C X C C C versus C X C C, the presence of the added C in the sequence causes an appreciable increase in the strengthening of the X (ten permilles with a probable error of two).*

The Spread or Scatter of the Influence of a Satisfying After-Effect to Connections Intimately Associated With the Rewarded Connection But Irrelevant to the Learner's Purpose

In experiment 1 the subject responded to each word by any number from 1 to 6 *and any letter.* The number was rewarded or punished, but concerning the letters no report was ever made to him and no requirement was made of him save that he should not repeatedly use the same letter nor use any system (such as using the letters in a fixed order). Subject to these rules he was to say the first letter that came to mind.† He had no interest in what letter he said for any word beyond fulfilling his obligation of saying some letter.

The connections word → letter or word + number → letter, which went with rewarded word → number connections were none the less strengthened more than those which went with punished word → number connections. The totals for all subjects gave a difference of 39 permilles (with a probable error of 3.4) in favor of the letters contemporaneous with rewarded connections. The average of the twenty-four individual differences is 40 permilles. Their median is 23 permilles.‡

connection, followed by a punished connection, followed by a rewarded connection, followed by three punished connections, followed by two rewarded connections, followed by two punished connections, and so on.

* See *An Experimental Study of Rewards,* p. 58.

† If he did occasionally use the same letter two or three times in succession no rebuke was administered.

‡ These results require confirmation. In spite of the fact that they were told that the letters could be neither right nor wrong and made no difference in the

The Restriction of the Spread or Scatter of a Satisfier's Confirming Influence by Time

In experiments Hb and Hc, in which the experimenter, after he had announced "Right" or "Wrong," waited about 2.25 sec. or 4 sec. before giving the next stimulus, the spread or scatter influence is not demonstrably less than in experiment Ha, where the same subjects learned the same sort of material under conditions otherwise identical, but with a time per unit of 2.25 sec. instead of 4.5 sec. or 6.25 sec.

In experiments A, B, C, and D, in which the time per unit was about 5 sec., the spread effect is as great as in experiments J, K, L, and M, where the times per unit were 1 sec. or 1.5 sec. These two sets of experiments differed in the content learned, but there is no reason to suppose that the content in A, B, C, and D was much more favorable to the spread phenomenon than the content in J, K, L, and M.

On the whole the spread or scatter phenomenon seems to be conditioned by remoteness in connections more than by remoteness in time, up to times of 10 or 12 sec.

A Theory of the Operation of After-Effects *

What evidence is available all goes to show that the strengthening or confirming influence of a relevant satisfying after-effect is as natural or biological a fact as facilitation, inhibition, diffusion, the refractory period, or any other fact of nerve physiology. The physiological processes constituting it and them are equally unknown, but it does not depend on interaction or any other doctrine of the relation of mind to matter, any more than they do. It does not act logically or teleologically any more than they do. Its influence does not pick out the 'right' or 'essential' or 'useful' connection by any mystical or logical potency. It is, on the contrary, as

score, some of the subjects sometimes said the number and letter to themselves when the former was called right, if they had time to do so before the next word was said by the experimenter. However, those who did not do so showed as large positive differences as those who did, and better controlled experiments will probably confirm the results quoted here.

* This section consists largely of quotations from an article by the writer which appeared in the *Psychological Review*, Sept., 1933, entitled "A Theory of the Action of the After-Effects of a Connection upon It."

natural in its action as a falling stone, a ray of light, a line of force, a discharge of buckshot, a stream of water, or a hormone in the blood. It will strengthen not only the connection which is the most preferred according to the principles stated above, but also to some extent connections which are wrong, irrelevant, or useless, provided they are close enough to the satisfier in the succession of connections.

One naturally asks first whether the action of a satisfier may be by stimulating the general circulation and thus causing the connections which happen to be in a state of excitement at or near the time of occurrence of the satisfier to be perferentially strengthened by some metabolic process. The facts seem to deny this possibility. The strengthening influence of a satisfier is probably in the form of a reaction of the neurones themselves. It is too rapid to be *via* an increase or decrease in the general circulation or by the liberation of a hormone. When a series $S \rightarrow R$ $\rightarrow$ Reward or Punishment, $S \rightarrow R \rightarrow$ Reward or Punishment, $S \rightarrow R \rightarrow$ Reward or Punishment is run at the rate of 3 sec. per unit, the action of each satisfier is localized at and around its point of application in the series with almost perfect clearness. And this is approximately true with rates of 1.5 sec. or even 1 sec. per unit. Moreover, remoteness in steps seems (though the data are not yet adequate) very much more important than remoteness in time in restricting its application.

This unknown reaction of neurones which is aroused by the satisfier and which strengthens connections upon which it impinges may be called the "Yes" reaction or "O. K." reaction or confirming reaction. Though its intimate histological basis and physiological nature are no better known than those of facilitation, inhibition, fatigue, strengthening by repetition, or any other forces causing temporary or permanent modifications in the brain, certain facts about it are known in addition to those already stated concerning its causes and results.

The confirming reaction is independent of sensory pleasures. A pain may set it in action, as Tolman, Hall, and Bretnall have recently demonstrated in a striking experiment.* The confirming reaction, though far from logical or inerrant, is highly selective. It may pick out and act upon the words one is saying, leaving

* E. C. Tolman, C. S. Hall, and E. P. Bretnall, *J. Exper. Psychol.*, 1932, vol. 15, pp. 601-614.

uninfluenced one's posture and gross bodily movements and all that one is seeing.

The confirming reaction seems often to issue from some overhead control in the brain, the neural basis of some want or 'drive' or purpose or then active self of the animal. This overhead control may be rather narrow and specific, as when a swallow of liquid satisfies thirst and the satisfaction confirms the connection which caused the swallowing and makes the animal continue or repeat that connection. This may happen while the main flow of his purposes concerns the work he is doing or the game he is playing or the book he is reading. It may be very broad and general, as when the purpose is to do well and win a game or to pass the time pleasantly and is satisfied by any one of many movements in response to some play of one's adversary or by attentiveness to any one of many sights and sounds. It may be stimulated to send forth its confirming reaction by a rich sensory satisfier, such as freedom, food, and companionship for an animal escaping from a cage, or by a symbolic satisfier, such as the announcement of "Right" in an experiment in learning. If what the overhead control wants is the announcement of "Right," that is what will most surely lead it to make the confirming reaction.

As suggested by the preceding paragraph, several wants or purposes or controls may be operative at the same time or in close alternation.

Arrangements may be made whereby certain events acquire power to cause the confirming reaction in the absence of anything that would ordinarily be called an overhead control. The reward or satisfier may then exert the confirming reaction directly upon the connection.

If an $S \rightarrow R$ connection has a satisfying after-effect which causes some control in the brain to send forth a confirming reaction, and if the S continues, the confirming reaction tends to cause a continuance or continued repetition of the R then and there, and often with more vigor and shorter latency. If the situation has vanished, the strengthening of the connection can only manifest itself when S recurs, which may be in a few seconds or only after months. There will then be an increased probability of repetition over what there would have been if no confirming reaction had affected the connection in question. In either case the strengthening causes the repetition, not the repetition the strengthening.

The potency of a confirming reaction may bear little relation to the intensity of the satisfier. A 'want' or 'purpose' or 'self' may as well be satisfied, and so issue as full and adequate a confirming reaction, by a moderate reward as by one much larger. There seems to be an upper point beyond which increases in a reward add only excitement. Toward the low end there is a range where the reward fails more and more frequently to arouse an adequate confirming reaction. There seems to be a point below which a confirming reaction is not evoked. A state of affairs below this degree of satisfyingness is satisfying to the extent of being tolerated, and nothing is done to abolish or evade it, or to replace the connection which caused it by some other connection; but also nothing is done to strengthen the connection and continue it longer than it would otherwise have been continued, or to repeat it in the future more frequently than it would otherwise have been repeated.

At the other end of this neutral zone begin states of affairs which are annoying to the animal and stimulate him to do whatever his repertory provides as responses to the annoyance in question. His repertory does not provide a general destructive or weakening reaction which is comparable and opposite to the confirming reaction and which subtracts from the connection upon which it acts. Any apparent subtraction is due to the increased strength of competing tendencies. The annoyer does not then and there destroy or weaken the connections of which it is the after-effect, but only causes the animal to make a different response to the S in question.

I do not think that this tendency to do something different in response to an S, the first response to which has resulted in an annoying state of affairs, is a unitary tendency applicable to any connection, and replacing it indifferently by any other connection than it. The confirming reaction set in action by a satisfier has, if my observations are correct and adequate, no comparable altering reaction set in action by an annoyer. The reactions in the latter case seem specialized and closely dependent on what the annoyer is and what state the brain is in.

Whether or not this is so, an annoying after-effect of a certain S → R has very different possibilities *according as the S remains or vanishes.* If it vanishes, the annoyer can do nothing, because it cannot change the response to an S which is not there. So, in multiple-choice learning in which each S vanishes as soon as it is responded to, punishments have zero influence upon learning and punished connections may do more harm to learning by occurring than they do good by being punished. If the S remains and the response to it is changed, the animal may benefit from the fact of changing and from the occurrence and the after-effects of the $S \rightarrow R_2$ which has replaced $S \rightarrow R_1$.

What sort of force acting through what sort of process or mechanism can be and do what the confirming reaction is and does? The answer which seems to me to fit all or nearly all the facts is that the force and mechanism of the confirming reaction are the force and mechanism of reinforcement, applied to a connection.

All explanations of reinforcement agree that one part of the brain can exert a force to intensify activities elsewhere in it and that processes or mechanisms exist whereby this force can be directed or attracted to one activity rather than promiscuously; and that is all that is required to explain the fundamental physiology of the confirming reaction. It is distinguished from other sorts of reinforcement by the fact that satisfaction sets the force in action and that the force acts on the connection which was just active in intimate functional association with the production of the satisfier, or on its near neighbors.

The Influence of the Confirming Reaction in Cases Where the Situation Continues or Reappears Very Soon

In our experiments each situation is quickly replaced by another as soon as the subject responds to it and a record of his response is made, and this situation does not appear again until a long series (usually about forty) of other situations has intervened. Such multiple-choice learning with only one response allowed to any one occurrence of a situation is very valuable for scientific analysis, and is a fairly frequent event in nature. But the case where the situation remains so that one after another response may be tried until one is found that produces a satisfying result and terminates the situation is much more common. And the case where the situation remains even after a satisfying result has been attained is perhaps even more common. We may call these Cases I, II, and III.

If the experimenter had permitted the subjects to give one response after another, until the right one was given, and had announced "Wrong" or "Right" for each as he did in Case I, and had proceeded to a new situation as soon as a "Right" was attained, we should have had Case II. The influence of the satisfying after-effect in such a Case II will be to strengthen the connection as in Case I.* Its influence will be complicated by that of the announcements of "Wrong."

If the experimenter had not only permitted the subject to try various responses until he had one whose after-effect was satisfying but had also permitted the situation to remain (suppose for example that, in the word-number learning, the word was printed on a card which remained before the subject for 10 sec.), what would a subject desirous of knowing the correct number for that word at the next trial have done? Upon saying, for example, *Six* at the sight of *bread* and hearing "Right," he would have made the connection again, saying *"six, six, six"* as he looked at or thought of *bread*. In Case III the confirming reaction not only strengthens *bread → six,* so that when *bread* recurs that connection will be more likely to act than before; it also causes that connection to repeat itself then and there, and if this repetition is satisfying, others will follow until the learner is bored with the procedure or has something more attractive to do, or until the situation vanishes.† In Case III with human subjects the confirming reaction thus not only adds strength to the connection though it occur but the once; it also adds occurrences of it, and adds more strength for each occurrence that it confirms. The same tendency, though less surely productive of repetitions, will be found in all animals that can learn at all.‡

---

* Whether the spread or scatter phenomenon and some of the other features of the after-effect's influence will appear to just the same extent in Case II as in Case I has not been determined.

† If the external situation vanishes before the subject loses satisfaction in the connection, he may set up some internal equivalent of it and respond to that, as by saying to himself *bread six, bread six.*

‡ The connection at the moment that it is made may be said to be of very great temporary strength, and it may lose very little of this if nothing happens to displace it or interfere with it. It is even possible to conceive that the con-

The experiments with human adults reported here and in *An Experimental Study of Rewards*, the classical multiple-choice experiments of Yerkes and his pupils with pigs, crows, and monkeys, and the experiments of Thorndike ['32] with chicks are instances of Case I. The well-known experiments with animals and children where freedom or food or some other desideratum is obtained by trial and successful choice are instances of Case II. Learning to lap milk, or gnaw bones, or play with a ball, or chew gum, or make a bell ring by shaking it are instances of Case III.

The confirming reaction makes the connection which it confirms stronger and thereby more likely to function. If the situation continues, the connection will often be made so much stronger relative to other competing connections at the time that it will repeat itself immediately or very soon and thus pile up strength. It is for this reason that the repetition of a connection having a satisfying after-effect seems more potent than it really is. Repetitions caused by the confirming reaction, and themselves in turn strengthened by it, are potent. But their potency is in the main due to the confirming reaction.

In some experiments of Case I, the confirming reaction causes an addition then and there of some inner equivalent of, or substitute for, the connection which had just been rewarded. Thus, in experiment 1, quoted as a sample earlier in this chapter, many subjects will often say to themselves the word and number when they hear "Right," or they will hear the word and number echo in their minds. Sometimes only the numbers will be repeated

firming reaction is primarily an influence causing the animal to continue or repeat the connection, and that its permanent strengthening influence is a secondary consequence of this when the situation vanishes so that continuance or repetition is impossible. Moreover, the influence of the confirming reaction may be augmented by the informative influence of the announcement of "Right." The connection may be echoing in the mind with some idea or expectation of "Right" attached to the echo so that it is readily available for choice and repetition. This is not the place to analyze the phenomenon, nor to assess the importance of these and other possible features of it. Our present concern is with two facts—the observed fact that continuance of the situation as in Case III gives a high probability of continuance or repetition of whatever the confirming reaction acts upon and the fact inferred from the results of experiments with Case I that the confirming reaction *must* act to cause such continuance and repetition (though probably not all of that observed, certainly not all of that observed in sophisticated learners whose minds, so to speak, seize, hold, and repeat any "Right" connection by deliberate intent).

internally. It would be more accurate to say that the words and numbers (or the numbers) repeat themselves. For the inner speech or hearing may be entirely unintentional, and unavoidable except by deliberately turning the mind to something else the moment "Right" is heard.

This consequence of the confirming reaction is a nuisance to the experimenter who is trying to discover whether a satisfier strengthens its connection directly and before and irrespective of such inner saying or hearing, but for many theoretical and almost all practical purposes, the additional strengthening which does or may occur as a result of unintentional inner repetition is indistinguishable from that which occurs irrespective of it. Both are set in action by the one satisfier. The key to learning by the force of either lies in the pressure of the confirming reaction upon the connection.

If the inner repetition is intentional, the case is very different. An inner repetition of this sort more nearly equals a repetition of the real situation by the experimenter, of the correct response by the learner, and of the "Right" by the experimenter. This is perfectly clear in the extreme case where a learner repeats the inner equivalents of the situation, correct response, and reward in sequence over and over again, say four times. There are then essentially four occurrences of the connection, each one presumably confirmed by its satisfying after-effect.

Such an intentional inner repetition of a connection and its satisfier may have a strengthening influence comparable in amount to an actual occurrence. Also it may require as much time as the latter. But the intentional echoing of a connection or of the response half of it as a secondary result of the confirming reaction is brief and adds relatively little strength to the connection. In one of our experiments (BBB) the learners were, in certain series, left to do whatever occurred to them in the fraction of a second between the experimenter's announcement of "Right" or "Wrong" and the appearance of the next situation. In other series, they were instructed never to repeat any situation and response or response alone. In still others they were instructed to repeat whenever they could before the next situation appeared. The loss under the second condition was slight and possibly no greater than could be accounted for by the interference due to trying not to let the response be repeated.

Relation of the Confirming Influence of Satisfying After-Effects to the Dynamics of Interest and Motives

Interests and motives may then influence life in two ways: by predisposing a person beforehand to connect certain responses with certain situations, and by modifying these connections when they have occurred. Interests and motives cause certain connections to occur, and also cause certain after-effects of connections to be satisfying. Recognition and use of the second potency is absolutely essential in an adequate theory of interests, motives, attitudes, or wants.

Chapter 4

THE ATTACHMENT OF REWARDS TO TENDENCIES

WHEN a satisfier happens in a man, it often is felt to belong to some connection or group of connections. So if one lifts a glass to his lips and drinks, the cool water going down his throat is felt to belong as a consequence to the connection which had the act of drinking as its end term. Hearing the teacher's "Excellent" may be consciously attached to the behavior that evoked it. But sometimes a satisfier may happen without being referred to any connection or connections, or with dubious and obscure reference. If I put my hand in my pocket to get a match and find to my surprise a ten-dollar bill, I probably will not refer the satisfier to the connection which ended in my putting my hand in my pocket.

A satisfier may, however, belong to, and exert its influence upon, a connection without any conscious reference of it to that connection and without any awareness on the part of the subject that it does or will influence that connection. This is indicated by the learning of young children and animals, who can hardly be supposed to consider the relations in question. It will be demonstrated by experiments to be reported later.

The fact that the satisfier belongs to a certain connection or connections, not the fact that the subject then and there knows or thinks that he knows what it belongs to, is the primary and important fact.

In the experiments reported in the previous chapter, the subjects, if they had had time to consider the matter and had an interest in it, could have consciously referred the satisfying "Right" to the connection which evoked it. They rarely did so, first because usually the next situation in the series of tasks was presented as soon as the reward or punishment had been conferred, and consequently they were occupied in listening to the next word. In the second place, they trusted their minds to use the reward in favor of the preceding connection rather than any other. If they had had time, they would not have spent it in

considering what connection the reward belonged to, but in repeating that connection or some equivalent for it and in thinking
that it was the right and proper connection. In these experiments
(and in all experiments) awareness of belonging is a secondary
and accessory feature, not essential to learning. The belonging
itself is what counts.

What then will be the difference in influence of two satisfiers
alike in all respects save that one belongs closely to a certain
connection $S_1 \rightarrow R_1$ out of the many that were active when, or
shortly before, the satisfier occurred, while the other does not?
Suppose, for example, that a subject is instructed as follows: "I
shall say a word, you will say some number from 1 to 10 and
also say some letter and tap one of these ten keys and draw a
line in one of these sixteen squares. Every time you say the right
number for a word, I shall give you one five-cent piece. Occasionally I shall give you five pennies. The circumstances which
will determine my gifts of five pennies I shall not tell you now
or ever. They may be regular; they may be fortuitous. They may
depend on something that you do; they may not. They may be
the same throughout the experiment; they may change." If then
the five pennies were always given if the subject leaned forward
and if this act occurred as often as a choice of the right number
in the first round of the series, how would the two satisfiers differ
in influence?

Before answering this question, we may best consider certain
facts which lead to a still more important question concerning
the comparative influence of relevant and irrelevant satisfiers.

Many satisfiers are such because they give the animal something which he then and there wants and is to a certain extent
trying to get. They may be said to fulfil a desire, or gratify a
craving, or relieve a tension (whatever a tension in a mind or
brain may be), or provide the attainment of a goal, or be the
object of a "drive." Possessing food if hungry, attaining company
if lonesome, and being relieved from pain or confinement are
samples of such relevant satisfiers that have figured largely in
experiments with animals. In our experiments, the "Right" and
the money rewards were relevant in this sense, that the persons
wanted them and were trying to get them, though there was no
deeper and more "natural" relevance, and no higher and more
logical relevance.

In the ordinary course of life of birds and mammals probably 90 percent or more of satisfiers are relevant. They ordinarily are moved by some want instigated by stimulation from without or within. The cat or dog or rat or chick or monkey does not simply sit around waiting for any passing satisfiers to come his way. He wants food or drink or sex-activity or exploration or fighting-play or pursuit or repose or company or something, and does whatever is in his repertory by original nature and training as responses to that want. (Of course he may be, and often is, moved by two or more wants at the same time.) The states of affairs which he attains from moment to moment as the consequence of his acts and environment are relevant satisfiers in the great majority of cases. Only rarely will the environment offer to an animal that is searching for food, sex enjoyment; or to one that is craving repose, a dainty morsel of food. In ten hours of exploration a dog will possibly encounter one tempting chance to fight.

Civilized man also is set to attain certain results in a large fraction of his waking life, and what the environment offers him in the way of satisfiers is usually relevant to some one of the wants which are responsible for the activity of the period in question. At meals the satisfiers are mostly the food, drink, company, and conversation which he goes to the table for. When he reads a book or newspaper, the satisfiers are the information, amusement, excitement, and the like which he seeks. Rarely do his meals provide thrills of pride at his physical prowess. Still less often does he find money hidden between the leaves of his book.

But satisfiers do, or at least may, occur at times when they are unexpected, unsought, out of harmony with the activity which absorbs the person. While hunting asses one may find a kingdom. We need therefore to know what difference there is between the effects of relevant and irrelevant satisfiers. More precisely, what will be the difference between two satisfiers, alike in all respects save that one is sought by the animal at the time whereas the other is not?

In the ordinary course of life, belonging and relevance are correlated; so observations and experiments that are instructive concerning one of our questions will usually be instructive concerning the other also.

In experiment 3 we study especially the restrictions due to different degrees of belonging, but one feature of the experiment measures the restriction due to incomplete belonging plus irrelevance plus (as it happened) lowered satisfyingness.* The nature of the experiment and its administration were as follows:

Twenty-four series of forty words were responded to by a number from 1 to 5. Each series was repeated five times in succession. The order of the series was rotated from subject to subject.

Twenty college undergraduates (all women) participated in this experiment during November and December, 1932. They did the entire series in six hours distributed throughout a single week. They were paid a basal minimum per hour plus whatever bonuses they may have earned. No session was longer than one hour.

The subject was seated comfortably, opposite, but screened from, the experimenter. The directions were read:

"This is an experiment in learning. I shall say a word. You will at once say a number from 1 to 5. Sometimes I will tell you whether you are right or wrong. Usually I will not. But I will tell you whenever you are doing specially well; and I will tell you after every eight responses how well you did in those eight. You will be paid a bonus of one cent for every two that you get right more than you would get by chance. There will be forty words in each series, and the series will be repeated five times. The first time you naturally will get the right numbers only by chance, but the second time you will do a little better, and the third time still better, and so on. Remember you are always to respond by saying 1 or 2 or 3 or 4 or 5 just as soon as I say a word."

The announcement of "Right" or "Wrong" was always made for the responses to seven or eight stimulus words in each series of forty. For the other thirty-two or thirty-three words the experimenter recorded whether the responses were correct or incorrect according to a key. No announcements of "Right" or "Wrong" were made for these thirty-two or thirty-three; but if the subject had two responses correct in sequence, the experimenter said, "You are doing finely now" in an encouraging tone. From time to time, also, but never three times in a single session, the experimenter handed the subject five cents in cash, saying, "Here is a bonus for faithful work." Also, after the eighth, sixteenth, twenty-

* The experiment was planned by the writer and carried out by Dr. Lorge, who also improved it in several particulars.

fourth, thirty-second, and fortieth words of each series, the experimenter said "You had . . . out of eight right," followed by "Very poor" if none right, "Not very good" if one right, "Good" if two right, "Very good" if three right, "Fine" if four, "Wonderful" if five, "Marvelous" if six or seven, "Perfect" if eight. The experimenter's tonal expression also changed from sad for none or one to joyous for the better performances.

At the end of each series the subject was told the total number of responses out of the 200 that were recorded as 'right' or 'correct' and was paid a cash bonus of one-half cent for each 'correct' or 'right' in excess of forty.

The Influence of Belongingness

In experiment 3 there were four sorts of satisfiers operating, each of which operated also in a different way. The ordinary announcement of "Right" was satisfying because it signified success and a definite money reward and so appealed to the person's desire to be competent and satisfied with himself and to win money. It operated mainly upon the connection which it immediately followed and to which it belonged (adding about 0.30 to its strength) but spread somewhat backward and forward to neighboring connections (adding about 0.045 to the strength of a connection one step removed). The announcement of "You are doing finely" made whenever the subject had two correct responses in succession was satisfying for the same reasons, except that the money outcome was less definite and less secure. It operated nearly as strongly upon the connections one step removed as upon the connection which it followed immediately (adding about 0.125 to each of the former and about 0.16 to the latter). It belonged logically only to past connections and could be reasonably applied to the two or three or four or five or even more of them that were nearest.

The announcements made after situations 8, 16, 24, 32, and 40 —"You had . . . right out of eight" plus "Good" if the number was two, "Very good" if it was three, "Fine" if it was four, "Wonderful" if it was five, "Marvelous" if it was six or seven and "Perfect" if it was eight—were satisfying because they signified success and definite money rewards.* Any one of them be-

* For none right out of the eight, the phrase "Very poor" was used; for one right, the phrase "Not very good."

longed logically to all the preceding eight responses, and as much to any one of them as to any other.

The efficacy of the announcement of "Right" for the first occurrence of a connection so rewarded is measured by the percentage of repetitions of the same connection in the next trial. For "Right" this percentage is 54.3. Similarly the efficacy of "You are doing finely" freed from the influence of spread from a "Right" is 34.6; for "No Announcement" freed from the influence of spread from a "Right," it is 27.7; for "You had . . . right" plus "Good," "Very good," or "Fine," it is 34.6. Whenever two of these announcements followed a connection, we can measure the effect of the two announcements in the same way.

"Right" + "You had . . . ," etc., and "Good," "Very
    good," or "Fine" 65.1
"You are doing finely" + "You had . . . ," etc., and
    "Good," "Very good," or "Fine" 45.8
"No announcement" + "You had . . . ," etc., and
    "Good," "Very good," or "Fine" 34.6*

All of these three satisfiers were perfectly relevant to the learner's purpose and activity, but varied in their logical and probably in their psychological "belonging." The gifts of five cents "for faithful work" are much less relevant and may belong logically to anything describable as "faithful work." They are satisfying or not according to the weights attached by the person to money receipts from the experiment and general commendation for industry and good behavior, on the one hand, and to the receipt of a nickel as one might receive a tip or charity, on the other hand. These gifts of five cents in the experiment had, on the whole, little or no strengthening influence upon the connections which they immediately followed, and presumably none on any other connections. They raised the probability of repetition in the following trial only 0.026 above that for "No announcement." (0.303 versus 0.277.) They may possibly have had such an influence in some individuals, which was counterbalanced by disturbance or confusion in others. They will be considered further in connection with the influence of relevancy.

The four sorts of satisfiers also had different values as sheer information. The "Right" said that the connection which had

* "Wrong" + "You had . . . ," etc., and "Good," "Very good," or "Fine"
gave 28.7.

just occurred was correct. The "You are doing finely now" said that an unspecified number of the connections which had just occurred contained a high proportion of correct ones. The "You had . . . right out of eight" gave the probability of correctness for each of the last eight connections. The gift of five cents said nothing about the correctness of any connection or group of connections.

The differences in the informative values of the three sorts of verbal satisfiers probably had very little to do with the differences in their strengthening influences, except in so far as they made satisfiers belong to different processes. The strengthening influences which are under consideration were from first occurrences only. With series of forty connections occurring at the rate of one every three seconds, there was only very, very rarely any memory at the next trial of what number one said for any word the first time one had it right, or of whether one had the number right or wrong. The "You are doing finely now" acted almost as strongly on the next following connection, concerning which it gave no information as on the next preceding connection, which it said was likely to have been correct.

From other experiments we may estimate the percentage of repetitions that would occur in experiment 3 as a result of chance plus the influence of favoritism in the choice of numbers as about 21. On this basis, "Right" belonging closely to its preceding connection causes a strengthening of 33.* "You are doing finely now," belonging less closely to its preceding connection, causes a strengthening of 14. A "Two, good," "Three, very good," or "Four, fine," belonging in logic equally to any of the preceding eight connections, strengthens the last one of them by 14. No announcement of any sort (which leaves the subject to whatever satisfaction his optimism may dictate) causes a strengthening of the connection just preceding it by 7.

There seems thus to be a real and substantial tendency for a satisfier to cause a confirming reaction, and for the latter to attach itself to the next preceding connection in the series, even though the satisfier does not belong to that one more than to others. We can surely say that the physiological influence of a satisfier

* Part of this strengthening may be due to actual inner repetition of the connections by the subjects, since this was possible to some extent in spite of the prompt presentation of the next situation by the experimenter.

is highly independent of logical belonging and somewhat independent of the belonging of which the subject is aware. Even when the subject has just been told the last preceding connection is wrong, the satisfaction of hearing "Four right out of the last eight. Fine" or the like does demonstrably strengthen it.

McTeer ['31] found no demonstrable advantage for learning from giving a shock in the finger when hits of wrong typewriter keys were made over giving a shock in the ankle. But presumably, after the first two or three occurrences, the shocks in the ankle belonged to the connections in question closely enough to satisfy all requirements of belonging. Moreover, neither sort of shock had a demonstrably beneficial influence on the learning. Shocks led the subjects to be more cautious and to memorize the un-shocked or right connections more thoroughly, so that they had fewer trials and errors, but made no saving in time. Consequently, McTeer's results do not help in our problem.

The Influence of Relevance

A gift of five cents for "faithful work" in experiment 3 had no observable influence upon the connection which immediately preceded it. But a similar gift of three or five cents in another experiment (experiment 4) did have. In this experiment, a series of cards numbered from 132 to 458 was prepared consisting of:

(A) Fifty-four cards containing well-written and interesting quotations.

(B) Seventy-three cards containing less interesting quotations.

(D) Eighty cards containing extremely uninteresting statements.

(J) Twenty-one cards containing jokes.

(P) Ten cards containing amusing pictures mostly from *Punch*).

(M) Ten cards containing the statement "Hand this to the examiner and you will receive three cents" (sometimes "five cents").

(N) In the case of seventy-nine of the numbers there were no cards.

The subjects at the start knew nothing about the constitution of the series. They were instructed as follows:

"Here are several hundred cards numbered from 132 to 458. Your first task is to choose cards by number until you get one that says something about death. You will say to the experimenter three times 'I want death. I choose 296' (or whatever number you select). The examiner will give you that card. You will read what is on it. If it says anything about death, you will hand it to the examiner. He will, if you are right, put it in the box marked 'Right.' If it does not say anything about death, you will put it face up in the box marked 'Wrong,' and choose again, saying as before, three times 'I want death. I choose . . . .' The examiner will give you that card. You will read what is on it. If it says anything about death, you will give it to the examiner as before. If it does not, you will put it in the box of wrongs as before.

"You will do just the same with each of the forty-four tasks. Then you will repeat them. Then you will repeat them again, and again, and again as often as time permits.

"You will be scored and paid according to the number of tasks you complete successfully. So the quicker you get the right card for each task the higher score you will get and the more you will earn."

The tasks of Series I were, in order:

SERIES I

1. Death ....
2. Roses ....
3. Spring or summer... .. ..
4. God or angels...... .. ..
5. Gold or silver....... .. ..
6. Morning, tuberculosis,
     or pneumonia..... .. ..
7. Evening, diphtheria,
     or suicide ....
8. Steel or golf........ .. ..
9. Winter or night..... .. ..
10. Love ....
11. Heaven or child..... .. ..

Series II, III, and IV comprised the same twenty-one tasks, but in different combinations.

These four series were repeated twice or more with each of nineteen young women (college students).

A card drawn from the file was put back into it after an interval of fifteen to twenty further choices. If a joke or picture was drawn, a new joke or picture with the same number was put into the file after such an interval. If a number was chosen for which there was no card, the experimenter said, "There is no card with that number."

The subject thus has, as the after-effect of choosing a number, some one of these:

Ac Reading a well-written and interesting quotation which contains some word or other expression of an idea which he wants.

Ax Reading a well-written and interesting quotation which does not contain some word or other expression of an idea which he wants.

Bc Reading a less well-written and less interesting quotation which contains the word or idea which he wants.

Bx Reading a less well-written and less interesting quotation which does not contain the word or idea which he wants.

Dc Reading a very dull statement which contains some word or other expression of an idea which he wants.

Dx Reading a very dull statement which does not contain the word or idea which he wants.

Jx Reading a joke (and never the same one again) which does not contain the word or idea he wants. In a very few cases, perhaps, one in a thousand, the joke did contain it, but these exceptions are disregarded in what follows.

Px Seeing a funny picture and reading its caption, which does not contain the word or idea that he wants.

M Receiving money (three cents or five cents) then and there.

N Being told "There is no card with that number."

Under the conditions of the game, *Ac, Bc,* and *Dc* are alike in the relevant reward of finding the wanted word or expression and unlike in the irrelevant reward of the literary value and interest of the content read. *Ax, Bx,* and *Dx* are alike in the relevant punishment (or lack of reward) of not finding the wanted word or expression and unlike in the irrelevant reward of the literary value and interest of the content read. The extent to which the literary value and interest are rewards depends, of course, upon the extent to which the subject is satisfied by literary quality and interest.

Jx and *Px* are like *Ax, Bx,* and *Dx* in the absence of any satisfaction by the presence of the idea or word then wanted, but unlike them in that they contain (with the exceptions noted above) no word or idea that *ever* can be wanted in the experiment. They are like *Ac* in the presence of a high degree of irrelevant interest.

M has, the first time that it occurs, an irrelevant satisfyingness, the amount of which varies with the subject's valuation of money. After *M* has occurred enough times to arouse the expectation that choices of numbers may result in money directly as well as by way of the score attained, M may become a relevant reward, the subject being desirous to get cards with the wanted words *or to get money directly*.

N is unlike all the above save Dx in producing no satisfaction whatever from reading the card and unlike all, including Dx, in lacking even the effect of reading the card.

We may study the influence of Ac, Ax, Bc, Bx, Dc, Dx, Jx, Px, M, and N upon the connections with the various situations such as "I want heaven or angels," "I want death," "I want roses," etc. We may also study the influence of Ac, Ax, Bc, Bx, etc., upon the connections made with the general situation of wanting an expression of this, that, or the other of these ideas.*

Both lines of evidence favor the decision that a satisfying after-effect strengthens somewhat the connection to which it is attached, even though it is irrelevant to the purpose in the interest of which the connection was made and highly incongruous with the cravings and expectations of the person at the time.

The failure of the gift "for faithful work" in experiment 3 to strengthen the connection which it followed may have been due only slightly to its irrelevance. If we may believe the subjects' reports, it was in some cases annoying, and in seven of the cases in which it was satisfying it did probably strengthen the tendency to which it belonged, namely to listen attentively and try hard to learn the correct numbers. Its failure to influence the preceding word → number connections may then be accounted for, regardless of irrelevance, by the fact that it did not belong to them closely enough.

In experiment 4, the drawing of a money card is less like receiving a tip and so is more often satisfying. Although irrelevant to the game, the reward belongs definitely and emphatically to the choice of a certain number in connection with a certain task. That choice in that connection was strengthened, and the choice of that number in connection with any of the tasks was also strengthened. The irrelevant rewards by Ax, Jx, and Px also exerted a strengthening influence.

* The evidence is reported in the *Journal of Educational Psychology*, vol. 24, pp. 1-15. It is too elaborate to be reported here and cannot conveniently be summarized.

Evidence on the Influence of Belonging and Relevance from Animal Experimentation

In much of the recorded facts of animal learning, the response whose connection with a situation is strengthened by a satisfying after-effect is one made by the animal when moved by a want for that after-effect. Furthermore, the after-effect occurs as a fairly prompt and direct sequent of the S → R in question, somewhat as a taste follows taking into the mouth or as capture follows a jump at the prey. The response belongs to the situation including and to the then active wants of the animal; the after-effect belongs to the situation → response connection; the after-effect is relevant to the then active want.

But there are indubitable cases where an after-effect strengthens a connection to which it belongs only exiguously. Such are (1) the learning of cats to lick themselves when put in a certain box and to scratch themselves when put in a certain other box, the door being opened by the experimenter, permitting escape and food when they did so. The opening of the door with the consequent freedom and food belonged to the licking or scratching at their first occurrences about as little as any one event could belong to any one act. Such also is (2) the learning of Roberts's rats to frequent a certain spot where they were likely to hit a hanging rod when put in a certain pen. When a rat touched the rod, the door was opened. Such also is (3) the learning of animals to step on a platform in the back of a certain pen, this act opening a door in the front of the pen. The act in the first and third cases was rather an accident, disturbing the responses set up by the external situation and the internal want, than a minor element among these responses. The after-effect came like a *deus ex machina*. In such cases it seems as if the satisfying after-effect strengthened the connection which it did strengthen because it was a strengthening force that had to influence something and, in default of anything to which it belonged, acted upon whatever connections were active at the time.

There are also cases where the after-effect causing learning has a very small amount of relevance to the then active want, if that is taken narrowly. To the want in the service of which a cat scratches or licks itself, escape and food are irrelevant satisfiers. To the particular want to break through the roof of a box, the opening of a door in its side (by pulling a loop of wire near the roof) is irrelevant. I do not recall any observations of the confirming influence of sex-gratification upon connections in animals wanting food or freedom, or of food upon connections in animals wanting sex-gratification or freedom, and the like. The experiments with water for hungry rats and dry food for thirsty rats cannot properly be used as evidence because the irrelevance is dubious and there may be a complicating after-effect in the possible satisfyingness of an unimpeded run to the food-box. Dr. Lorge has attacked the problem of whether the reward of access to food and indulgence therein will strengthen the connection (in the rat) of washing its face, scratching itself, standing upright, or standing half upright and peering forward, if it is provided whenever one of these acts is performed. He has shown that it unquestionably will.*

Indeed, the rats learn to escape from a box by these acts nearly or quite as quickly and as well as by digging through sawdust or gnawing through a barrier or choosing an effective exit rather than a blind alley or by pushing against a door or by running to a certain spot or by exploring a certain cranny. A hungry rat that stops "trying to get out of the box and to the food outside" by running, etc., and washes its face will, if the door then opens, quickly learn to wash its face as soon as it finds itself in that box.

Lorge's results are strong evidence that a connection made to satisfy want A may be strengthened by an after-effect which satisfies want B, and that an after-effect which satisfies want B will confirm a connection to which it belongs only to the extent of being its close sequent in time and of belonging still less to any other connection. They support the hypothesis that a satisfier of the want for escape, access to food, and eating may strengthen any connection that may occur in a hungry animal, no matter how little relevance and belonging there may be.

On the whole, we may safely draw two conclusions. A satisfying state of affairs exerts a strengthening influence without perfect relevance. This strengthening influence will operate on connections to which the satisfier does not in any logical sense belong. So much seems established. For a complete adjudication of the restrictions set by relevancy and belonging one can as yet only set up hypotheses.

* I. Lorge. Unpublished study.

I suggest the simple, though extreme, hypothesis that any satisfying state of affairs tends to arouse a confirming reaction. A state of affairs which would ordinarily be satisfying will not be when it is so irrelevant to any then active wants that the creature does not enjoy it when it comes. It will then not arouse a confirming reaction. A state of affairs unsought, unexpected, and intruding as a shock, though an agreeable one, will be much less likely to arouse a confirming reaction than the same state of affairs sought and attained as a normal part of the animal's primary behavior.

I suggest as a hypothesis to account for what and when the confirming reaction will strengthen, that the confirming reaction will strengthen modifiable connections in accordance with the temporal nearness of their excitement and the closeness with which they and the satisfying state of affairs belonged together. It may expend all its force on the one connection closest to the want and after-effect in question. It may dissipate its force over a hundred connections if all belong equally to that want and after-effect. As the belongingness approaches zero, temporal nearness may be decisive.

If these hypotheses are used as working hypotheses, we should proceed to study the limitations and restrictions to a satisfier's action by various sorts and degrees of irrelevance and isolation. It may be more prudent, however, to use the hypothesis that no satisfier strengthens anything until there is specific proof that it does and to extend the typical cases of the previous chapter very cautiously.

Chapter 5

UNCONSCIOUS LEARNING

IT is important to know whether connections can be strengthened without awareness on the part of the $\left\{\begin{array}{l}\text{subject}\\\text{person}\\\text{learner}\end{array}\right\}$ that they are being strengthened. It is still more important to know whether connections can be strengthened without awareness on the part of the $\left\{\begin{array}{l}\text{subject}\\\text{person}\\\text{learner}\end{array}\right\}$ that the connections exist or even that he is responding in any way to the situations in question.

The former is certainly the case. A person may increase the probability that certain situations will evoke certain responses without knowing at the time that he is doing so or afterward that he has done so. This is evidenced both by experimental records and by facts of ordinary life. No competent psychologist would now dispute it. There is no direct consciousness of learning paralleling the fact of learning and revealing it to the learner.

The latter also seems to be the case. A person may respond to situation $S_1S_2S_3S_4$ by $R_aR_bR_cR_d$ and increase the probability that the feature S_4 will evoke R_d from say 0.1 to 0.3 and all the time be unaware that he is connecting R_d with S_4 or even that he is responding to anything more than $S_1S_2S_3$ or by anything more than $R_aR_bR_c$. He may indeed be unaware of $S_1S_2S_3S_4$ and $R_aR_bR_cR_d$ *in toto*. But this is relatively rare, the commoner case being that the person thinks he is forming a certain habit or is doing a certain thing in certain circumstances when he is really forming a more complex habit, or doing more things than he wots of in a richer set of circumstances than he consciously envisages.

It seems to be the case often in the learning of animals and infants—and in certain habits and prejudices of learners in general—and more definitely in experiments 49 to 70 reported in Chapter X of *The Fundamentals of Learning* [Thorndike *et al.*,

'32]. These experiments tested also the power of a satisfier following upon the $S_4 \rightarrow R_d$ to strengthen it. They consequently justify
the expectation that rewarding good tendencies will strengthen
them regardless of the learner's knowledge about the tendency or
ability to identify, describe, or control it.

The matter is so important for the teaching of subtle attitudes,
interests, desires, and aversions that we have carried on two additional experiments (5 and 6), which may be called the 'Association' experiment and the 'Four Quadrants' experiment.

The 'Association' Experiment

In the former, the subject is instructed as follows:

"I shall say 'Ready' and then say a word. You will say the first
word or words that you think of. I will record the time in fifths of
a second. Then I will say another word. You will say the first
word or words that you think of. I will record the time as before.
We will continue this. At the end of the experiment, you will
receive a money bonus depending upon how quickly you respond
on the average. Also I shall say 'Right' if the word that you say
is one of ten or more that we have arbitrarily decided to call right
as responses to the word in question. I shall say 'Wrong' if the
word that you say is one of ten or more that we have arbitrarily
decided to call wrong as responses to the word in question. Sometimes I shall say nothing because the word that you say is in
neither our list of rights nor our list of wrongs for the word in
question. At the end of the experiment, you will receive a money
bonus depending on a system of credits for rights and penalties
for wrongs."

In all, 320 words or 640 words are then read to him, one
at a time. In each case if his response is clearly due to the
sequential connections used in speaking and writing (such as
*yours—truly, achieve—success, across—the street, absurd—
statement, up—stairs*), he is rewarded by the announcement of
"Right." If his response is clearly due to connections used in
getting the word's meaning (such as *yours—mine, achieve—get,
across—over, absurd—unreasonable, up—down*), he is punished
by the announcement of "Wrong." Thus for *adverb* any of the
following would be called right: *and, of, in, of time, of degree,
meaning, used, is, was, will be, that, which,* etc. Any of the following would be called wrong: *verb, adjective, noun, plainly,
slowly, quickly.* For *achieve* any of the following are right: *success,*

much, little, results, good, good success, more, what, what he desires, etc. Any of these would be called wrong: *win, accomplish, get, obtain, do.* For *across* the following are right: *the, the street, the river, the sea, oceans, deserts (person, child, boy, girl*—these being due to hearing *across* as *a cross*), etc. Any of these would be called wrong: *near, away, over, sideways, about, toward, over.* Further illustrations of words called "Right" and "Wrong" are given in Table 9.

If the experimenter cannot decide immediately which tendency is operating, no announcement is made. As was shown in *The Fundamentals of Learning* (p. 379) over 90 percent of the first words that come to mind in the free-association experiment are due to one or the other of these two tendencies. But the subject knows nothing about this.* If he thinks about the experiment at all, he probably thinks of it as a test of his sanity, complexes, interests, or speed of reaction, or he expects the same words to recur. If he did anything voluntarily, he might repeat to himself the stimulus word and his response in cases where he had it right. He has, however, little time to do this.

To prevent the subjects from inferring that opposites were always or nearly always wrong, certain opposites which might well come by the action of the tendency to operate the connections used in speaking and writing were always called right. Such were *far→near, true→false, good→bad, eat→drink, give→take, hand→ foot.* To make the administration of this rule easy, any response whatsoever to *far, true, good, eat,* etc., was called right. There were two such words in each forty.†

If the subject became aware of the principle according to which the rewards and punishments were allotted or of the two classes of connections, he would, after a little experimentation, change from a moderate percentage of successes to nearly 100 percent. If the subject gradually increases his percentage of responses that manifest the one tendency, it is evidence that that tendency is strengthened without his being aware that there is any such tendency.

The experiment is a good one because the rewarded tendency

---

* At the time of the experiments the book was still unpublished.

† In the case of the first fifteen of the subjects a different rule was used to the same end. One opposite out of each successive forty responses was arbitrarily called right.

and the punished tendency are real, are distinct, and are ready to act, though the subject is ignorant of their existence.

There is learning. The total number of right responses in the first ten was 80 and in the last ten, 204. In the first forty it was 358 and in the last forty, 720. Little, if any, of this learning can be ascribed to awareness of the distinction.

TABLE 9

Samples of responses probably due to these two types of connections and so treated in the experiment

Stimulus word	Responses, probably due to speech-writing connections, called "Right"	Responses, probably due to connections of meaning, called "Wrong"
among	bushes, friends, many, neighbors, others, people, the forest, them, the men, the people, those, us	amidst, between, in, together, with, within
balmy	air, breeze, day, evening, ocean, seas, summer, weather	airy, calm, clear, foolish, nice, rainy, soft, sweet, warm, wet
bargain	counter, house, on the table, sale, sales, with	cheap, contract, money, sell, trade
begin	here, life, now, over, saying, some, story, the day, the experiment, the lesson, the work, work	end, start
cheap	and not good, apples, furniture, goods, house, literature, wares, woman	bargain, dear, expensive, high, inexpensive, little, meager
decent	behavior, book, clothes, company, gentleman, girl, looking, man, person	clean, good, immodest, indecent, respectable, right, upright
defer	a little, business, our payment, payment, to	postpone, put off, stalling, wait
gift	of talk, to, to men	giver, present

The detailed individual records show that there was awareness of the general distinction in probably only one out of thirty-one subjects. Subject R did shift fairly suddenly from a mixture of connections of both sorts to nearly 100 percent of such sequential connections as are common in speech and writing. This subject had learned slowly and gradually as the others did during the first 120 responses, with scores of 0, 2, 0, 0, 2, 1, 3, 2, 3, 4, 4, 4. In the next ten she used eight speech-writing connections and in

TABLE

Number of responses attributable to the speech-writing

Group	A	B	C	E	F	G	H	I	J	K	L	M	N	O
I	4	1	6	3	2	1	7	4	3	0	0	2	2	1
II	7	4	7	9	4	1	6	5	2	1	4	2	1	3
III	7	0	10	6	4	1	9	6	0	0	2	0	0	1
IV	3	1	10	4	3	1	6	2	0	1	2	0	2	1
V	9	2	10	6	5	1	6	7	1	2	9	0	5	7
VI	8	3	10	7	6	0	1	4	5	1	10	0	6	7
VII	7	1	10	8	7	0	0	8	5	2	10	4	9	7
VIII	10	0	10	8	7	0	2	6	4	0	6	1	7	8
.	.	.	.	.	.	.	.	.	.	.	.	.	.	.
.	.	.	.	.	.	.	.	.	.	.	.	.	.	.
.	.	.	.	.	.	.	.	.	.	.	.	.	.	.
XXIII	9	1	10	6	4	1	10	7	10	2	9	5	7	4
XXIV	6	5	9	8	5	0	5	9	9	1	9	6	7	7
XXV	9	8	10	9	8	5	8	9	10	2	9	6	9	7
XXVI	7	4	10	3	5	3	6	5	8	0	8	9	5	7
XXVII	4	9	10	8	2	1	10	7	6	1	10	7	9	9
XXVIII	8	5	10	8	5	4	9	9	9	0	9	9	6	6
XXIX	9	2	10	10	7	7	7	10	9	3	9	9	9	8
XXX	10	5	10	10	8	2	8	9	10	1	9	10	9	7
First 80	55	12	73	51	38	5	37	42	20	7	43	9	32	35
Last 80	62	39	79	62	44	23	63	65	71	9	72	61	61	55

the next 10, nine. From then on, all but eight of her 260 responses can be attributed to speech-writing connections. The eight were *soft→hard, whistle→noise, fell→feather, adverb→adjective, darling→dear, immoral→bad, whiskey→ale,* and *simple→difficult.**

The learning was then, except possibly in R, not due to awareness of the distinction. Our next precaution must be to learn whether it was due in part to other sorts of awareness, such as notions that "of" is often right, "and" is often right, "it" is often right.

I have inspected all the responses made by all the individuals who showed the slightest evidence of such special conscious awareness. One subject did use *of* and *me* much more frequently in late than in early responses. But she did not shift suddenly, and such special insights cannot account for much over a third of her learn-

---

* It may be argued that even this subject was not clearly aware that any sequential speech or writing connection would be called right, since, if that were so, the connections should have been *soft → bed, whistle → loud, fell → down, darling → child,* or the like.

sort of connections in the first 8 tens and the last 8 tens

P	Q	R	S	T	U	V	W	X	Y	Z	AA	BB	CC	DD	EE	All
2	1	0	1	2	2	7	3	6	2	0	1	1	1	10	5	80
7	1	2	3	1	2	9	4	9	3	1	1	1	0	9	5	114
0	1	0	1	1	2	9	1	8	0	1	2	0	4	8	5	89
0	0	0	1	2	1	5	1	9	2	0	1	0	6	9	2	75
4	3	2	3	2	4	4	2	9	2	2	1	0	4	9	1	122
5	2	1	3	3	1	7	2	7	2	2	1	1	5	9	1	120
5	4	3	3	2	4	7	3	6	0	0	1	0	5	9	3	133
6	2	2	2	4	3	5	4	7	1	1	2	0	2	9	3	122
.	.	.	.	.	.	.	.	.	.	.	.	.	.	.	.	.
.	.	.	.	.	.	.	.	.	.	.	.	.	.	.	.	.
7	2	9	4	1	2	6	5	9	3	2	0	2	5	9	5	156
10	3	10	1	5	2	10	3	10	2	0	3	1	4	9	6	165
9	2	6	1	5	1	4	3	6	3	1	2	0	3	9	4	168
6	1	9	2	4	0	5	4	8	0	0	1	0	4	9	3	136
10	3	7	4	2	1	4	2	9	2	2	1	0	6	8	2	156
9	1	9	5	5	2	8	5	9	2	2	1	1	.3	10	5	174
8	2	9	2	5	1	9	10	10	1	0	2	0	4	9	5	186
10	6	10	5	7	3	10	10	10	0	2	1	0	5	10	7	204
29	14	10	17	17	19	53	20	61	12	7	10	3	27	72	25	855
69	20	69	24	34	12	56	42	71	13	9	11	4	34	73	37	1345

ing. For the subjects in general, the increased use of *and, of, to, me, up,* and the like was due to the same unconscious confirmation as the increased use of speech-writing connections in general.

Table 10 presents the results in early and late parts of the series for all subjects except D (who early formed the habit of very often responding by *and,* but who undoubtedly learned also, and unconsciously, to favor the speech-writing connections).*

The 'Four Quadrants' Experiment

The rewarded response in this experiment was to hit within a certain distance from a point *and also in a certain quadrant or direction from the point.* That is, a constant error of direction was rewarded, provided it was not too great in amount. The subjects knew nothing of this, thinking they were rewarded for general precision. The essentials of the apparatus and procedure were that the subject put his left forefinger on a point on the under surface

* For more detailed information see the article by E. L. Thorndike and R. T. Rock, Jr. ['34].

of a block, and then tried to put a pencil point on the corresponding point of its top surface (which was hidden from his vision by a screen).

A description of the conduct of the experiment together with the instructions to the subjects is given in Rock and Thorndike ['34]. Its plan and execution are due to R. T. Rock.

The learning is very variable among individuals and within the same individuals, as is shown by the detailed scores of Table 11. There can be no doubt, however, that the tendency to make a certain systematic error is in general strengthened. The average percentage of dots within the chosen quadrant rises from 24 to 48 from the first to the sixteenth fifty. They run in order, 24, 27, 35, 37, 39, 41, 39, 43, 41, 45, 44, 45, 44, 49, 47, and 48. There was no adequate evidence that a single subject of the thirty-four subjects discovered the system. There are sudden rises in the percentage of right responses, but there are equally sudden drops. At all events, we find learning still present if we omit the records of all individuals who might conceivably have learned by inferring the basis for the announcements of "Right." After omitting I. He. and A. Gr., the average percentages for the first and sixteenth fifties are 24 and 45.

The most likely explanation of the results in these experiments and in experiments 49 to 70 of *The Fundamentals of Learning* is that making $R_aR_bR_c$, etc., a response to the situation $S_1S_2S_3$, etc., and being satisfied as a consequence strengthens not only the connection $S_1S_2S_3{\rightarrow}R_aR_bR_c$, but also to some extent the connections $S_1S_2S_3{\rightarrow}R_a$, $S_1S_2S_3{\rightarrow}R_b$, $S_1S_2S_3{\rightarrow}R_c$, $S_1S_2{\rightarrow}R_a$, $S_1S_2{\rightarrow}R_b$, $S_1S_2{\rightarrow}R_c$, $S_1S_3{\rightarrow}R_a$, $S_1S_3{\rightarrow}R_b$, $S_1S_3{\rightarrow}R_c$, $S_2S_3{\rightarrow}R_a$, $S_2S_3{\rightarrow}R_b$, $S_2S_3{\rightarrow}R_c$, $S_1{\rightarrow}R_a$, $S_1{\rightarrow}R_b$, $S_1{\rightarrow}R_c$, $S_2{\rightarrow}R_a$, $S_2{\rightarrow}R_b$, $S_2{\rightarrow}R_c$, $S_3{\rightarrow}R_a$, $S_3{\rightarrow}R_b$, $S_3{\rightarrow}R_c$, $S_1{\rightarrow}R_aR_b$, $S_1{\rightarrow}R_aR_c$, $S_1{\rightarrow}R_bR_c$, $S_1{\rightarrow}R_aR_bR_c$, etc.

The satisfier may, in the subject's mind, belong only to $S_1{\rightarrow}R_a$ and still operate upon $S_2{\rightarrow}R_b$ or $S_3{\rightarrow}R_c$ or $S_4{\rightarrow}R_d$.

We may then expect that rewarding any tendency will have some chance of strengthening it, even when we cannot make the subjects aware of what the connection is that we are rewarding. For example, suppose that we wish to teach a person to like modest elegance without liking ostentatious display or to like classic simplicity without liking commonplace statements or to like sentiment but not sentimentality or to cultivate purity in

TABLE II

'FOUR QUADRANTS' EXPERIMENT

Number 'right' in each successive fifty trials for each individual

SERIES	INDI-VID-UAL	NUMBER OF DOTS IN A 2″ BY 2″ SQUARE FORMING ONE OF THE QUADRANTS ABOUT THE POINT AIMED AT, IN 16 SUCCESSIVE SETS OF 50 TRIALS															
		1	2	3	4	5	6	7	8	9	10	11	12	13	14	15	16
2	1	0	12	16	23	21	22	12	23	13	12	7	6	8	6	7	13
	2	0	0	0	4	1	2	1	0	0	0	0	5	0	0	0	0
	3	1	4	16	8	8	21	19	17	21	32	22	22	33	36	38	28
3	4	7	3	27	24	36	49	23	34	12	30	47	49	46	48	44	44
	5	29	24	28	20	41	30	27	34	38	26	31	39	34	36	31	23
	6	20	36	33	37	34	39	38	35	30	27	27	30	41	47	36	28
	7	27	32	31	31	39	28	20	34	26	28	16	25	29	37	33	32
	8	11	11	42	47	48	48	48	45	30	37	48	49	49	49	49	48
4	9	33	29	34	21	37	32	44	32	46	44	41	42	47	45	47	47
	10	0	11	26	31	20	7	24	22	11	22	20	12	12	16	12	9
	11	1	0	1	0	2	2	0	14	36	32	30	32	16	25	7	14
	12	3	4	2	3	10	14	8	8	14	8	5	1	4	2	2	0
5	13	43	41	38	45	40	40	37	40	46	41	41	39	33	30	25	29
	14	6	0	0	0	0	0	0	0	39	48	50	45	49	48	48	46
	15	14	7	13	29	24	17	22	15	38	43	49	41	42	34	41	41
	16	28	31	25	24	21	34	30	30	27	19	17	12	8	8	9	10
6	17	30	29	20	16	13	18	16	33	13	25	18	15	22	32	34	37
	18	1	0	4	6	8	11	6	1	4	3	9	6	6	21	20	38
	19	25	43	45	49	48	47	44	48	28	42	49	44	46	48	48	49
	20	3	8	30	39	35	37	34	35	18	36	31	34	19	5	22	11
	21	19	11	12	30	17	28	22	28	32	33	36	29	31	28	28	12
	22	8	12	7	11	15	14	23	30	22	29	17	32	17	14	28	34
	23	0	2	0	4	4	6	0	2	9	10	8	16	12	22	45	39
	24	24	22	28	32	39	37	43	40	37	49	39	38	38	44	44	39
	25	0	2	9	0	0	0	10	18	25	18	10	15	23	26	24	31
	26	0	3	2	6	12	12	14	14	0	0	3	5	6	5	8	2
	27	3	1	10	0	1	3	0	0	3	2	2	0	0	1	2	0
	28	20	14	28	13	16	15	16	12	2	1	8	1	3	0	3	1
	29	0	1	0	2	0	0	0	3	18	26	7	5	13	36	7	29
	30	19	28	21	24	25	32	32	28	7	14	22	39	45	44	39	40
	31	1	0	1	0	1	0	0	4	4	0	1	0	0	0	0	0
	32	9	12	18	11	12	17	11	16	19	31	25	36	14	40	16	21
	33	2	0	0	0	0	0	0	0	0	0	0	0	0	0	0	0
	34	13	20	28	41	29	36	43	43	26	20	8	8	0	8	5	12
Average		11.8	13.6	17.5	18.6	19.3	20.5	19.6	21.7	20.4	22.3	21.9	22.7	21.9	24.7	23.6	23.9
Percent		24	27	35	37	39	41	39	43	41	45	44	45	44	49	47	48

speech without purism or to be dignified without being cold, stilted, or pompous. It is difficult for him to identify the features to be liked in the first three cases, isolate them, and connect them with enjoyment. It is difficult for him to summon the responses to be made in the last two cases and connect them with the situations of communication and social intercourse. We may hope that arousing and rewarding any connection containing one of the desired tendencies as a component may strengthen the desired tendency.

We should, of course, make the situation identifiable and the response available when it is practicable to do so. Unconscious learning is relatively undependable and slow. But it is not mystical or fortuitous.

Chapter 6

THE INFLUENCE OF PUNISHMENTS

OUR discussion may best begin where a similar discussion in *The Fundamentals of Learning* left off. The conclusions there (p. 311 f.) were:

"First, a satisfying after-effect which belongs to a connection can be relied on to strengthen the connection.

"Second, an annoying after-effect under the same conditions has no such uniform weakening effect. In certain cases, known by general observation or displayed in experiments such as those of Hoge and Stocking and of Warden and Aylesworth, an annoying after-effect does weaken the tendency which produces it.

"Third, when it does so, its method of action is often, perhaps always, indirect. That is, the person or animal is led by the annoying after-effect to do something else to the situation which makes him later less likely to follow the original connection.

"Fourth, what he is led to do indirectly is often (1) either to make a native or acquired response to the particular annoyance in question (as when he responds to annoyance at a certain place by leaving that place, or to annoyance by a certain object by avoiding that object, or to annoyance in the mouth by spitting out the mouth's contents) or (2) to have an idea or other awareness of the undesirability of such and such behavior (as when he responds to a 'Wrong' heard after saying that 9 × 8 are 78 by thinking '78 is not good to say for 9 × 8').

"Fifth, what an animal is led to do directly by an annoyer need not make him later less likely to follow the original connection. For example, let an animal that has learned to choose exit A rather than B or C or D from a certain pen nine times out of ten because A has meant rest and food whereas B, C, and D have meant only rest, be given, the next time it enters B, a violent electric shock, producing a panic of agitation and terror. Then in later trials the animal may be so agitated and panic-stricken when put in the pen that it is as likely to go to exit B as to exit A, increasing the frequency of that error from 0.10 to 0.25.

"The influence upon learning of both satisfiers and annoyers depends upon what they cause the animal to be or do. A satisfier which is attached to a modifiable connection always, or almost always, causes the animal to be or do something which strengthens the connection to which the satisfier is attached; but we do not know what this something is. It may be to maintain relatively undisturbed the physiological basis of the connection; it may be to retain it longer than would otherwise be the case; it may be to confine it by some metabolic effect; it may be to alter it in some more mysterious way.* An annoyer which is attached to a modifiable connection may cause the animal to feel fear or chagrin, jump back, run away, wince, cry, perform the same act as before but more vigorously, or whatever else is in his repertory as a response to that annoyer in that situation. But there is no evidence that it takes away strength from the physiological basis of the connection in any way comparable to the way in which a satisfying after-effect adds strength to it."

Since this summary was written, experiments by Lorge, Tuckman, Stephens, Rock, and the writer have provided facts which may be summarized as follows:

In multiple-choice learning by human subjects where the situation vanishes immediately after the choice, is replaced by another, and recurs only after interval of 50 to 200 sec. filled by other (usually thirty-nine) situations and responses, a connection 'punished' by the announcement of "Wrong," or "Wrong" plus one or more electric shocks, or "Wrong" plus a money fine, is (practically without exception) strengthened by the occurrence in spite of the annoying after-effect. The subject who has to learn to connect each of a list of words with a number from 1 to 4 or 1 to 5 or 1 to 6 or 1 to 10 and says "3" for a certain word and is told "Wrong" and shocked, is actually more likely to say "3" for that word when it recurs than he would otherwise have been† [Lorge,

---

* The satisfying after-effect obviously often causes the animal then and there to continue or repeat the connection. But this influence *via* immediate continuation or repetition is different from that with which we have been concerned.

† For example in an experiment of Tuckman ['33] in which mere chance would give a probability of 0.250 that the connection operative in any trial would be repeated in the next trial, we have the following percentages of repetition for connections punished by the announcement "Wrong" and a fine of 0.4 of a cent. The subjects were 100 boys.

Occurring once, 34 percent recurred in the next trial
Occurring twice in succession, 45 percent recurred in the next trial
Occurring three times in succession, 48 percent recurred in the next trial

The punishment being the announcement "Wrong" and four electric shocks, the percentages of repetition in the cases of ninety-six boys were:

'33a and '33b; Thorndike, '33; Thorndike and others, '33; Lorge and Thorndike, '33; Tuckman, '33; Rock (as yet unpublished)].

If, in such experiments, some connections are followed by no announcement of "Right" or "Wrong" and by no payment or fine or shock, but only by a click or other signal which is neutral as to satisfaction versus annoyance and adds no information, these connections are strengthened much less than rewarded connections and but little more than punished connections. [Lorge and Thorndike, '33; Stephens (as yet unpublished).]

Rexroad ['26] used multiple-choice learning with five possible responses. He used only five situations (colored lights) each of which continued until the right connection occurred. Then another of the five situations appeared. After as many rounds of trials as were made in two and a half minutes, there was a rest of one minute and a new response was called right for each of the five colors. The learner had thus to form new habits against possible interference from the old. After two and a half minutes of work with this learning and another rest of one minute, there was a new shift making a still different response right for each of the five colors. And so on. In some of these two-and-a-half minute learning periods, the wrong responses were punished by an electric shock, in another series they were not. The average number of correct responses and the average number of wrong responses were as follows for the first half-minute and last half-minute of the punished and unpunished series:

	First ½ Min.	*Last* ½ Min.	
Correct, shock series....	13.94	20.58	Gain in correct, 6.64
Correct, no shock series.	13.68	20,27	Gain in correct, 6.59
Errors, shock series.....	12.07	4.89	Drop in errors, 7.18
Errors, no shock series..	12.86	6.08	Drop in errors, 6.78

There is thus probably a slightly more rapid learning with punishment than without it.

Bunch ['28] and also Vaughn and Diserens ['30] found a gain

Occurring once, 32 percent recurred in the next trial
Occurring twice in succession, 41 percent recurred in the next trial
Occurring three times in succession, 42 percent recurred in the next trial

Occurrence plus punishment is harmful and the more frequent it is, the more harm is done.

from using moderate or slight shocks in human maze-learning, but since there were only two choices at each point of learning, so that the absence of a punishment may act as a reward, and since punishment for going into an alley caused the response of going out from it, their findings are not evidence concerning the potency of punishment *per se*. They may be evidence of the potency of reward, or rather of the potency of two rewards, namely, absence of a shock when entering a right alley and relief from shock when backing out from a wrong alley.

Valentine ['30] found a gain from using shock with rats in maze-learning. But for the reasons stated above her results may be and probably are measures of the potency of reward rather than of punishment.

The greater strengthening of the connections with neutral after-effects may be explained by the hypothesis (a very likely one) that the neutral after-effect permitted an occasional confirming reaction, whereas punishment never did.

In all these experiments, useful learning occurs almost or quite exclusively by the strengthening of certain connections by satisfying after-effects. Indeed, wrong choices on the whole do more harm by occurring than punishing them repairs.

If the situations had not vanished and if the subjects had been permitted then and there to try another response after the failure of their first one (or first two, or first three, etc.), guided by their memory that such and such choices made a few seconds ago had been punished, these human subjects would presumably have profited more (or suffered less) from the punishment. Its informative value would have established ideas leading them to repeat the same wrong choice less often than they otherwise would have done, not more often as in the experiments with vanishing of the situation. It would also have led them to form then and there the habit of turning to a different choice.

With chicks, however, although the situation persists, or reappears after only thirty seconds (spent in solitary confinement without the insertion of interfering situations), the punishment of a connection by solitary confinement or by thwarting of a tendency to go through a certain hole does not weaken it. Freedom, food, and society as an after-effect strengthens connections notably, but the annoying after-effect just described has zero influence, in the results of some thousands of observations [Thorndike, '32]. The chicks apparently lack the capacities needed to get and use ideas of the connections and of their consequences. The informative value of the after-effects is consequently nil or nearly nil; and the direct strengthening of the connections by the rewards is not paralleled by any direct weakening by the punishments.

On the whole, it now seems certain that annoying after-effects influence behavior only in specialized ways. Whereas attaining what satisfies an active want directly strengthens any connection which the attainment follows and to which it belongs, failure to attain such satisfaction or the occurrence of something definitely annoying certainly does not weaken the corresponding "punished" connection directly. Nor does it do so by strengthening whatever connections other than the punished connection are capable of being made under the conditions effective at that time. An annoying after-effect simply makes the animal do what is in his repertory as a consequence of that particular annoyance in those conditions. This may be useful, as in retreat from a blind alley which thwarts, or avoidance of an object which shocks or burns, or spitting out what tastes nasty. It may be of zero or nearly zero value, as in sulking at failure or crying at a shock. It may be actually harmful, as in paralysis, negativism, or extreme terror.

The utility of an annoying state of affairs may be by causing the animal to do something useful in the premises, as when confinement evokes struggles to escape. It may be by counteracting a satisfying after-effect of undesirable behavior and so reducing the net total after-effect to zero or to annoyingness, as when a child who grabs another's toy has the satisfaction of success and possession counterbalanced by the pain of being spanked and deprived of the toy. Roughly speaking, the former sort of utility is predominant in learning matters of intellect and skill, and the latter in matters of moral conduct.

If the person or animal has the capacity to get and make use of the information that such and such responses to such and such situations produce such and such consequences, an annoying after-effect is potentially useful as a giver and impresser of information, but this informative value may bear little relation to the amount of annoyance. A mere "Wrong" after $3 \times 9 = 28$ may be as useful in teaching a child that $3 \times 9 = 27$ as a severe beating; and when he has learned that $3 \times 9 = 27$ he may be no more likely to revert to $3 \times 9 = 28$ if it once produced the gentle annoyance than if it once produced the severe beating. Doubtless the latter will be more memorable, but memories of the tragic consequences of an error concerning 3×9 may not recall what the error was, much less what the right connection was. Inducing the child to think $3 \times 9 = 27$ and rewarding that connection will be at least as good informatively and much better for learning as a whole.

It would be useful to have an inventory of the commonest annoyers, and of their results, temporary and lasting, on the strands of behavior along with which the annoyer occurs and on the subject's total nature or personality, for persons of both sexes, various ages, and various sorts of mentality. Such an inventory would aid us in choosing annoyers as incitements to change a connection to one more suitable or as counterbalances to the satisfying after-effect of an undesirable connection.

As a provisional beginning of such an inventory, I suggest the list shown below. It is neither logical nor biological, but it does cover the common annoyers in a way convenient for memory and discussion.

A. Injuries to the body
B. Diseases and imperfect functioning of bodily organs (including excessive stimulation of any sense organ)
C. Work without rest
D. Certain sensory stimuli, such as bitter tastes
E. Deprivations of:
    1. Food.
    2. Water
    3. Movement
    4. Sleep
    5. Society
    6. Attention
    7. Affection
    8. Sex activity
    9. Parental activity
F. Thwartings of any purpose
G. Social treatment by:
    1. Dislike, enmity, hate
    2. Disapproval, scorn, derision
    3. Aversion, repugnance, loathing
    4. Domination, bullying
H. Conditions, variously caused, of:
    1. Fear, dread, anxiety
    2. Disgust or repugnance

3. Shame
4. Inferiority
5. Sadness
6. Irritation
7. General ill-being

It is obvious that the influence of many annoyers varies greatly amongst individuals in the immediate reaction produced and in the wider and more lasting effect on the person. But the nature of these differences is not well enough known to justify an attempt to describe them here. I will only give two illustrations.

Suppose that we have chambers built with four slits all of the same size, but identifiable by their positions and marks of one sort or another. Each of them is wide enough for the animal in question (chick, child of three, man) to insert his head, but not to pass his body through. All but one are backed by an immovable wall. One (call it slit C) has in place of the wall a perfect imitation of it (to vision) which will easily give way if the chick, child, or man pushes against it vigorously. Beyond the wall are freedom, food, and other chicks, children, or men. The animal is put in the chamber when in a state such that solitary confinement there without food will annoy him and freedom, food, and society will satisfy him.

Consider the result when connection is made with the act of trying to push through slit A (or B or D), the connection being followed by thwarting of the effort and continuance of S. The influence on the chick will be substantially zero. If it ever learns to escape from S, it will learn because, in the chance up-and-down in strength of the tendencies to try to push through slit A, slit B, slit C, slit D, etc., the tendency to push through C becomes temporarily the strongest. The thwarting in and of itself will not weaken S$\rightarrow$ push at A (or B or D). It may evoke harder pushes, irritation, and peeping. The child may be moved by the thwarting to harder pushing, angry behavior, kicks at the wall, screams, and the like. A specially intelligent one may be moved to try the other slits in order. A specially hysterical one may be prejudiced against slits for a long time. The man presumably will try the other slits. But he will probably have a modicum of anger or irritation at each failure. Only in so far as the punishment leads child or man to try sooner or later slit C will it benefit the special learning. It may have a share in teaching general lessons of considering all possibilities, of the possible differences among things that look alike, etc.

Compare next the results of food swung down behind in easy reach when the face enters slit C versus a blow on the face when it enters slits A, B, D, etc. The influence of the food will be much the same as that of escape. But the blow will probably cause surprise, retreat, and fear behavior in the chick and in timid children, and surprise, temporary or partial retreat, and angry behavior in the man or in an aggressive child. A psychologist employing this experiment with certain subjects would find the bar that delivered the blow torn from its fastenings. The retreat will be beneficial if it is attached to slit A, B, D, etc., and not to all the slits, the tendency to pull the head out of A indirectly weakens the tendency to put the head in at A. The value of the fear and anger for the immediate task at hand is probably negative. For the general task of life it is also probably negative, fear and anger being inappropriate responses to most of the mechanical contrivances of civilization.

The best results are obtained from punishments when the annoying state of affairs then and there causes or encourages or at least permits the animal to operate a right connection and receive satisfaction therefor. So in the experiments of Warden and Aylesworth the annoyance of receiving a shock in the wrong alley may provoke the animal to run back out of it and enter the right alley. So in *Umweg* experiments the annoyance of being thwarted in efforts to go through an obstacle may provoke the profitable response of running around it. So if a child after being punished by a "Wrong" for spelling *red* "r-e-d-e," may be led to try "r-e-d" and win success. So a player whose shots fall short may be led by the failure plus the special information to use more force and get the satisfaction of hitting the mark.

In much learning in which the annoyingness due to a certain connection causes the person to change to a more successful connection, there is an element of special information besides the information that the first connection had bad results. Thus, in the simplest case of all, if there are only two responses possible, one learns from the failure of one that the other is right. One often learns something about the direction and magnitude of one's error, which gives his next trial a greater probability of success.

In all cases the benefit of the punishment lies in its power to provoke a change to or toward the desired behavior. I venture the prediction that with sufficient ingenuity ways can usually be found to evoke the desired behavior more directly and economically.

There are two cases of the use of punishment which are so common as to deserve special discussion. In the first the punishment is simply the failure to attain a want, occurring typically in learning by trial and error (better named learning by trial and success). In the second the punishment acts by associating fear, repulsion, shame, or some other strong negative attitude with certain responses to certain situations.

As things now are, an enormous amount of learning in homes, schools, and shops consists in doing one thing after another with some guidance from physical circumstances, models, explanations, and directions. Each item is a case of multiple-choice learning with usually very many possible choices. The learning progresses by the selection of the connections which have satisfying after-effects. The connections which fail to do so may vary from neutrality to a very annoying degree of failure and frustration and may have various punishments *ab extra* attached to them in the form of disapproval, ridicule, physical pain, etc. The child flounders in this way and that until he learns to swim. The scholar makes this, that, and the other sound until he attains a tolerable pronunciation of the French *u*. The writer does this and that to his essay or story until it seems fit. All is largely on the basis of "Try, try again," with expectation that out of the welter of wrongs and rights improvement will somehow manifest itself. Improvement will come from the rights if they are rewarded, but the less confidence we put in the utility of the wrongs the wiser we shall be in most cases.

Teachers have sought to reduce the waste from the "Try, try again" procedure, but they have too often tried to cure it by some doctrinaire method or one-sided set of exercises based on erroneous psychology. One after another of such methods is tried and found little or no better than the haphazard self-education it was supposed to eliminate. What is needed is a method which will get learners to make the right connections and be satisfied thereby with a minimum of practice in error and with due regard for other educational desiderata.

The most striking case of the use of punishment is our second case where a certain response to a certain situation is punished by pain, ignominy, ridicule, or some other consequence which attaches a potent negative tendency to that connection. If the situation recurs, the idea of making that response or the impulse to make it then tends to arouse a memory of the punishment and fear, repulsion, or shame. This is relieved by making no response to the situation (more properly speaking, by responding to it by neglect) or by making a response that is or seems opposite to the original punished response. Whatever the original attractiveness was in the punished behavior, it is submerged or neutralized by the unattractive prospect of a repetition of the punishment.

A very important variant of it, much used in schools and industry, is the one in which the failure to make a certain response to a certain situation or to attain a certain status is punished. Unless a child knows his lesson he is beaten. Unless the slave does his work he is not fed. In such cases the person concerned may well have a pronounced satisfaction at learning his lesson or doing his work. The absence of the punishment may be psychologically as positive a reward as words of praise or a money payment. When anything but a certain specified behavior is punished, that behavior is in a true and important sense rewarded.

Punishment by pain, blame, disgrace, ridicule, etc., is an almost universal feature of most human societies, and perhaps of many animal groups. It has been a pillar in family life, was until recently the corner-stone of school discipline and industrial management, permeates law and penology, and is essential to most religions. It deserves study in all its aspects, including its origin (of which vengeance is only a minor fraction), its kinship with other social consequences of behavior, its theoretical justifications, and its obvious misuses. We shall return to a consideration of it after the general facts concerning the operation of ideas of after-effects have been presented.

Chapter 7

THE DYNAMICS OF IDEAS OF SITUATIONS, OF RESPONSES, AND OF AFTER-EFFECTS

IT is natural to assume that the idea of an act plus the ability to perform it plus the will or desire to perform it will produce it. Psychologists, like ordinary folk, have usually accepted this apparent induction from the observation of human behavior. Their modifications of it have been chiefly to note that the will or desire to perform it may be absent, the mere idea of an act that is within a person's repertory being often adequate to produce it. It is also natural to assume that the idea of an act plus the idea of desirable consequences attached to it will be potent to produce it, if it is within one's repertory. The idea of desirable consequences attached to it will, it is assumed, arouse desire to perform it or incline the person toward it in other ways.

So long as we are sufficiently liberal in our definition of "idea of an act" and "idea of desirable consequences," and so long as we restrict our field of observation to the sophisticated behavior of man, these assumptions work fairly well. I have ideas of drinking a glass of water, reading a certain book, taking off my coat, turning on the electric fan, etc., etc., and ideas of the satisfying consequences of so doing, and do so, all as per the doctrine. Yet the doctrine is fundamentally unsound. Unless we mean by the "idea of an act" an idea that will produce that act if not prevented from doing so by some contrary force, the idea of an act will no more produce it than the idea of an earthquake will produce it. Ideas do not produce acts which they are ideas of (in the sense of "images of" or "representatives of" or "mental parallels of" or "equivalents of") by any features whatsoever of their internal constitution. Ideas produce acts which they—or parts of them or wholes containing them—or states of mind like them have produced, not acts which they picture or resemble. Their productive power lies in the connections leading from them, not in some sympathetic magic of the mind.*

Ideas of desirable consequences by the same token are impotent save by the connections which they make. Let the reader summon and contemplate the fame and enhanced self-respect that would accrue if he should write a dozen sonnets surpassing Shakspere's and Milton's. Let him picture the joy of his friends, listen to the praises of reviewers, and smell the incense of collegians and literary clubs. Yet he will not move his hand an inch toward his pen or his mind one iota toward poetic creation unless these daydreams, or some fraction or compound of their neural equivalents, have connections leading toward such acts. We must not be deceived into the fallacy that because certain ideas in the ordinary course of life often evoke certain behavior, the inner constitution of an idea determines what behavior it will evoke. On the contrary, its dynamic power depends upon the past dynamic history of it and other things like it.

It may be objected that this puts an intolerable burden upon the sciences of man. Instead of the relatively easy task of inventorying a man's ideas of what is desirable, it compels science to inventory also the habits and tendencies (that is, the connections) associated therewith. Instead of a relatively simple apparatus of calling up ideas of acts and adding to (or subtracting from) their

---

* This seems to be the view of Hull, who writes, for instance ['33, p. 397]: ". . . A true suggestion response is one in which the subject's own symbolic processes, instead of becoming active either in facilitating or in resisting the tendency to action naturally arising from the experimenter's words, remain passive so far as the particular act suggested is concerned. It seems reasonable to assume that this passivity is facilitated by the suggestions usually given for the subject to relax and not to think of anything but sleep. This withdrawal of the subject's symbolic activities would naturally leave his muscles relatively susceptible to the symbolic stimulation emanating continuously from the experimenter.

. . . .

"A continuous stimulation by words associated with a particular act will bring about the act, whether these words are those of the subject himself or of some other person.

. . . .

"According to the present hypothesis, the physical substance of an idea is a symbolic or pure-stimulus act. The proprioceptive stimuli arising from such acts, usually spoken words, are assumed when combined in certain patterns to have acquired during the previous history of the subject, through the process of association or conditioning, the capacity to evoke the reactions of which they are the names."

potency by attaching ideas of desirable (or undesirable) consequences to these ideas of acts, there is required an apparatus of
millions of connections coöperating and competing in millions and
millions of combinations. This may be objectionable to a logical
mind, but it is not intolerable to the brain. On the contrary, it is
precisely what the brain seems' capable of and useful for. In any
case, the sciences of man must deal with man as he is, not as he
has been supposed by erroneous popular observation to be.

We have then to study the history—that is, the development—
of ideas, whether of consequences or of anything else, and the
connections they have acquired in order to understand their
powers.

When a situation evokes a response and an after-effect with
ordinary conditions of belonging and relevance, this event leaves,
or tends to leave, certain traces, disposition, residua, relics, or
whatever one chooses to call them. Lacking any knowledge of the
physiology, biophysics, or biochemistry of these relics, we shall
study only their results in behavior.

These may include, besides the strengthening of connections so
often mentioned, expectations, images, memories, and judgments
or unnamed tendencies comparable to expectations, images, memories, and judgments. Thus if the situation (S) of being in a
certain place evokes the act of opening a certain door (R), with
the after-effect (E) of obtaining a banana enough times, there
may result not only a strengthening of the real S to evoke the
real R, but also tendencies as follows:

A. (1) For the real S to evoke an expectation of R
   (2) For the real S to evoke an image of R
   (3) For the real S to evoke a memory that R occurred after
       that S
   (4) For the real S to evoke a judgment that R occurred or
       that R is likely to occur after that S

B. For the real S in connection with the real R to evoke (1) an
   expectation of E, (2) an image of E, (3) a memory that E
   was a consequence of R or of S→R, or (4) a judgment that E
   was or might be a consequence of R or of S→R

C. and D. (1) For the real R alone or the real S alone to evoke
          an expectation, image, etc., of E
   a. (2) For an image or idea of S to evoke an image of R
      (3) For an image or idea of S to evoke a memory that R
          occurred

(4) For an image or idea of S to evoke a judgment that R occurred or is likely to occur after S

b. (2, 3, 4) For an image or idea of S evoking R to evoke an image of E, or memory that E occurred after S→R or judgment that E occurred or is likely to occur after S→R

c and d. For an image or idea of S alone or of R alone to evoke an image, memory, etc., of E

There are still other tendencies left as relics of the event S→R producing E, but instead of exhausting these, we may best return to the history of the simplest developments. These are, first, to leave no relic at all save the change in the S→R strength and, second, to leave only an embryonic sort of expectation shown by disturbances of one or another sort when S→R does not produce its normal E. The first event or something approximating it seems to occur in much of the learning of the lower animals and infants and in some of the learning of motor skills by older children and adults. Roberts' rats, for example, learned to hit a suspended stick (after which behavior he immediately opened a door for them) when put into a certain enclosure, in the sense that they did so in a far shorter time than originally and in a few seconds after being put in the enclosure, but they did not give evidence that the training had produced any tendencies for being in the enclosure to arouse any ideas of hitting the stick or for hitting the stick to arouse any expectation that the door would open or that they would escape from the enclosure. A swimmer or tennis-player may make some of his responses without any ideas of what he is going to do or expectations of what will be the result.

The second event occurs widely in animal learning and in the comparable trial-and-success motor learning of man. The animal gives evidence by signs of 'surprise' or 'disappointment' (when the banana of our illustration is replaced by a stone, spinach, or nothing) that he had expectations at least to the extent of readiness to deal with the normal E. A tennis-player may have no ideas of what his stroke will produce and still be set to certain readinesses, so that he will be upset if, for example, the racket should be pulled out of his hand, or if the ball should assume ten times its normal weight or vanish into thin air when he hit it.

The case of S→R leaving as a relic a tendency for S to arouse not only R but an accessory expectation of R or readiness for R is somewhat different. So far as I am aware, there are no observations of what happens when, by some disease or accident, an S evokes something other than its habitual R, all other things being equal. The after-effects usually change also. It seems highly probable that if a chick seeing a worm on the ground should jump into the air and then find the worm in its mouth as it would have been had the chick snapped it up, the chick would still be somewhat disturbed in its mind. But perhaps it would leave this substitution of an irregular R unnoticed. Let us therefore restrict the argument for the present to expectations of after-effects.

Expectations of After-Effect

If S→R resulting in E can produce as an accessory a tendency of S→R to arouse an expectation of E, there should be no difficulty for an animal that has images to have an image of E (a banana, for example) as part of the expectation. There should be no difficulty for an animal that has memories of events to have a memory that E occurred (that he got a banana) after S→R as part of the expectation, nor for an animal that has language and makes judgments to have a verbal judgment that E is likely to result from S→R as a part of the expectation. These developments will be natural consequences of the general developments in question.

Whatever be the detailed nature of his expectation, its potency will depend on its connections, and our main problem is to observe or infer what the expectation that E will occur will connect with and tend to evoke as a result of its occurrence, after, or along with, the real S→R. We have no sure evidence from animal observations that it tends to evoke anything, except perhaps an acceptance and toleration of R as a response to S, and a certain peace, equilibrium, or maintenance of the status quo when E is a satisfier. Violating or thwarting or non-fulfilment of it tends to evoke behavior described anthropomorphically as irritated, disappointed, vexed, or angry. Popular observations suggest that expectation of an annoying E tends to evoke behavior of escape and avoidance.

A priori one would infer that expectation of a satisfying E would, by being a part of a total process that evokes the confirming reaction, acquire power to evoke it, and reports from human subjects indicate that it does. The facts of animal behavior are in harmony with this. By similar reasoning the expectation of an annoying E would acquire power to evoke whatever behavior the total process containing that expectation had evoked.*

If the expectations of satisfying after-effects E_1, E_2, E_3, . . . E_n have in each case acquired power to evoke the confirming reaction, there may be built up a tendency for the expectation of the common element of these E's, satisfyingness in general, to evoke the confirming reaction.

If then any form of expectation of any satisfying after-effect is attached to any connection, it may strengthen that connection as truly as the real after-effect would.

Ideas of Situations

Consider now how relics of experiences of situations acquire power to influence connections with behavior. Consider a real situation S with a strong connection with a real response R, the occurrence of R being prevented and S never reappearing, but in its stead and after a time, some part of S, or precursor of S. Under

* There is no common consequence of the total behavior which includes an expectation of an annoying E comparable to the confirming reaction in the case of behavior including an expectation of a satisfying E. The annoying after-effect (and so later and indirectly the total event leading to and including it) may arouse retreat, fear, repulsion, anger, struggling, blows, tears, wails, shame, chagrin, the repetition of the very responses producing it (often in more violent form), or whatever else inherited and acquired tendencies have associated with that after-effect, or possibly with annoyances or unpleasantnesses in general. Any behavior which relieves the annoyance will tend to be favored in later experiences. As the expectation of the annoying E develops, the situation will tend to form connections which abolish or prevent the annoying E, so that the expectation of E may be modified by the new expectation that doing so and so will prevent E.

In particular the expectation that a certain response will produce an annoying E may lead the person then and there to avoid that response and to seek for some other, since those are common and often beneficial outcomes of total events containing an expectation of an annoying E.

Often, however, nothing within the person's repertory can abolish the after-effect, and continued experiences leave as their commonest element of response to it a sullen misery, sense of impotence, panic fear, violent resentment, or the like.

The result of these and other facts is that what any given expectation of an annoying after-effect will evoke in the case of any given person is very hard to prophesy. Did the reader's expectation of a visit to the dentist (in the old days when dentistry was really painful) make him nervous or angry or frightened or cause him to invent reasons for postponement? How do a teacher's threats influence the various children in the class? There is a predominance of avoiding and rejecting behavior, but with a bewildering variety of other acts and feelings.

certain conditions, in man and in some of the lower animals, the part of S or precursor of S will then evoke R though it would not have done anything of the sort except for the earlier occurrence of S. Thus a monkey sees food put in a certain can, is strongly moved to obtain what he has seen go into that can, and is prevented from doing so by being removed. When later he is brought back, he goes to the can and looks for the food. His second presence in the room in sight of the can is the part of the earlier S or precursor of the earlier S. It operates by evoking some relic of S, some expectation or image or idea or representation or meaning corresponding to *food in the can,* which endows the part or precursor with a tendency it would not have had otherwise. Such a case differs from the expectation of after-effects discussed above, because there has been no real after-effect. A relic, not of an earlier after-effect, but of an earlier situation, determines response.

What now does such a relic of a situation have power to evoke? In the case of the delayed-reaction phenomena, when the animal is left to its own devices, it often evokes the continuance of the posture (and probably of the inner attitude) of readiness to make to the remaining part of the situation the response which the real situation would evoke. If the animal is removed from the part of the situation or if it is removed from his field of awareness, the relic may cause for a while behavior indicative of irritation or impulses to seek the attractive lost situation, and then nothing overt until the real part or precursor of the real situation appears again, when the relic of the past experience acts to give that part or precursor a power it would otherwise not have had.

What it would evoke if it occurred by itself alone in the mind of a rat or monkey, I do not know. It very probably does not occur there alone as a free image or memory.

In a man, such a relic of a situation, if it occurs alone, will evoke whatever it or some part of it or some total containing it or something like it (that is, some total containing part of it) has evoked. It may float through his mind in a dream and evoke only momentary contemplation. It may 'seek expression' in words, as "food in the red can." It may suggest ideas about the contents of the big green can and the little shiny can, or about bananas in boxes or bananas in fruit-stands. It may help determine the plan for breakfast, or it may rouse a clean-up of all receptacles in the house. Even in man its best-known activity is to coöperate with the precursor or part of the real situation when that occurs.

But in human behavior the relic, especially in the form of a memory or judgment, enters the stream of inner ideational life and planning as well as the stream of more direct responses to external situations. Any thinking about that banana or that can or bananas in cans is likely to evoke the memory or judgment that So-and-so put a banana in a can or the partial form that a banana was put in that can or the mutilated form that somebody put something in that can or the very attenuated form that something happened about that can. Indirectly by its action on the stream of thought it may react upon the stream of responses to external situations in multifarious ways.

It should be noted that in all these phenomena such imaginal or representational relics of after-effects or of situations do not operate by being confused with the occurrence of the real after-effect or situation. The rat does not try to enter the expectation of a food-box; the monkey does not during the period of delay chew at the imaginal relic of the banana. The relic of a situation does not itself arouse the response which the real situation would arouse. It causes some real situation to do so (ordinarily some real situation which was a part of or precursor of the real situation). The relic of a satisfier does not arouse the confirming reaction because the person's brain mistakes it for the real satisfier but because the relic is part of a total condition which arouses the confirming reaction.

There may be exceptions to this. The first experiments to show the existence of "free ideas," from which the work of Hunter and others on the delayed reaction developed, may seem to be an exception. In them, a signal was given, then after ten seconds a situation was presented (approach of the experimenter with food) to which the cats' response was climbing up the wire front of the cage. After a sufficient number of occurrences, the animals climbed up the cage or went to a certain spot on the floor at the signal or before the approach. One simple interpretation would be that the oft-repeated sequence *signal—ten seconds of life* (often spent in close observation of the experimenter)—*approach—climbing up—receiving a bit of meat or fish* caused the signal to evoke a relic of the approach in imaginal form which the animal mistook for the real approach and responded to just as it did to the real approach.

I think, however, that the animals did not mistake the relic for the real situation, and I am sure that they did not respond to it in just the same way. In man surely the action of such relics is very rarely as illusions, and the few exceptions to the description of the preceding paragraph are such as prove it to be the normal procedure.

Ideas of Responses

Some responses have little or no ideational representation. The reader probably cannot imagine a lengthened pulse rate or the movements of his eyes in reading or how it feels to write his name. A response may be made thousands of times but leave no relic save a readiness to be made under similar circumstances. Emotional responses often thus lack imaginal parallels.

Two classes of responses in man, however, are usually widely supplied with ideational parallels. These are responses in the form of *do one thing or another until result X is attained* and verbal responses. For the former the inner content that parallels and identifies the responses is, or at least includes, an image or idea of the result. For the latter there is a variety of parallels, ranging from the actual response mutilated only by the absence of actual voicing (and other abbreviated and slurred forms of soundless speech) to kinesthetic and auditory images of words, and perhaps to imageless thoughts of words.

The events of life provide many of these ideas (of action till X is attained and of saying words) with power to evoke the responses in question. For the events of life establish connections, often very strong ones, leading from these ideas to the responses which they are ideas of. When for example a child of two responds to food by putting it in his mouth and has, as a part of the total event, the idea of *doing one thing or another until the food is in my mouth,* he is connecting the response not only to the sight of that food but also to that idea. The idea thereby acquires power to evoke it. Also in many commands, directions, and recommendations, some verbal description of a response evokes an idea of it and then its actual occurrence, as when a child hears "Put your hat on your head" and is induced to do so. In the case of words, practice at making sounds like those one hears, repeating heard words in inner speech, saying aloud or in inner speech the words one sees in books, thinking of what one is to say before saying it, finding words to express facts and then uttering them, and the like connect ideas of words with saying them aloud or to oneself. Moreover, one of the commonest forms of an 'idea of' a verbal response is merely that response shorn of voicing and of some other features. Inner speech of this sort (not kinesthetic images of words) of course easily evokes its normal accompaniments and becomes actual speech.

It is this elaborate provision by the experiences of life of bonds linking ideas of attaining results and ideas of words as causes to the actual responses of attaining the results and saying the words that tempts one to think that the idea of any response tends to produce it by some general power.

In respect of evoking ideas, a real situation and an idea that represents or means that situation to the person can substitute the one for the other. If hearing "yours" makes him think of "truly," or "mine," thinking of "yours" may do the same; if thinking of "good" makes him think of "morning" or "bad," actually seeing or hearing "good" may do the same. In respect of evoking acts and feelings this is not the rule, and it happens rarely and for special reasons. The idea of an apple and a real apple may evoke the idea of a tree equally well, but the idea of an apple will not evoke the desire or the grasping and eating which the real apple evokes.

The first of these propositions is not self-evident, though probably no psychologist would dispute it. Perhaps a qualifying *usually* should be inserted between "can" and "substitute." I shall not try to justify it here nor to state in detail what the conditions are which cause a real situation to evoke an idea which has been evoked only by the idea of it, nor those which cause an idea to evoke an idea which has been evoked only by the real situation. One main condition is that the brain process which corresponds to the percept *via* which the real situation has its connective potency and the brain process which corresponds to the relic or image or memory are alike. Another is that the same experiences which give verbal ideas their meanings give situations the power to evoke the verbal ideas corresponding to them.

Ideas of After-Effects

Ideas of after-effects have two sorts of potency. In the special form which includes expectation that the after-effect will occur they have power to arouse whatever behavior original nature and past experience have associated with that expectation, as described in the earlier pages of the chapter. In the form of mere ideas of the satisfying or annoying state of affairs such as a gustatory image of a sweet taste or a day-dream of receiving a million-dollar legacy or a memory of the fact that one had a severe headache, ideas of after-effects have only the power to evoke what they or parts of them or totals including them or totals including parts of them have evoked. The memory of the headache may thus evoke pleasure and the day-dream of receiving a million dollars may evoke regret. *"Nessun maggior dolore che recordarsi del tempo felice nella miseria."*

We may now summarize the main essentials for explaining the dynamics of ideas of situations, responses, and after-effects and understanding when and how anticipations, plans, promises, and threats operate.

(1) Any form of expectation of a satisfying after-effect tends to arouse the confirming reaction and to strengthen the connection to which it is attached.

(2) Any form of expectation of an annoying after-effect tends to evoke the particular behavior which previous experience has attached to it.

(3) Any relic of the experience of a situation may coöperate with some part or precursor of that situation to evoke the behavior which the real situation would evoke.

(4) Ideas of responses of the type *doing something until X is attained* and of verbal responses usually easily evoke these.

(5) A situation can (at least usually) evoke an idea associated with an idea of the situation.

(6) An idea of a situation can (at least usually) evoke an idea associated with the situation.

(7) The stream of ideational life operates with images, memories, ideas, and judgments of and about situations, connections, responses, and after-effects as it does with any others. It attaches them to others, and others to them, plans about them, tries out its plans in thought, and reaches conclusions.

When man uses ideas of situations, responses, and after-effects rather than the corresponding realities to influence behavior, it is through commands, suggestions, arguments, promises, threats, and the like. To illustrate the dynamics involved, we had best take a connection where the real situation in and of itself would be utterly powerless to evoke the response, say causing a man when he next sees the word *harmony* to draw three circles underneath it. We may secure the mental set of obedience and simply say, "If you see the word *harmony* on this sheet draw three circles under it." The command avails because the description or prophecy of the real situation identifies it when it appears and attaches the verbal idea of drawing three circles below *harmony* to it and because the verbal idea of drawing three circles below *harmony* easily evokes movements which attain that result. Yet except for our command there would not have been a probability of 0.000000001 that the person would have drawn three circles under the word. We may suggest to some young musician that "Both Beethoven and Debussy had the odd habit of drawing three circles under the word *harmony* and two under the word *melody,* whenever they saw it." We may promise a child "If you draw three circles under the word *harmony* wherever it occurs on this page, you will receive five cents. If you mark all but one, you will receive three cents." The promise attaches the expectation of a satisfying after-effect to the idea of making that response to the situation and attaches this idea to a verbal idea meaning the situation. When the situation occurs, it evokes this idea. The idea is able to evoke the response. The expectation of a satisfying after-effect strengthens its tendency to do so.

Chapter 8

THE INFLUENCE OF DIFFERENCES IN THE AMOUNT OF REWARDS AND PUNISHMENTS

IF, in a series of connections alike in other respects, some connections are rewarded by a mere announcement of "Right," whereas others are rewarded by "Right" plus a money bonus of 1, and others by "Right" plus a money bonus of 2, and others by "Right" plus a money bonus of 4, what will be the difference in strengthening? The answer to this question has been found by R. T. Rock * for cases where amounts of reward varied from connection to connection in a series of twenty, being the same for any two successive connections only occasionally by chance.

The learning was of two sorts, code-learning and tossing balls at a target. In the code-learning the connections favored were between the sight of lines each containing one nonsense word followed by four English words and the underlining of one of the English words. Two of the English words were arbitrarily called 'right' and two of them 'wrong,' in each line. The money rewards were 0, 1, 2, 3 and 4 tenths of a cent.

In the ball-tossing the connections were between sitting on one of several stools with a ball of a certain weight and tossing over one's shoulder at an unseen target. The money rewards were 0, 1, 2, and 4, their absolute values being left unknown.

The subjects in the code-learning were 50 educated adults and 75 school-children twelve or thirteen years old in grades 6, 7, and 8. The subjects in the ball-tossing were 125 educated adults. For the children at least the mere satisfaction at success in these dull tasks was presumably small in comparison with the satisfaction at even the smallest money reward; and the increments of satisfaction with increases in the money reward were presumably large.

* In a study as yet unpublished.

93

The answer found by Mr. Rock is that neither the addition of a money reward nor the increase in its amount causes a demonstrably greater strengthening over that found for the mere announcement of "Right." The summary of his results is as follows:

For the 125 subjects in the code-learning * the average improvement in percentage of correct responses from trial 1 to trial 8 was:

> 7.8 for reward 0 (from 52.4 to 60.2)
> 18.2 for reward 1 (from 48.2 to 66.4)
> 20.5 for reward 2 (from 43.0 to 63.5)
> 14.9 for reward 3 (from 53.1 to 68.0)
> 19.2 for reward 4 (from 48.3 to 67.5)

These results are complicated by the fact that all 'right' responses are counted. Using the more rigorous technique of computing the frequency of repetition of the particular response that was rewarded, Rock finds this to be:

> 41.2, or 16.2 above chance, for "Right" $+$ 0 units money
> 40.4, or 15.4 above chance, for "Right" $+$ 1 or 2 units
> 44.1, or 19.1 above chance, for "Right" $+$ 3 or 4 units †

For a response punished by "Wrong," the corresponding percentage is 33.5 or 8.5 above chance.

For the 125 educated adults in ball-tossing the average improvement in percentage of correct responses from trial 1 to trial 5 was:

> 13.4 for reward 0 (from 30.2 to 43.6)
> 12.6 for reward 1 (from 31.1 to 43.7)
> 11.2 for reward 2 (from 31.4 to 42.6)
> 13.8 for reward 3 (from 30.8 to 44.6)
> 13.6 for reward 4 (from 30.8 to 44.4)

Using the more rigorous technique of computing the influence of one rewarded connection in trial 1 or trial 2 in causing a repetition of that connection in the next trial, Rock finds:

> 50.9, or 20.0 above chance, for "Right" $+$ 0 money
> 48.4, or 17.5 above chance, for "Right" $+$ 1 or 2 units
> 50.6, or 19.7 above chance, for "Right" $+$ 3 or 4 units

* The data from the children did not differ significantly from those for adults, so the two sets are combined.

† All these percentages are for the influence of one occurrence, in trial 1 or trial 2.

In the code-learning there is a slightly greater strengthening for "Right" + 1 or 2 than for "Right" alone, and for "Right" + 3 or 4 than for "Right" + 1 or 2. In the ball-tossing there is no difference.

In considering these facts one must keep in mind that there is some "spread" or "scatter" of the influence of each sort of satisfying after-effect which would to some extent equalize their respective strengthenings. This, however, could not be a large influence, and allowing for it would raise the excess strengthenings over that due to a connection rewarded by "Right" alone by only a small amount.

The experiments of Rock measure the strengthening influence of different amounts of satisfaction upon the particular connections to which they are attached. Their more diffuse effect in arousing interest and attention for the learning as a whole is deliberately equalized by the conditions of the experiment. They measure chiefly the differences in the direct immediate forces exerted upon a connection by its after-effect. There may also be, in the code experiment, an indirect influence *via* self-teaching by the learner in the form of a retention or repetition of some equivalent of the connection after the announcement of "Right" is made. He may keep his glance fixed on a word if it is called "Right," but not if it is called "Wrong," for a second or so before going on to the next line. He may occasionally say to himself ". . . is right for. . . ."

The most probable interpretation of the results is, in my opinion, (1) that the essential thing is, in each case, whether the confirming reaction is set into action by the satisfier; (2) that a satisfier having less than a certain amount or intensity fails occasionally to do this and fails oftener the less it has; (3) that a satisfier having more than this amount or intensity will never fail (except for causes outside itself) to set off the confirming reaction; (4) that the amount or intensity which is required to ensure occurrence of the confirming reaction is moderate (five cents being as good as five dollars for a school-boy in one of these experiments, for example); and (5) that variations in the potency of the confirming reaction itself are slight and largely uncorrelated with the intensity of the satisfier which sets it off.*

* A reasonable substitute for element 5 would be the hypothesis that, though the confirming reaction can vary greatly in potency in certain respects, it can

Moreover, a satisfying after-effect may cause the learner to hold in mind the fact that so-and-so is right or to repeat it to himself in inner speech. Larger rewards would presumably be more rather than less likely to do this than smaller rewards. The slight apparent advantage of the larger rewards in the code-learning of Rock could be so explained. In his ball-tossing the response cannot be easily held in mind and cannot be repeated in inner speech, so that there is little or no advantage from the larger rewards.

If all the correct connections in one series of twenty or forty tasks are rewarded by a mere announcement of "Right," whereas all the correct connections in another series of twenty or forty are rewarded by "Right" plus a money bonus of 1, all those in another series are rewarded by "Right" plus a bonus of 2, all those in another series by "Right" plus a bonus of 4, and all those in another series by "Right" plus a bonus of 8, what will be the difference in strengthening? The answer to this question, especially as regards the differences between the four amounts of money, has been found by Thorndike and Forlano ['33] for cases where the subjects were boys ten to sixteen years old, the money units were 1, 2, 4 and 8 tenths of a cent, and the multiple-choice learning concerned (a) the selection of one from five English meanings of Spanish words, (b) one from six parts of pictures, and (c) a number from 1 to 6 as a response to an English word. The answer is that the learning is more rapid the greater the money reward up to 4 units but is less rapid with 8 units than with 4. A summary of the facts is as follows: The gain from "Right" + 0.1¢ is 1½ times that from "Right" alone. The average gain from "Right" + 0.2¢, "Right" + 0.4¢, and "Right" + 0.8¢ is 1¾ times that for "Right" alone. The gains from "Right" + 0.1¢, "Right" + 0.2¢, "Right" + 0.4¢, and "Right" + 0.8¢ in a combination of all experiments are in these proportions: 85, 92, 114, and 108.

The clearer influence of the differences in the amount of reward in these experiments than in Rock's is presumably due to the

vary little in its power to improve learning directly (as in these multiple-choice experiments, where the situation vanishes as soon as it is responded to). For example, the confirming reactions in a hungry dog due to one gram of meat and ten grams of meat might cause great differences in the dog's zeal, but not in the actual addition of strength to the connections rewarded.

continuation of the same reward throughout each series and so to differences in interest and effort between the series. The drop in learning for rewards of 8 tenths of a cent below that for rewards from 4 tenths of a cent is presumably due to interference from excitement and strain.

In the experiments of Thorndike and Forlano several degrees of reward were used at one sitting, though never in the same series. There was consequently a contrast effect possible as the subject changed from a series with rewards of one unit or two units to a series with greater rewards and conversely. If the series are remote in time, or are performed with different subjects, this contrast is reduced or eliminated.

We have some such experiments. Certain subjects (educated adults) learned to select the correct meaning for 200 Spanish words, in each case from five English words with no reward other than the announcement of "Right." Certain other educated adults learned the same tasks, but with "Right" plus a money reward which was of real consequence to them. There was no demonstrable superiority in their learning.

In the experiments of Stephens ['31], the intensity of a shock which was the signal for "Wrong" was altered from one 'set' to another. In Stephens' experiments, the subject did not have to wait until nineteen or thirty-nine different situations had been responded to before having a chance to repeat or alter his response. He could repeat it or alter it in his very next response, the situation remaining (so far as he knew) the same.

The percentage of repetitions of hits on the same square after a mild shock was 19.31 ± 0.74; after a medium shock it was 20.66 ± 0.74; after a heavy shock it was 16.86 ± 0.68. There is thus a stronger tendency to change response after the heavy shock than after either of the others.

Since in Stephens' experiments the absence of shock was the reward, we may also perhaps regard the absence of a shock in the sets where it was strong as a greater reward than its absence in the sets where it was weak. On this basis the greater reward caused 44.88 percent of repetitions in the next trial (±0.89); while the two lesser rewards caused 42.76 ± 0.86 (for absence of mild) and 44.79 ± 0.92 (for absence of medium). Here again there is a slightly greater influence of the greater reward.

The question answered by Rock for amounts of reward has

been answered by Tuckman ['33] for amounts of punishment. He gave one, two, three, or four shocks in certain experiments. He took away from the subject one, two, three, or four tokens, each worth 0.1¢ in other experiments. A summary of his results follows.

Using the same code-learning as was used by Rock (choice of one word from a line containing a nonsense word followed by four English words two of which were arbitrarily scored "Right" and two, "Wrong") the influence of one occurrence rewarded by "Right" appears in a percentage of repetition in the following trial of 53.67, or 28.67 above mere chance ($n = 8453$). The influence of one occurrence punished by "Wrong" plus 0, 1, 2, 3, and 4 shocks respectively appears in percentages of repetition in the following trials as follows:

Wrong and 0 shock, 35.75 or 10.75 above mere chance ($n = 2403$)
Wrong and 1 shock, 34.49 or 9.49 above mere chance ($n = 1409$)
Wrong and 2 shocks, 36.17 or 11.17 above mere chance ($n = 1352$)
Wrong and 3 shocks, 36.06 or 11.06 above mere chance ($n = 1001$)
Wrong and 4 shocks, 32.25 or 7.25 above mere chance ($n = 1442$)

In a similar experiment, but with deprivations of money as the annoying after-effects, the comparable percentage for the influence of one occurrence rewarded by "Right" was 53.18, or 28.13 above mere chance ($n = 8613$). The influences of one occurrence punished by "Wrong" plus the withdrawal of 0, 0.1, 0.2, 0.3, or 0.4¢ from the learner's possession appear in percentages of repetition in the following trials as follows:

Wrong + withdrawal of 0¢, 37.99 or 12.99 above mere chance .... ($n = 2632$)
Wrong + withdrawal of 0.1¢, 39.24 or 14.24 above mere chance .... ($n = 1455$)
Wrong + withdrawal of 0.2¢, 38.28 or 13.28 above mere chance .... ($n = 1429$)
Wrong + withdrawal of 0.3¢, 35.76 or 10.76 above mere chance .... ($n = 1032$)
Wrong + withdrawal of 0.4¢, 33.65 or 8.65 above mere chance .... ($n = 1416$)

The greater punishments leave only a slightly greater influence upon learning. The averages of the two percentages are, in order, 36.8, 36.9, 37.2, 35.9 and 33.0. This is borne out by the study of the influence of two successive occurrences of each sort, of three successive occurrences of each sort, and of four successive occurrences of each sort, in these two experiments. As grand total weighted average influences, Tuckman finds the following excesses over mere chance:

For one occurrence rewarded by "Right".................. 25.77
For one occurrence punished by "Wrong" + o shock or
    deprivation 12.35
For one occurrence punished by "Wrong" + 1 shock or
    deprivation 11.51
For one occurrence punished by "Wrong" + 2 shocks or
    deprivations 11.17
For one occurrence punished by "Wrong" + 3 shocks or
    deprivations 10.35
For one occurrence punished by "Wrong" + 4 shocks or
    deprivations 7.88

The results of two similar experiments in learning to choose the right part of each of ninety-eight queer pictures each made up of six parts are summarized in the following excesses over the repetition due to mere chance (which is here 16.67):

One occurrence rewarded by "Right".................... 11.79
One occurrence punished by "Wrong" + o unit of shock or
    deprivation 6.76
One occurrence punished by "Wrong" + 1 unit of shock or
    deprivation 4.70
One occurrence punished by "Wrong" + 2 units of shock or
    deprivation 6.84
One occurrence punished by "Wrong" + 3 units of shock or
    deprivation 5.52
One occurrence punished by "Wrong" + 4 units of shock or
    deprivation 5.43

The numbers of observations of each sort run to several thousands. The differences here are very small.

It may be that a certain amount of favoritism for certain positions in the line and for certain parts of the queer pictures should be allowed for in interpreting these results. It would, however, be practically impossible to determine this and allow for it in the case of the 100, 96, 68, and 40 subjects used in the four experiments. The number of choices for any one subject is not large enough to distinguish true position favoritism from chance variations accurately enough to measure the former.

For twenty of Tuckman's subjects chosen at random, the average percentage of repetitions expected from chance plus favoritism for certain positions in the line in the code-learning was 27.4 instead of the 25.0 which mere chance would give. In an extensive experiment with code-learning by nineteen adults the average expectation of a repetition in the following trial from chance plus favoritism for certain positions in the line was 27.0. If 27.4 is used instead of 25.0, the weighted average results expressing the amount of strengthening in the two code experiments of Tuckman become 23.4 for a "Right" and 10.0, 9.1, 8.8, 8.0, and 5.5 for the various intensities of punishment.

For fifteen of Tuckman's subjects chosen at random, the average expectation from chance plus favoritism for certain positions in the experiments with queer pictures was 18.2. If we use 18.2 in place of 16.7, the weighted average results expressing the amount of strengthening in the two experiments with queer pictures become 10.3 for a "Right" and 5.3, 3.2, 5.3, 4.1, and 4.1, respectively, for the various intensities of punishment from "Wrong" $+$ none to "Wrong" $+$ four units of shock or deprivation.

By any reasonable allowances for position favoritism two things remain sure from Tuckman's work. One is that even the severe punishment of receiving four shocks or losing 0.4¢ did not have enough weakening force to counterbalance the strengthening force due to occurrence. For example, a connection so punished in three successive occurrences will be far more likely to occur in the next trial than chance plus position favoritism would permit. (The percentages were 47.98 and 42.36 for the two code-learning experiments. They were 39.39 and 32.10 in the two experiments with pictures.)

The other is that the differences in influence between the slight and the intense punishments are small.

As a reasonable and very simple hypothesis to explain the facts found by Tuckman, I suggest the following. Punishment of any sort prevents the setting-off of any confirming reaction. It also encourages the learner to use any form of inner self-teaching that "so-and-so is wrong" which occurs to him. The greater punishments would be more likely than the less to stimulate such inner repetition. In the code-learning, this is more natural and feasible than in the marking of the queer pictures. Consequently the intensity of the punishment has more influence in the case of the former.

In the experiments of Rock and Tuckman the learners were

urged on to make a quick response to the next line, picture, etc., as soon as they had received each after-effect. If they were encouraged to stop and indulge in self-teaching to any extent that they desired, the money rewards might cause much more self-teaching than the mere "Right," and the larger amounts of money might cause much more self-teaching than the smaller. The shocks and deprivations might cause much more self-teaching than the mere "Wrong"; and the larger amounts of shock or withdrawal of money might cause much more than the smaller. Presumably they would, since it would pay a subject to spend much more time to win the greater rewards and avoid the greater punishments. With such problems in economics we are not concerned here.

Poets and proverb-makers, and many psychologists, would not be satisfied with rating satisfiers and annoyers by amount alone. They would assert that among those equal in amount there were important qualitative differences. Money and love, for example, or hunger and fear, they might regard as incomparable. Two, at least, of the qualities in respect of which they would differentiate motivating after-effects deserve some consideration here. In the interest of brevity, we shall describe them vaguely and in figures, as they are usually described.

We may grade satisfiers and annoyers as narrow or pervasive according to the amount of a person that they satisfy or seem to satisfy. Thus, if a person is walking downstairs in the dark, it is satisfying to have each step meet a stair or the floor, as expected, and annoying to meet air when one expects the floor, or to meet the floor when one expects a drop to a stair, but the satisfaction or annoyance does not penetrate deep or spread wide. But if a young man receives a smile or a sneer from a girl whom he loves, large areas of his soul seem to be thrilled or mortified.

We may also grade them as superficial or penetrating according to the depth of the impression which they make or seem to make. Thus, the announcement of "Right" in one of our experiments, or by a teacher to a child in school, usually affects only the surface layer of the person, so to speak, whereas the announcement of "Not guilty" to a person on trial for murder would strike into the depths where pride, hope, fear, and self-respect abide.*

* Differences in scope and poignancy of satisfaction would be correlated with amount of satisfaction as rated by any reasonable procedure, but the correla-

There is some reason to believe that greater pervasive and penetrating power in a satisfier may cause a stronger confirming reaction. For example, suppose that instead of multiple choices of the number from 1 to 10 that is attached to a certain word, the subject is choosing (with some infallible oracle as a guide) which of ten careers he shall follow, which of ten stocks he shall spend his last dollars for, which of ten girls he shall woo, or the like. Would not the "Right" of the oracle, by virtue of its wide and poignant appeal, arouse a stronger confirming reaction than the "Right" of the experimenter? Would not one occurrence of it raise the strength of the connection which it followed and to which it belonged from 0.10 to 0.95 or 1.00 instead of from 0.10 to 0.45 or 0.50? To neither question is the answer known; and the answer to the first need not be 'yes' if the answer to the second is.* Nor is an affirmative answer to the second so likely as the experiences of life seem to suggest. In the experiences of life the connections which produce these broad and deep after-effects are likely to be dwelt upon longer or to echo in some inner equivalent oftener. What would happen if forty such momentous choices were made one after another in 120 sec. or less cannot be prophesied with certainty.

It does, however, seem probable that a connection whose rightness or success was of interest to many and deep segments of a person would be more strengthened thereby than less vital connections, even if everything else save its different interest were kept equal. This could happen by an increased potency of the one confirming reaction, or it could happen by a summation of two or more confirming reactions. The second alternative seems to the writer the more likely.

The magnitudes of the satisfiers in our experiments were all of a relatively low order, though little or not at all below that of the average after-effect operating upon the average connection in schools, offices, factories, and the like. If the amount of satisfaction is greatly increased, the nature of the satisfier is often changed toward greater scope and penetration. Consequently the facts and possibilities stated in the last half-dozen paragraphs

---

tion might not be perfect so that cases could occur where equally rated amounts of satisfaction would be unequal in scope or poignancy.

* The second terms in these momentous connections are of high identifiability, and the first terms are very impressive.

are applicable to any estimate of what would happen to the strengthening of a connection by a great increase in the magnitude of its satisfier. If to "Right" alone, "Right" + 0.1¢, "Right" + 0.2¢, "Right" + 0.4¢, we should add "Right" + $100, we should for many persons be changing our motive from *desire to do well* + *desire to appear well* + *desire to make a fraction of a cent* to *desire to do well* + *desire to appear well* + *desire to be° forever free from financial worries* + *desire to give a struggling relative an education* + *desire to be one's own master,* etc. We are likely to appeal to more of the person and to deeper parts of his nature.

General Principles Concerning the Influence of the Amount or Intensity of Satisfying and Annoying After-Effects

Variations in the amount of a satisfier or annoyer certainly do not influence learning logically or by a simple law of direct proportion. They operate through physiological processes which are like neither bookkeepers nor gas-engines.

We may separate their influence into several components. The first and second are the direct, immediate influences of the satisfying and annoying after-effects respectively on the connections to which they are attached. The third is the indirect and slightly delayed influence by continuance or repetition of a rewarded connection with a continuing situation or by the repetition of some inner equivalents of the situation and response. The fourth is a similarly indirect and slightly delayed influence by the continuance or repetition of the new behavior (such as flight, fear, immobility, or cries) aroused by an annoying after-effect. The fifth is a more extended and protracted strengthening of attentiveness, effort, or other features of the total behavior in the course of which the satisfying after-effect occurs. The sixth is a similarly extended and protracted influence of annoying after-effects upon such general features of the total behavior in the course of which the annoying after-effect occurs.

Concerning the first influence it appears probable that the main and perhaps the sole difference lies in whether the confirming reaction is or is not aroused. Very moderate satisfiers can do this as well as any, and very moderate annoyers may fail to arouse it as surely as any. Extremely intense satisfiers may swamp the confirming reaction in a general flood of excitement.

Concerning the second, the influence is nil, whether the annoyance is little or great.

Concerning the third we have little exact quantitative evidence, but some experiments of a practical nature which will be reported in chapters 9 and 10 and general observations lead me to think that very moderate satisfiers will do nearly or quite as well as any. If they are adequate to make the animal or person continue at all or repeat at all, this continuance or repetition, bringing the satisfier anew, will cause a second, and so on, until the connection is well established. So a child who nibbles once at a new variety of candy or cooky and finds it good will probably learn to eat it as perfectly if it is moderately sweet and good as if it were the nectar of the gods.

Concerning the fourth influence, the case is different. Rather, the cases are different, since there are many sorts of "negative" behavior which may be caused by different annoying after-effects. The snow-ball effect that can occur as a result of the confirming reaction causing continuance or repetition cannot occur as a result of running away, fear, drawing back a part of the body, and many other common consequences of punishment.*

The potency of the punishment, in respect of this third sort of influence, can rarely, if ever, add to itself. Running away does not lead the animal to approach and run away again, and, if it did, the value for learning would be problematic since it would be learning to approach as well as to run away. Consequently a mild punishment which made a child back off slowly a step from S would, so far as influence 3 goes, not be as potent in teaching retreat from S as an intense punishment which made the child jump back vigorously. A gentle fear aroused by a mild rebuke would not be so potent in teaching avoidance as the terror due to a severe shock.

In respect of the fourth sort of influence we should then expect an increase in some accordance with the magnitude of the punishment up to a point where the punishment produced an emphatic

---

* Something of the sort might occur in some, as where the punishment was a general wretchedness which grew by what it fed on to produce more general wretchedness and somehow attached this to the S $\rightarrow$ R in question or to some inner equivalent of it. But this would still be essentially different from the true snow-ball effect of a reward.

connection of flight or fear catalepsy, with the situation such as would surely outweigh the connection which was punished and would leave a relic of memory or expectation surely adequate to outweigh that connection in the future. From that point on any increase would follow a law of diminishing returns. If the intensity of the punishment was so great as to cause very great excitement and confusion, it might actually lose in potency.

In using punishments, there is danger that the retreat, fear, or other response aroused by the punishment may become attached to a situation other than the particular one to which the punisher wishes it to be attached. An animal shocked in a certain sort of alley may avoid all alleys; a child ridiculed for using incorrect language may refuse to speak at all. This danger is probably greater with intense punishments, there being a wider diffusion and less restriction by belonging.

Investigations are very much needed in the case of the fifth influence, whereby a satisfying after-effect strengthens the whole mental set and behavior in which the particular connection rewarded is imbedded, and strengthens it more than momentarily. According to general observation, the course of affairs is after the following pattern:

The person is moved by some want to enter upon a course of behavior consisting of (1) very general features such as a set toward gratifying that want, the exclusion of irrelevant thoughts and acts, etc.; (2) more special features, such as maintaining a certain posture or routine of movement, the direction of effort toward a series of tasks, etc.; (3) very special and detailed features such as occurrences of identifiable situations and the responses to each. His behavior is guided largely by the satisfactions he obtains or expects to obtain. Unless the initial momentum is very great, he will abandon or modify the course of behavior or be less likely to respect it in the future, if he is not from time to time encouraged by some satisfactions or expectations thereof. Some of these satisfying events or expectations are surely consequences of the special and detailed features; and these contribute to making the total course of behavior satisfying, or at least tolerable. But general observation does not reveal how they do so at all fully, precisely, or surely.

It does indicate that an intense satisfaction contributes more to the satisfyingness of the total course of behavior than a moderate one. A professional humorist would thus be better satisfied on the whole with a speech which convulsed his audience a score of times than with one which drew forth only moderate guffaws. A reader would be better satisfied by reading the first half of a book, more likely to finish it, and more likely to read a second book by the same author, if his reading of the first half resulted in spells of thrilling entertainment, than if it resulted in an equal number of spells not far above the threshold of boredom. Presumably the subjects in Rock's experiments were more influenced to engage in a similar experiment again by a "Right" plus four units of money than by a "Right" plus no or one unit. Experiments are needed to discover how the intensity of a reward for a particular item in a total course of behavior strengthens the tendency to maintain or repeat that course of behavior or something like it.

The sixth sort of influence requires even more investigation than the fifth because of the variety of behavior to which annoying after-effects of being thwarted, pained, frightened, etc., may lead, at the time and in memory. There can be no doubt that greater intensity of punishments up to a certain point tends to weaken the tendency to pursue the general course of behavior in which the punishments occurred. But experiments are needed to separate the influence of the punishments from the influence of their relics in memory and expectation and to determine the operation of each.

In the case of any total course of behavior of any considerable length, there is likely to be a mixture of influences of type 5 and influences of type 6. How the neurones of man strike a balance so as to predispose him for or against that course of behavior in the future, and how strongly for or against it, is unknown. Sometimes the balance is registered in a fairly clear judgment. John Doe may know that he *will* play billiards under certain conditions and that he *will not* play the piano, as he knows that he is six feet tall and does not have three hands. Sometimes the balance is so emphatic as to be always operative (except for extraordinary circumstances), but the subject is unaware of it. So Richard Roe may always read the newspaper or listen to the radio, though convinced that, "I wish I had time to read one good book a month." Sometimes no stable balance is achieved, and the person may reach a temporary balance pro or con according to the momentary dominance of certain relics of the past. Sometimes there are alternations, perplexities, attempts to eat the cake and have it too, and many sorts of compromises. In no case is the psychology of the causation known. The principles of Chapter 7 doubtless apply, and the general laws of reinforcement, facilitation, interference, and inhibition would doubtless apply if we knew what these were.

We come nearest to knowledge of the causation in the most deliberately controlled and aboveboard compounding of the influences, or of ideational equivalents, representatives, or symbols of them, as when a person observes and records the satisfactions and annoyances (or recalls them in memory), judges the influence of each as best he can, and forms a double list of weighted values or 'motives' or 'reasons' which he then examines. His decision after such an examination of one or more such double lists that he wishes to do so and so, or prefers this course of behavior to that, is in a sense caused by the weighted values. Just as logical minds are strongly moved to reach a certain conclusion from certain evidence, so prudent minds are strongly moved to make a certain choice from certain 'reasons.' On the other hand, just as logic is the science of proof and not the science of reasoning, so the calculus of 'reasons' is not the same as the causation of choices. Even in the most deliberately controlled compounding of influences, the fundamental causation is hidden.

Such rational compounding of influences is, of course, very rare. The compounding is ordinarily done on a deeper level. Its psychology and physiology should be a fascinating subject for study. In the simple cases of the direct immediate strengthening of a connection by occurrence and satisfying after-effect we have uncovered the principles of the impressiveness of the situation, the belongingness of the response to the situation, the belongingness of the after-effect to the connection, the confirming reaction, and the spread or scatter phenomenon. In the complex case of the influence of satisfying and annoying consequences upon the total course of behavior the prospects for experimental analysis are very hopeful.

Chapter 9

INTRINSIC AND EXTRINSIC INTERESTS: LEARNING AND DOING WHAT SEEMS UNINTERESTING OR VALUELESS, OR BOTH UNINTERESTING AND VALUELESS

LEARNING and work in homes, schools, and shops is, and perhaps always will be, loaded with many items which have little or no intrinsic interest to the learner or worker. He is induced, or induces himself, to learn them by appeals to pride, self-respect, love of parents, desire for approval, prudence, and the like.

The general view of a hundred years ago was that any one interest would do about as well as any other, that, example, the interest in avoiding a beating would lead one Latin about as well as an interest in linguistics. The a iew of to-day is that an intrinsic interest in the activity ss of ulterior consequences is an enormously superior means of learning. It is doubtless a safer bet, but whether its advantage is 1000 percent or 500, 200, 150, 100, 50, 40, 30, 20, or 10 percent has never been shown. Moreover, one logical corollary of the view approved to-day would be that, no matter how earnestly a person tried to learn something that seemed dull or valueless to him, he simply could not learn it save at enormous cost. This is not so heartening. The doctrine is less attractive as a handicap dent effort by persons whose reason and foresight tell th at they should learn this or that uninteresting thing than as re- ventive of pedagogical cruelty to children.

Knowledge concerning the relative efficiency of activity which is in and of itself alluring in contrast to that to which one is bribed by some external consideration may in the future be as important for economics and business as for morals and education. Wages and profits are typical cases of artificial, external, and remote motives compared with those that stimulate the activities of the hunter of game. There is a growing tendency to try to adapt men and productive labor by vocational guidance and improvement of methods of work.

We have sought to increase such knowledge by conducting extensive and varied experiments in learning interesting and uninteresting, useful and useless, valuable and harmful things. Our subjects were in all cases educated adults or college students; and what seemed interesting or valuable to them would not necessarily be to others. We are concerned with the general issues only, and for such a group we used:

(1) The birth years of celebrities in art, letters, etc., versus the birth years of nonentities (tailors, cobblers, etc.)

(2) The real birth years of celebrities versus years stated to be years when they were *not* born

(3) The real meanings of rare English words versus words stated to be what the words *do not* mean

(4) The reading of one's first choice among Fraser's *Golden Bough*, the Bible, and the Book of Mormon versus the reading of one's third choice among them

(5) Writing with the left hand with eyes open versus writing with the left hand with eyes closed

(6) Typewriting of the ordinary sort versus typewriting in which each word was spelled backward (*The man had* being typed as *ehT nam dah*)

The essential facts concerning these experiments follow.

Learning Valued versus Valueless Facts

Lists of names of persons plus the occupation and year of birth of each were prepared. Each list contained twenty names. Lists 1 to 8 were of persons eminent in music, art, writing, statesmanship or affairs, and science or philosophy. Lists 101 to 118 were of nonentities (blacksmiths, cobblers, drivers, farmers, and tailors). Lists 1 + 102 A, 1 + 102 B, 2 + 101 A, 2 + 101 B, etc., were each composed half of eminent persons and half of nonentities, being made by division of tests 1, 101, 2, 102, etc.

Such a list was read to a subject two or more times.* Then the names alone were read, and he was required to supply the year of birth.

* In some experiments, always in the same order; in others, always in a different order; as noted later. There were also variations within some of the lists in that sometimes the name was said twice, sometimes the date, etc. These variations were equalized between famous persons and nonentities and do not concern us here.

The instructions before the experiments were as follows:

For 1, 2, etc.: I shall read the name, occupation, and year of birth of certain persons famous in art, music, writing, statesmanship or affairs, and science or philosophy. You will listen and try to remember the date for each name.

For 101, 102, etc.: I shall read the name, occupation, and year of birth of certain persons of no importance, blacksmiths, cobblers, drivers, farmers, or tailors. You will listen and try to remember the date for each name.

For 1 + 102 A, etc.: I shall read the name, occupation, and year of birth of certain persons, some famous in art, music, writing, statesmanship, or affairs and science or philosophy, and some persons of no importance. You will listen and try to remember the date for each name.*

Consider first experiments 7, 8, 9, and 10, in which the subjects were all women college students of psychology; the lists were all read three times in different random orders; each name, occupation, and date was read without duplication of any part at a rate of one unit per four seconds; and the celebrities and nonentities in the lists to be compared were born within the same time limits of the same century. All subjects were pledged to try just as hard to remember the nonentities as the celebrities, and those who reported that they did not do so were nearly equally divided between greater and less attention to the celebrities.

The average number of birth years of celebrities known apart from the training was 5.5 per thousand. The correction for this is so small relatively to the number learned that it may be disregarded.

Eighteen subjects who were trained with one list of celebrities and one of nonentities averaged 7.8 for the former and 4.4 for the latter. The median of the eighteen individual ratios (Celeb/Nonent) was 2.0. Its probable error is 0.2.

Eighty-five subjects had either three or four mixed sets each containing ten celebrities and ten nonentities. One of them remembered twelve celebrities and thirteen nonentities. In every other case more celebrities than nonentities were remembered. The averages for those having three sets were 13.1 for celebrities and

---

* Additional instructions in some experiments concerned the fact that sometimes the name was repeated, sometimes the date, and sometimes both. But these do not concern us here, since all these variations in the presentation were equalized for the famous persons and the nonentities.

5.0 for nonentities. For those having four sets, they were 12.2 and 4.3. About 2.75 times as many celebrities as nonentities were then remembered by the group. The median Celeb/Nonent ratio for all was 3.0. Its probable error is about 0.1.

In spite of attempts to attend and retain equally, the more valuable connections are strengthened much more than the less. A study of the connections most strengthened among the valuable ones confirms this. I list in Table 12 (I) those of the celebrities studied in the mixed sets who were remembered at least twice as often as the median celebrity of those studied by the subjects in question and also (II) those who were remembered less than half as often as that median. All the subjects, it should be remembered, were college girls.

TABLE 12

CELEBRITIES WHOSE BIRTH YEARS WERE REMEMBERED MOST (I) AND LEAST (II)

Group A	I	Garibaldi, Dickens, Longfellow, Tennyson, Lincoln
	II	Agassiz, Liebig, Wundt, Cézanne, Alma Tadema, Gegenbaur, Fortuny
Group B	I	Trotski, Freud, Galsworthy, Kipling, Mussolini, Jefferson, Edmund Burke, Joshua Reynolds, Cowper, Smollett, Lessing, Washington, Goldsmith, Benjamin Franklin, Warren Hastings
	II	Leoncavallo, Masaryk, Humperdinck, Van Gogh, Zorn, Zuloaga, Detaille, Röntgen, Fragonard, Hartley, Gluck
Group C	I	Coleridge, Beethoven, Rossini, Keats, Byron, Washington Irving
	II	Fichte, Gauss, Marat, Alfieri, Goya, Candolle, Ingres, Chamisso, Meyerbeer, Corot
Group D	I	(including those 1.9 times the median) Jefferson, Washington, Benjamin Franklin
	II	Haydn, Fragonard, Gluck, Cuvier, Fichte, Marat

Consider next experiments 26 to 29 in which thirty educated adults or adolescents over seventeen were subjects; the lists were read four times in different random orders; each name and date was read at a rate of one such unit per three seconds; the dates in any list of twenty were within the same time limits of the same century. These subjects knew that they would be paid bonuses depending on how much they learned. Eight subjects who reported greater effort to learn the birth years of the celebrities were excluded from the computations. Two lists of twenty celebrities, two lists of twenty nonentities, and four lists, each containing ten celebrities and ten nonentities mixed in a random order, were used.

The average number learned for celebrities in separate lists was 9.3 out of twenty; for nonentities in separate lists, it was 4.5 out of twenty. The useful/useless ratio was thus 2.07. The median of the twenty-two individual ratios was 2.5 with a probable error of 0.3.

When the celebrities and nonentities were mixed, all learned more celebrities. The number of celebrities learned was 2½ times as great as the number of nonentities. The median of the twenty-two Celeb/Nonent ratios was 3.6. Its probable error in the downward direction is about 0.3.

In both sets of experiments there is a superiority in strengthening for the connections with celebrities when dates for celebrities and nonentities are learned in separate lists (median Celeb/Nonent ratio, 2.0 and 2.5). There is a still greater superiority when the two are learned together in mixed tests (median ratios then being 3.0 and 3.6).

These facts are confirmed by other experiments (11 to 16) reported in Appendix II.

Learning Useful versus Harmful Facts

In experiments 18, 19, 20, and 21 we compare the learning of the birth years of famous persons with the learning of a date for each which was stated *not* to be the birth-year, and the learning of the meanings of rare English words with the learning of a word for each which was stated *not* to be the correct meaning.

Twenty-eight educated adults received the following instructions after preliminary experiments which acquainted them with the nature of the experiment:

Experiment 18

I shall read the names of twenty men and the year of birth for each. I shall read them four times. Then I will read the names alone and you will write the last two figures of the year of birth for each (the first two figures will be the same for all). If you are sure you do not know the birth year, just draw a dash-line. Use the first column of the test sheet.

Experiment 20

I shall read twenty words and the meaning of each. I shall read the list through twice. Then I shall read the words alone and you will write the meanings in column 2 of the sheet. If you are sure you do not remember the meaning, make a dash-line. We want to be sure to have all twenty spaces filled.

Experiment 19

This time I shall read a name of a person and a date when he was *not* born. You are to listen, to try to remember the year in which I told you he was *not* born. I shall read the twenty names and dates four times and then read the names alone. You will write the last two figures of the date that you heard (the first two figures will always be the same). If you are sure that you do not remember the date, just draw a dash-line. Use column 3 of the sheet.

Experiment 21

I shall read twenty rare words and a word for each which is *not* its meaning. You are to listen and try to remember the words which I told you the rare words did *not* mean. I shall read the words and incorrect meanings twice, then I will read the words alone and you will write the incorrect meanings in column 4 of the test sheet. If you are sure you do not know the incorrect meanings that I read, you may draw a dash-line.

The names and dates or words and meanings were read at the rate of three seconds per unit in the training. The names or words were read at the rate of five seconds per unit in the test. Four sets of the experiments were made on four successive days, useful and harmful content being equalized in respect of order.

The subjects understood that they would be paid bonuses dependent on their success in the learning. They also had the usual desire to achieve which moves educated people in such tasks. Consequently, their status in learning the harmful dates and meanings represented a balance between these motives and the motives of avoiding misinformation and of saving their energy for useful learning.

The results of the experiments were as follows:

They learned 900 of the correct dates and 859 of the wrong dates, 761 of the correct meanings and 459 of the wrong meanings. We correct for the dates and meanings known or partly known before the training from the facts for a control group.* The corrections change the numbers stated above to the following:

Correct dates, 890; wrong dates, 859. The useful/harmful ratio
is thus 1.04
Correct meanings, 721; wrong meanings, 459. The useful/harmful
ratio is thus 1.57

There is a slight superiority for the correct dates and a large superiority for the correct meanings. The superiority for the correct meanings is found in twenty-seven of the twenty-eight persons.

In Appendix II evidence is presented to prove that the results of experiments 18 to 21 would remain closely the same if we had cross-examined each subject in regard to his fidelity in trying equally hard to learn the false dates and meanings and had excluded any whose inclusion caused a balance of effort on the true dates and meanings.

The results of experiments 18 to 21 are also corroborated by those of two other sets of experiments with right and wrong dates and meanings in Appendix II. The average useful/harmful ratio in all three experiments is 1.07 for dates and has high reliability. The comparable average useful/harmful ratio for words is between 1.60 and 2.00.

In comprehensive memory tests after from one to five days the Celeb/Nonent ratio is higher than in the immediate memory test, the useful/harmful ratio for dates is much higher than in the immediate memory; so also is the useful/harmful ratio for meanings.

The comparison of such ratios is a troublesome matter, but by any reasonable treatment the useless and harmful facts suffer more than the useful ones from the destructive forces due to the lapse of time.†

* Seventeen individuals comparable to those who were subjects in experiments 18, 19, 20, and 21 were tested to provide an approximate estimate of the knowledge of the correct dates and meanings possessed apart from the training. Four knew the date for Washington; one that for Wundt; one that for Kipling. The allowance for dates is thus one third of a date out of eighty. In the case of the words, there were twenty substantially correct meanings and nine that showed acquaintance with the word such as might facilitate the learning of its meaning. If we count these nine as equal to four fully known meanings, we have about one and a half words to be subtracted from a person's score for eighty, to attain comparability with the learning of incorrect meanings.

† The essential facts are presented in Appendix II.

If printed lists containing sixty names and dates are used and enough time (fifty minutes) is allowed so that the best learners can learn almost or quite all, the superiority of the scores for celebrities is notably reduced. In our experiment 17, reported in Appendix II, the average number correct in tests at the close of the fifty minutes of study was 35.8 for the celebrities and 29.4 for the nonentities, the Celeb/Nonent ratio being 1.22. Long doses of learning content that has no intrinsic interest did not accentuate, but rather alleviated, its deleterious influence. The mind does not grow intolerant of the useless facts as the period is changed from about four minutes to fifty, and as the facts are repeated or recalled many times instead of three or four.

The fact noted in the previous paragraph and the fact that the wrong birth-date of a celebrity is much easier to learn than the real birth-date of a nonentity show that the potency of intrinsic interest is due to something more than a simple mechanism and other than a reasoned purpose.

Experiment 35

One of us (Woodyard) prepared tests on approximately 100,000 words each of the Bible, the Book of Mormon, and Frazer's *The Golden Bough*. The Bible excerpts included the books of Exodus, Joshua, Judges, Nehemiah, Daniel; those for the Book of Mormon included First and Second Nephi, Jacob, Enos, Jarom, Omni, Words of Mormon, Mosiah; those for *The Golden Bough* included chapters 1 to 17 in the one-volume edition.

Twenty-eight educated adults were asked to rank their interest in reading these three selections among other interests.* On day 2 they read or studied their first choice among these three for three hours. They took the test on it on day 3. On day 4 they read or studied the book which was their third choice for three hours. They took the test on it on day 5. Three hours were allowed for each test. The test on the Bible is shown in Appendix III.

The Bible was first choice with seven, third choice with nine. The Book of Mormon was first choice with six, third choice with thirteen. *The Golden Bough* was first choice with fifteen, third choice with six. The average scores in the tests were as follows:

---

* *The Golden Bough* was described as "one of the most important books on anthropology ever written."

Bible as first choice, 112; as third, 96
Book of Mormon as first choice, 94; as third, 84
The Golden Bough as first choice, 99; as third, 74

The 1st choice/3rd choice ratios were thus 1.17, 1.12, and 1.34.
The differences in favor of the scores for the preferred books were thus 18, 10, and 25, or 17 percent, 11 percent, and 19 percent of the average of the two means in question. The average of these percentages is 16 with a probable error of 3. If we assume that scores of 104, 88, and 87 in Bible, Mormon and *The Golden Bough,* respectively, represent equal learning, the excesses of the scores made by reading one's first choice over those made by reading one's third range from −32 to +51 for the twenty-eight individuals, with an average of 14 and a median of +11.5. The probable error of the +14 is 3.

We may then estimate that if educated adults were allowed a fifth or sixth more time on their third choice than on their first, they would have learned about as much from one as from the other.

We may then conclude that the difference in interest causes a real difference in learning, by more intense or continuous attention or by more potent or frequent action of the law of effect, or by both, but that this difference is moderate in amount.

Experiment 36

True biographies each containing about 1,200 words were prepared by quotation or adaptation from the *Encyclopædia Britannica* for twelve famous persons. False biographies were prepared by Dr. Woodyard duplicating the true ones in length, in the number of incidents and characterizations, and the like. Samples are shown below. Tests intended to be equal for each pair of biographies, so far as subjective planning could make them so, were also prepared. Samples are shown below.

Three of the false biographies (those of Milton, Napoleon, and Wesley) were read slowly, twice each, to a group of thirty subjects (the same group that participated in experiments 26 to 34) at such a rate as to require fifteen minutes each in the reading. Immediately after the reading of each biography, the subjects spent eight minutes upon the test, which was presented to them in printed form. Twenty-four hours later, the true biographies of three different persons (Wagner, C. W. Eliot, and Rembrandt) were read in precisely the same way, and precisely similar testing took place. Forty-eight hours later one true biography (that of Gladstone) and one false biography (that of Horace Mann) were read and the memory of each tested.

On the eighth day of the entire experiment (seven days after the use of the first three false biographies, five days after the use of the first three true biographies, and three days after the use of the fourth false and fourth true biographies), a comprehensive test of all the eight biographies was made in which six minutes were allowed for each of the eight tests.

Rembrandt: True

Rembrandt Harmens van Rijn, Dutch painter, was born in Leyden on July 15, 1606. He was the fourth son of Gerrit Harmens Van Rijn, a well-to-do miller. His parents resolved that he should enter a learned profession and so sent him to the High School at Leyden, but the boy disliked the prospect and determined to be a painter. Accordingly for three years he studied under Swannenburch, then under Lastman of Amsterdam, with whom he stayed only six months. During the early years he devoted himself entirely to studies, painting and etching the people around him, the beggars and cripples, every picturesque face and form he could get hold of. Life, character, and above all light were the aims of these studies. He painted nine portraits of his father, numerous ones of his mother, and several of a sister, as well as fifty to sixty self-portraits. His earlier pictures were made at Leyden where he resided, with his sister for housekeeper, from 1627 to 1631. Typical of this period are heads of old men, firm and hard in workmanship and full of detail, the effects of light and shade being carefully thought out.

Lovers of art in Amsterdam now being attracted to his work, he was invited to move to Amsterdam; urged by their calls, he went into residence, remaining there for the rest of his life. He became immediately popular as a portrait painter. In his early years there he painted at least forty portraits, all firm and solid in manner and staid in expression. There he painted also "Simeon in the Temple" and, in 1632, "The Lesson in Anatomy," which is made a great picture by the grouping of the expressive portraits and the completeness of the conceptions.

In 1634 Rembrandt was married to Saskia van Wylenbooch, a beautiful, fair-haired Frisian maiden of good connections. Till her death in 1642 she was the center of his life and art, and she lives for us in many a canvas other than her portraits. She was painted as the Queen of Artemisia or Bathsheba, and as the wife of

Samson. She brought him a marriage portion of 40,000 gulden as well as a circle of influential friends. She bore him four children, three of whom died in infancy.

By the year 1640 Rembrandt's characteristic style was fairly well fixed. His shadows are more transparent, his blending of light and shade perfected; his marvelous golden-brown tones have appeared. His self-portrait of that year shows a strong, robust man, with powerful head, firm and compressed lips and determined chin, heavy eyebrows, separated by a deep vertical furrow, and eyes of keen penetrating glance.

The year 1642 saw the painting of the "Night Watch." In that year also his wife died. Later his affairs became involved and he borrowed considerable sums to keep going. He kept up an extraordinary activity in order to earn enough to free himself of debt. In 1654 he was involved in the scandal of having a child by his servant Hendrickje Jagers or Stoffels. He recognized the child and gave it his mother's name, Cornelia, but apparently he did not marry its mother, though she continued to live with him. It is even supposed that the Venus and Cupid now in the Louvre is Rembrandt's portrait of Hendrickje and her child; it is more sure that the "Rembrandt's Mistress" in the Edinburgh National Gallery is her portrait. In 1656, Rembrandt's financial affairs became more involved and the Orphans Court transferred the house and grounds to his son Titus, to whom his mother had willed it under the trusteeship with full use of the funds of Rembrandt. In July of this year he was declared bankrupt, an inventory of his estate being ordered. The sums realized from these forced sales were but a fraction of the value of the pictures. Driven thus from his house, stripped of all possessions even to his table linen, he took lodgings in the Keizerskroon Hotel. This same dark year however saw the production of some of his greatest work: "John the Baptist," now in the Berlin Gallery, "Jacob Blessing the Sons of Joseph," "Lesson in Anatomy of Johann Deyman," and probably also the portrait of Jan Six, "Master of the Vineyard," and "Adoration of the Magi." His skill in color is mature and masterful, his drawing forceful. It is worthy of note that the Six family was closely connected with Rembrandt's artistic life. In 1641 Rembrandt painted with consummate skill the portrait of Anna Wymer, the mother of Jan Six. In 1647 also he executed the beautiful etching of Six standing by a window reading his tragedy of *Medea*, the illustrations for which Rembrandt made. In 1655 or possibly later he paints the portrait of the man in his prime and also in the same year paints the "John the Baptist" for him. Six, if he could not avert Rembrandt's financial disaster, at least stood loyally by him during it.

As old age came on, Rembrandt returned to the painting of his own portrait, a subject which had intrigued his skill as a young man. These early pictures, however, are often the outburst of exuberant fantasy, and were adorned with scarfs and feathers and gold chains and colorful dress. The late ones, of which there are at least twenty, still show the self-reliant expression of earlier days, though broken by age and care and subdued by sorrow and penury. About 1663 he painted the "Jewish Bride," now in the Ryks Museum in Amsterdam, and the "Family Group," the last and in some respects the most brilliant works of his life, bold and rapid in execution and marvelous in the subtle mixture and interplay of colors. The women and children of the latter picture are done with such affectionate touch that the impression is conveyed that they represent a group intimately known to him, but we do not know who the originals may have been.

In 1668 Titus, the only surviving son of Rembrandt, died leaving one child and on the eighth of October, 1669, the great painter himself passed away. Curiously enough he had outlived his popularity and was no longer in favor with a people who had come to admire the smooth trivialities of Van der Werff and Mieris.

Usually Rembrandt is thought of only as a painter, but his achievements in etching were also first-class. He excelled by his technical skill, his mastery of expression, and the lofty conceptions of many of his great pieces, such as "Death of the Virgin," "Christ Preaching," "Christ Healing the Sick," "Crucifixion," and the like. So great is his skill as an etcher that one is apt to overlook the nobleness of the etcher's ideas and the depth of his nature, a tendency confirmed by the enormous premium in money terms put upon those which are rare. The single impression of "Rembrandt with a Sabre" realized £2000 at the Holford Sale in 1893. The great etching period of his life was from 1639 to 1661, and in these twenty years he produced also his greatest works in portraiture, landscape, and Biblical story, all of which are instinct with the personal genius of the artist.

Rembrandt: False

Harmens Rembrandt Van Rijn was born in Brussels, January 2, 1608. He was the son of the earliest of the Belgian painters to achieve more than local renown and was from babyhood urged to the use of his pencil and trained for an artistic career. The boy wished, however, to go to sea, and ran away from home when he was twelve years old as cabin boy on a fishing schooner. His one experience of a month at the banks was sufficient to cure him of romantic desire for the sea, at the same time that it furnished him experiences which he later capitalized in his great sea pictures. Upon his return, he willingly set himself at his art studies. His father wished him to be a portrait painter, but it was soon evident that his skill lay in depicting the moods of nature rather than the characters of men. The only portrait he ever made of more than mediocre excellence is the well-known one of his mother.

At the age of twenty, he was urged by his father to travel and study in Italy to perfect his art. Setting out in the customary manner of the poor traveler, on foot, with his money concealed on his person, he journeyed through northern France, Luxembourg, and southwestern Germany into Italy. Travel was slow and dangerous. A distance of twenty miles per day was a maximum, not an average journey. For his protection he carried a well-whetted, leather-encased dirk strapped to his left side and a thick cudgel. His Nordic build and bulk of stature made him seem a formidable antagonist. To this fact in addition to his inconspicuous dress and unobtrusive manner it is doubtless due that he met with no serious misadventure by the way. He arrived in Firenze on Mayday, 1628, having passed through Mons, Neufchatel, Luxembourg, Mainz, Mannheim, Stuttgart, Innsbruck, Verona and Bologna in addition to numerous villages and farming communities. Fortunately also, practically all his funds were intact, since he had frequently paid for his lodging by painting tavern signs for his hosts. He carried in his knapsack, besides the change of clothing provided by his housewifely Dutch mother, sheets of drawing paper and a few crayons. When some noteworthy scene intrigued him, a few quick, bold dashes of the pencil served to fix it for later study and use. The great variety in the backgrounds of some of his famous pictures can doubtless be traced to the use of these sketches.

For two years he stayed in Firenze studying painting, color, distemper, and drawing. He frequented the rooms of all the artists, watching them at their work, asking occasional questions, soaking himself in the atmosphere of the greatest art center in the world. Drawn to return to his native North, he wished first to visit Rome. Curiously enough, he found it, after Florence, lacking in charm. So after only two weeks' stay he started to return to Belgium through Switzerland and France. The grandeur of the Alps moved him profoundly. As with his earlier love of the sea, however, the hardships of certain of his mountain-climbing exploits daunted him. To the end of his days, however, the massive peaks jutting into the sky, the gush of the waterfalls, the brilliance of the Alpine flowers, the grace of the mountain goats and other animals, the purity of the vast snow fields remained in his thought and added to the depth of his artistic creation.

His sojourn in Paris was intended to be for a month only. But one night in a cafe frequented by artists he met the Duke de Guise. Attraction was mutual. Soon the Duke commissioned him to design six paintings for wall decoration in his palace. In a twinkling, the pent-up resources of his years of study gushed forth. Two of the finest of all his sea pictures, "The Flying Dutchman," and the "Wreck Off Cape Lomax," and two mountain reminiscences, "Twilight in the Alps," and "Sunrise in Switzerland" were speedily executed. The two remaining spaces were unusual in shape and called for bold treatment. For one he executed a long, narrow horizontal panel in which a single long ocean swell just at the breaking point but showing in perspective a far expanse of sea is a masterpiece of utilization of necessities. For the other, a very long, narrow oval was needed. As subject for this he used a mountain lake with encircling peaks falling away to a valley stream. So great was the success of his work that other orders came to him in quick succession. For three years he was busy finishing these commissions. All of them were of the sea or the mountains—great green waves breaking over bleak rocks, great pines against the mountains, Alpine villages surrounded by their everlasting hills, masses of living rock, icefields in the moonlight, but in them all tremendous power and vitality, strength and tempest. Only one of all his Parisian pictures has the note of peace and rest—a tropical lagoon of soft blue water surrounded with lush vegetation in pompon-like masses, but showing the restless ocean beyond the breakers.

In October, 1634, aged twenty-six, he arrived in his native city. Settling at once to work, he produced in the next five years some of the most famous of his canvases. With each succeeding year his technique matured, his comprehension widened, his appreciation of the vast forces of nature deepened. In 1635 he married Julia van der Heyde, his second cousin. Her tragic death with her babe and her two-year-old son by fire in 1639 changed the whole current of his life. For months he could do no work. Only the sea and the woods seemed to solace him. For hours he would tramp along the shore, or, taking boat, row out beyond the breakers and let the tide sweep him in to land, or else he would wander through the forest, stopping now and again to measure some great tree with appraising eyes. Then came a request from the city council for a large canvas twelve by fifteen feet in size, to decorate the chamber of deputies. For six weeks he delayed reply, hoping for inspiration. Finally it came, and he portrayed the majesty of a great peak against which the storms of the ages beat only to succeed in piling upon it great depths of eternal snow, which in turn feeds life-giving sluices of torrential waters. No other great artist has so symbolically portrayed the fructifying power of tragic experience, and in no other of his works has Rembrandt been so tender and poignant.

After this picture was finished, a year of idle travel ensued, during which time he visited most of the great forests of Germany and France. Returning to Brussels in the spring of 1643, he busied himself with his paintings of trees and forests. Twelve canvases of great beauty were the outcome. Then he seemed definitely to have decided to abandon painting and began etching, turning, curiously enough, to architectural subjects exclusively. Oriel windows, balconies, bits of streets, doorways remembered from his French and Italian travels, Dutch roof-lines became his models.

In the ten years from 1646 to 1656 he executed some 300 different etchings, many of superb conception and workmanship. Once more he seemed to come to a pause in his creative power. His thoughts turned to Italy, and again he set out for Florence. While in Dresden he caught a severe cold which quickly developed into pneumonia. His death occurred November 15, 1656.

Test on Rembrandt (*True*)

Name ....
  1. Who was Rembrandt's first painting teacher?..............
  2. Rembrandt's technical individuality ripened to maturity by the time he was 20 25 30 35 40 years old................
  3. Rembrandt's father was a (write the number here).........
     (1) cobbler (2) lawyer (3) pastor (4) tailor (5) miller
  4. What was Rembrandt's family name?......................
  5. Rembrandt's wife was of (write the number here)...ancestry.
     (1) Bavarian (2) Frieslander (3) Prussian (4) Flemish (5) Danish
  6. Did Rembrandt survive his wife?........................
  7. Famous pictures painted by Rembrandt include (1) "The Fair" (2) "The Night Watch" (3) "The Lesson in Anatomy" (4) "The Fall of Man" (5) "The Annunciation" (6) "The Family Group" (7) "The Young Bull" (8) "The Syndicalists." Write here the numbers of as many as seem appropriate answers ....
  8. Rembrandt's early work was in (write the number here.....
     (1) genre (2) portraiture (3) landscape (4) still life (5) tempera
  9. Rembrandt was born about 1600 1605 1610 1615 1620.......
 10. What was Rembrandt's wife's family name?...............
 11. The Christian name of Rembrandt's son was..............
 12. Rembrandt at different times lived in (1) Copenhagen (2) Brussels (3) Hamburg (4) Leyden (5) Haarlem (6) Amsterdam (7) Rotterdam (8) Utrecht (9) Lille (10) Mannheim (11) Oslo (12) The Hague
     Write here the numbers of as many as seem appropriate answers ....
 13. Rembrandt was the father of 1 2 3 4 5 children..........
 14. What was Rembrandt's mother's Christian name?..........
 15. Rembrandt lived to be about 60 63 66 69 72 years old......
 16. Name a friend of Rembrandt's who was loyal to him during his financial difficulties...............................
 17. Rembrandt's marriage brought him (1) cares (2) fortune (3) unhappiness (4) children (5) commissions (6) penury (7) a model (8) enemies (9) divorce (10) illness (11) domestic afflictions (12) family scandals

Write here the numbers of as many as seem appropriate answers ....

18. By whose authority was Rembrandt's wife's property taken out of his control? ....

19. Rembrandt's portraits of himself painted after 1662 show him (1) somber (2) aged (3) ill (4) vacillating (5) sad (6) meditative (7) bitter (8) revengeful (9) self-reliant (10) smiling (11) egotistic (12) pugnacious
Write here the numbers of as many as seem appropriate answers ....

20. Rembrandt's bankruptcy was a legal means of (1) preserving his wife's fortune for his son (2) loss of his home (3) forced sale of his canvases (4) salvaging his reputation (5) humiliation of his son (6) rescuing him from a vampire (7) setting his time free for art work.
Write here the numbers of as many as seem appropriate answers ....

21. The most disastrous year financially for Rembrandt was 1653 1654 1655 1656 1657..............................

22. The subjects of Rembrandt's etchings were largely (1) landscape (2) Bible stories (3) waterscapes (4) old men (5) Dutch streets (6) fairy tales.
Write here the number of the best answer.................

Test on Rembrandt (*False*)

Name ....

1. What was Rembrandt's family name?...................

2. Rembrandt's father was a (write the answer here).........
(1) author (2) artist (3) voyager (4) general (5) printer (6) syndic

3. Rembrandt ran away to sea at about age 10 11 12 13 14 15 ....

4. On his first trip to Italy, Rembrandt passed through (1) Zurich (2) Innsbruck (3) Dresden (4) Mainz (5) Padua (6) Verona (7) Rheims (8) Vienna...................

5. On his first journey to Italy, Rembrandt often secured his food and lodging by (1) singing (2) waiting tables (3) painting portraits (4) playing the flute (5) painting signs (6) stealing
Write here the number of the best answer.................

6. Rembrandt's painting subjects were chiefly (1) women (2) mountains (3) villages (4) peasants (5) officials in uniform (6) farming scenes (7) roads (8) valley streams (9) ocean (10) cathedral spires
Write here the numbers of as many as seem appropriate answers ....

7. Rembrandt's first visit to Florence lasted about 1 2 3 4 5 6 years ....
8. Rembrandt's first paying commission was executed in (write number here) ....
   (1) Rome (2) Firenze (3) Brussels (4) Copenhagen (5) Paris (6) Geneva
9. What was the cause of the death of Rembrandt's wife?.......
10. Rembrandt had 0 1 2 3 4 5 children ....
11. For the city council of Brussels, Rembrandt painted a picture of (1) a forest in the wind (2) an ocean storm (3) a snow-covered peak (4) a field of corn in the sun (5) moonlight on an Alpine village (6) a camel train in the desert
    Write here the number of the best answer...................
12. What was Rembrandt's wife's maiden name?...............
13. Rembrandt worked in Paris about 0 1 2 3 4 5 years......
14. Rembrandt was married about 1630 1633 1636 1639 1642
    ....
15. Rembrandt began to etch about 1640 1642 1644 1646 1648
    ....
16. The subjects of Rembrandt's etchings were (1) marine (2) landscape (3) figures (4) architecture (5) still life (6) animals.
    Write the number of the best answer here ....
17. Rembrandt's death was due to (write the number here).....
    (1) exposure (2) fire (3) accident (4) violence (5) pneumonia (6) fever (7) old age
18. After the death of his wife, the subjects of Rembrandt's chief paintings were (1) hills (2) women (3) men (4) forests (5) lakes (6) streams (7) woods (8) villages
    Write here the number or numbers of as many as seem appropriate ....
19. Rembrandt's first visit to Rome was in 1628 1630 1632 1634 1636 ....
20. Rembrandt's painting for the Chamber of Deputies in Brussels is (1) portrait (2) still life (3) symbolism (4) miniature (5) genre (6) bucolic
    Write here the number of the best answer.................

The four false biographies were better learned and better retained than the five true ones. In the first test the average score for the false was 32.0; for the true, 26.1. In the memory test, the corresponding averages were 25.6 and 18.5. In one false and one true, tested only once, the average scores were, respectively, 25.8 and 21.4.

The reports were of equal effort in the two sorts except for three persons who thought that they had tried harder in learning the false biographies. If any allowance should be made for pre-knowledge, the difference would be increased. There can be no doubt that the worthlessness of the false biographies was little or no hindrance to learning them. They may have unwittingly been made a little more exciting and memorable, but allowance for this could surely do little more than equalize the above scores.

Experiments 37 and 38

In experiment 37 twenty-seven educated adults practised writing with the wrong hand for fifty periods of five minutes each. In periods 1, 3, 4, 7, 8, 11, 12, 15, 16, etc., they wrote with eyes open. In periods 2, 5, 6, 9, 10, 13, 14, 17, 18, etc., they wrote with eyes closed. Periods 1 and 2 came on day 1, the next eight on day 2, the next eight on day 3, etc. There were rests of two minutes between periods 1 and 2, 3 and 4, 5 and 6, etc. There were intervals of thirty minutes filled by other activities between periods 4 and 5, 12 and 13, 20 and 21, etc. Each subject wrote always with the same kind of pen, ink, and paper. The copy was the first verse of "My Country, 'Tis of Thee," *Sunday, Monday, Tuesday, Wednesday, . . . Saturday,* and the words *one, two, three, . . .* to *twenty.* The subjects were told, "You are going to learn two things, to write with your left hand (or wrong hand) and to write with your eyes shut or bandaged. Learning to write with the left hand may be very useful to you. Learning to write with eyes closed is of no practical use to you, but has a scientific interest for us." Other instructions were given to secure uniformity by the subjects in what they wrote with the eyes closed. The assumption is that the intrinsic interest will be much greater in the writing with eyes open which is, as stated, a useful art and which was enlivened by constant easy visual observation of how well one did, than in the writing with eyes closed. The latter of course lacked the guidance from easy visual observation.

The results showed average gains as follows: From period 1 to period 49 (i.e., left-hand, eyes open), 27.1 letters per minute (from 39.3 to 66.4), 1.63 in quality score (5.61 to 7.24 in units of the Thorndike handwriting scale). From period 2 to period 50 (i.e., left-hand, eyes closed), 29.3 letters per minute (from 37.0 to 66.3), 0.59 in quality score (2.19 to 2.78).

The useful work thus showed a little less gain in speed and about 2.66 times as much gain in quality. Besides the possible difference in intrinsic interest, the useful work had the advantage of continuous knowledge of results, but the useless work had the possible advantage of transfer effect of abilities gained with eyes open. We hoped to make allowance for this latter by means of two other experiments, in one of which students of psychology with a keen interest in both sorts of work would practise the two functions and in the other of which subjects would repeat the experiment described here but with the valueless work done before and after the valuable, not dovetailed into it. But this has not been possible, and the result is thus uncertain.

In experiment 38 we compare learning to typewrite in the ordinary way with learning to typewrite each word backward (*eht* for *the*, *yob* for *boy*, etc.). In the ordinary learning, we have (a) the interest in achievement + (b) the desire to earn a large bonus + (c) the interest in acquiring a useful ability. In learning the backward typing, we have (a) + (b) + (d) the desire to avoid possibly harmful habits and save energy for useful ones.

Twenty-eight educated adults practised at ordinary typing for ten minutes daily for six days, and also at typing in which each word was typed with the order of the letters reversed. Preliminary instructions and practice in the use of the machine were given on the day preceding the six practice days. The instructions were as follows:

"In the first period of each day, you are to practise ten minutes at ordinary typewriting. You will typewrite the first verse of 'My Country, 'Tis of Thee,' *Sunday, Monday, Tuesday, Wednesday*, . . . to *Saturday*, and *one, two*, . . . to *twenty*, and then repeat all. If you do not know how to use the machine at all, one of us will show you now.

"In the second period (also of ten minutes) you are to typewrite each word backward. That is, you are to write the words in their order, but the letters of each word in the reverse order. For *my* you will write *ym;* for *country* you will write *yrtnuoc;* for *one* you will write *eno* and so on.

"We will not do any typing to-day but will begin to-morrow at this time. To-day those who do not know how to use the machine will be instructed."

Each person was given a sheet containing the first verse of "My Country, 'Tis of Thee," the days of the week, and the words *one, two*, etc.

The number of letters typed minus 3 for each mistake was

used as the measure of achievement.* The allowance of 3 was such as made the course of practice, as shown by the corrected score for those with widely different numbers of errors on the first and on the last day of regular typing, resemble closely the course of practice for those who had nearly the same number of errors on day 6 as on day 1. Any reasonable allowance for mistakes would leave the general conclusions which we shall draw unaltered.

The first of these is that there is unquestionably learning in the useless backward typing, and much more than would be expected by transfer from the ordinary learning. The facts (shown in detail in Table 13) for three groups, selected in accordance with their scores in ordinary typing on the sixth day, are as follows: Group I, averaging 140 letters per minute in ordinary typing on day 1, averaged 190 on day 6. In the backward typing their averages for day 1 and day 6 were 53 and 115. Group II, averaging 88 letters per minute in ordinary typing, averaged 125 on day 6. In the backward typing their averages were 35 and 65. Group III, averaging 39 letters per minute in ordinary typing on day 1, averaged 68 on day 6. In the backward typing their averages were 22 and 39.

The chief abilities required in the backward writing are (1) keeping track of the copy by vision and memory, (2) general knowledge and management of the machine, (3) ability to hit the right key quickly when one thinks of any letter, (4) abilities to hit the right keys quickly and in the right sequence when one thinks of certain sequences of letters (as *yad*, which comes in *Sunday, Monday,* etc., the *eno* for *one,* or the *owt* for *two*), and (5) abilities to think of the reverses for the various words or parts of words of the material to be copied (as *yrtnuoc* and *sendew* for *country* and *Wednes*) quickly and accurately.

The persons of Group III might have improved in the backward writing even if their direct practice in it had little or no value, by transfer, i.e., by the improvement of abilities which

---

* It would perhaps have been better to have assigned values also to each space between words and to each shift from one line to a new line. But we were in doubt about the magnitude of the value and thought it wise to have the score in the backward typing as free as possible from useful elements. Anybody desirous of determining what the results would be from such a scoring can make the necessary computations from the data of Table 13.

TABLE 13

IMPROVEMENT IN ORDINARY TYPING AND IN TYPING EACH WORD WITH THE LETTERS IN REVERSE ORDER

GROUP AND SUBJECT	SCORE FOR 10 MIN. FORWARD TYPING			SCORE FOR 10 MIN. BACKWARD TYPING		
	Day 1	Day 6	Gain	Day 1	Day 6	Gain
Group I, Indiv. 1	2203	2880	677	854	1836	982
2	1611	2042	431	914	1753	839
3	1489	1917	428	253	801	548
4	1275	1894	619	511	1144	629
5	1189	1702	513	342	1142	800
6	1205	1695	490	553	867	314
7	1098	1553	455	411	917	506
8	1168	1526	358	440	765	325
Average	1405	1901	...	535	1141	...
Group II, Indiv. 1	1065	1453	388	189	468	279
2	811	1446	635	361	627	266
3	909	1382	473	420	794	374
4	806	1370	564	334	906	572
5	989	1207	218	381	543	162
6	844	1167	323	353	793	440
7	838	1161	323	469	681	212
8	876	1116	240	310	766	456
9	835	1081	246	403	471	68
10	789	1075	286	306	456	150
Average	876	1246	...	353	651	...
Group III, Indiv. 1	510	877	367	305	456	151
2	654	876	222	256	341	85
3	530	838	308	224	395	171
4	585	732	147	270	399	129
5	387	689	302	192	396	204
6	362	615	253	245	556	311
7	199	598	399	121	424	283
8	292	580	288	236	369	133
9	337	548	211	225	366	141
10	37	405	368	87	222	135
Average	389	676	...	216	392	...

were practised in the regular typing, notably abilities 1, 2, and 3 above. But in the persons of Group I these abilities were at so high a stage the first day that they could hardly have improved at all, and certainly not enough to account for more than a very small fraction of their gain in backward writing. In Group I, all, or nearly all, of the gain in backward writing must have come from improving the almost useless abilities to tap out *yrt, nuoc, sruht,* and the like, or the still less useful ability to know that

Monday is to be written *yadnoM*. To a less extent and less surely this is true of Group II.

Our second conclusion is that there is no evidence of any inferiority in the learning of the useless backward type. If we compare the improvements in the two functions on the assumption that the changes from writing twenty letters correctly to writing thirty letters correctly, from writing forty letters correctly to writing fifty letters correctly, etc., all represent equal increments of gain and differ each from the next by an equal amount, we find that the gains in regular typing and in backward typing for Groups I, II, and III total 116 and 109.

If we used percentile gains, the improvement would seem much greater for backward than for ordinary typing, but there is here, as usually in psychological measurements of improvement, no reason to assume that a gain of 1 on 1 equals a gain of 10 on 10 or 20 on 20 or 100 on 100.

Another reasonable, though complicated, comparison may be made as follows: In ordinary typing in our experiment those scoring 38.9 on day 1 gained 28.7; those scoring 87.6 on day 1 gained 37.0; those scoring 140.5 on day 1 gained 49.6. We may then expect that, in a similar experiment with a similar sort of subjects, those scoring 67.6 on day 1 would gain about

$28.7 + \left(\dfrac{37.0 - 28.7}{87.6 - 38.9} \right) \times 28.7$. This is 33.6. Similarly we may expect that those scoring 101.2 on day 1 would gain about

$37.0 + \left(\dfrac{49.6 - 37.0}{140.5 - 87.6} \right) \times 13.6$. This is 40.3.

We then may make a curve composed of three parts, the first showing the actual gain of the ten subjects of Group III, the second the estimated gain of a group that began at 67.6 where Group III left off, and the third the estimated gain of a group that began at 100.3 where the assumed group left off. This curve is shown as the continuous line of Figure 4.

The facts for our three groups for the backward typing were:

Group III began with 21.6 and gained 17.6, reaching 39.2
Group II began with 35.3 and gained 29.8, reaching 65.1
Group I   began with 53.5 and gained 61.8, reaching 115.3

A group of similar subjects beginning at 39.2 would reach 69.0 if they gained as Group II did. They would reach 101.0 if

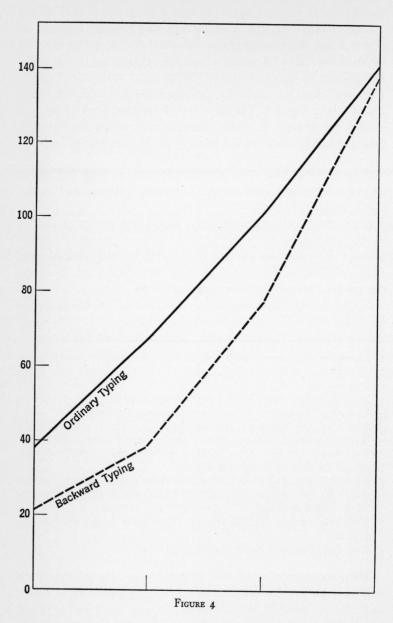

FIGURE 4

they gained as Group I did. They would reach 85.5 if they gained as Group II did till they reached 53.5 and thereafter gained as Group I did. We may set 77 as the score that would be reached by them on day 6. A group of similar subjects beginning at 77 and gaining at the same rate as Group I did would reach 138.8. The curve made by combining these three sections is shown as the dotted line of Figure 4. The curve for the backward typing reaches in the end almost the same height as the curve for forward typing. Since it starts from a lower level, the amount of learning is greater for it as judged by this method.

It appears then that these subjects were able to learn the useless letter-reversing and typing queer letter sequences as well as the useful acts.

Experiments 39 and 40 used boys and girls in grades 10 and 11 as subjects, extended the time of study for each individual to fifty minutes daily for five days, and provided for five choices from eight possibilities. They thus serve as an independent check on the results obtained in experiments 7 to 38.

In experiment 39, twenty-eight pupils spent two hours a day for five consecutive days in learning and being tested upon work *chosen by them.* There were eight sorts of work as follows:

1. Learning the correct meanings of 100 rare English words
2. Learning certain wrong meanings of 100 (different) rare English words
3. Learning the correct birth years of 100 famous men
4. Learning the correct birth years of 100 nonentities
5. Learning the dates of 100 important events (such as when Turner painted "Rain, Storm and Speed," when Brooklyn Bridge was opened, when Stevens invented the screw propeller, when Beethoven composed *Fidelio*)
6. Learning the dates of 100 utterly trivial and useless events (such as that Edgar built a fire, Peter began studying Latin, Max found a dollar, Mr. Ames's horse ran away)
7. Learning twenty bits of poetry (four lines each) by famous authors
8. Learning twenty bits of doggerel or trash

These varieties of work were described, and the subjects were told that the pay for learning would be 1/3¢ per word in No. 1 and 2/3¢ per word in No. 2, 1/3¢ per date in No. 3 and 2/3¢ per date in No. 4, 1/3¢ per date in No. 5 and 2/3¢ per date in No. 6, 1/3¢ per line in No. 7 and 2/3¢ per line in No. 8. Each subject then chose what he would work at on day 1. On day 2, he chose from the other seven. On day 3 he chose from the six not yet used, and so on. Each day, at the close of fifty minutes of study, each person had twenty-five minutes to spend on a test of what he had learned. Samples of the instructions, material studied, and tests used are presented in Appendix IV.

We first compare the learning of the valuable material with that of the same sort which is useless but paid for at twice as high a rate. The latter was learned better. The average scores after correction for pre-knowledge were*:

Right meanings, 37; wrong meanings, 26; diff. 11
Dates of celebrities, 23; of nonentities, 35; diff. —12
Dates of important events, 19; of trivial events, 34; diff. —15
Good poetry, 38; bad poetry, 33; diff. 5

The totals stand 117 to 128. The extra 1/3 of a cent then clearly outweighs whatever greater stimulus to learning the materials of Nos. 1, 3, 5, and 7 had.

We next compare the learning of certain material by persons for whom it was a first or second choice with the learning of it by persons for whom it was a third, fourth, or fifth choice.† There is a little difference in favor of the later choices, but this may be due to general practice in learning. The average scores were as shown in Table 14.

These pupils certainly showed no signs of learning what they themselves chose much better than what they took more or less by imposition.‡

---

*Allowance for pre-knowledge is made on the basis of results from sixty other pupils in the same grades of the same schools who were tested for the right meanings and good poetry without any opportunity for study. The meanings called right in scoring experiment 39 were given on the average for eight tenths of a word per person, but there was evidence of such knowledge as might make the learning easier in 4.2 other words per person. By estimating the saving for each such case, we have 1.9 words, making 2.7 as the probable total allowance. It cannot be more than 5.0. The allowance in the case of the poetry is approximately zero. From our studies with adults we know that the allowance for pre-knowledge of dates is almost zero.

† But for No. 6 (trivial events), which was never first choice and only once a second choice, we compare second and third choices with fourth and fifth.

‡ It is of some interest to know the general trend of the 137 choices (three subjects were absent on one day). There were fifty-three of useful material and eighty-four of useless. Of the useful, 35.8 percent were word-meanings, 20.8 percent birth years of celebrities, 17.0 percent dates of important events, and 26.4 percent bits of poetry. The useless were divided nearly equally (25.0, 22.6,

TABLE 14

THE RESULTS OF LEARNING ACCORDING TO THE ORDER OF PREFERENCE

Material learned	Average score when first or second choice	Average score when third, fourth, or fifth choice	Difference
1	41	37	— 4
2	21	33	+12
3	20	24	+ 4
4	34	35	+ 1
5	16	26	+10
6	31	35	+ 5
7	42	36	— 6
8	36	31	— 5

Experiment 40 was a test given to twenty-seven of the twenty-eight subjects of experiment 39 seventy-two hours after the fifth day's work, in which each individual had seventy-five minutes to write all they could remember on five test sheets identical with those which he had used at the end of the work of each day. He was instructed to go through these in the same order as that of the previous week, but this was not enforced. After allowance for pre-knowledge of the right meanings, dates, etc., the averages were *:

Right meanings, 13; wrong meanings, 9; diff. 4
Dates of celebrities, 6; of nonentities, 10: diff. —4
Dates of important events, 7; of trivial events, 8; diff. —1
Good poetry, 23; bad poetry, 23; diff. 0

The losses over the three days were as follows:

24 out of 37 for right meanings; 17 out of 26 for wrong meanings
17 out of 23 for celebrities; 25 out of 35 for nonentities
12 out of 19 for important dates; 26 out of 34 for trivial dates
15 out of 38 for good poetry; 10 out of 33 for bad poetry
In all, 68 out of 117 for the useful, and 78 out of 128 for the wrong or trivial, were lost.

The results of experiments 7 to 40 present a picture very clear in its two main features, but indistinct and puzzling in some details. There can be no doubt that our subjects could and did learn facts and skills that were useless and even harmful to them,

23.8, and 28.6) among wrong meanings, birth-dates of nonentities, trivial events, and trashy poetry.

* The method of allowance used here may not be the best, but any reasonable method will give almost the same result.

except for the money rewards and good repute as learners in the eyes of the experimenter and their own consciences. Probably never before in all their educational and vocational history had they spent time so profitlessly to themselves as in learning the false dates, false biographies, writing with eyes closed, and typing words backwards. Yet their minds learned this pernicious rubbish almost as well as the true dates, true biographies, and normal typing.

There can be no doubt also that the operations of interests, even in these intelligent and specially trained persons, are notably unreasonable. Their minds revolted at the useless birth-dates of cobblers, tailors, and other nonentities much more than at the wrong birth-dates of celebrities. They lost more by being shifted from *The Golden Bough* to the Bible (or vice versa) against a moderate handicap of interest than by being shifted from a true biography of an eminent man to a batch of empty falsehoods about him. Their minds are lured by the famous names regardless of the value of what is said about them, and by novelty, surprise, romance, and the like in the biographies regardless of truth.

When the useless or harmful material does reduce learning, reduction is not by a general dulling of activity or a persisting unreadiness to attend. On the contrary, twenty useless or wrong things in a series by themselves are better attended to than when they occur mixed, ten and ten, with useful facts.

So far as our results go, there is no cumulative action from learning the useless or harmful. There is no evidence of greater difference at the end of an hour than in its first five minutes. On the contrary, our long periods of study show smaller advantages of the useful over the useless or harmful. There is reason to believe that if our subjects had studied true and false biographies and so on for two-hour or three-hour sessions instead of one-hour sessions, they would have maintained their ability to learn the trash as well as the worthy facts.

In all of this, some of the adult learners may have been somewhat inspired by the thought that they were participating in experiments useful for science and education. It would be instructive to check the influence of this by a parallel experiment in which the learning was announced as paid for by an insane man. I do not think the results would be altered greatly. The high school pupils were surely little influenced by any such ideas.

Chapter 10

EVIDENCE ON THE INFLUENCE OF REWARDS AND PUNISHMENTS FROM THE HISTORY OF EDUCATION AND INDUSTRY

Rewards and Punishments in Education *

AN endeavor has been made to find what has been the effect of rewards and punishments used as educational instruments. It was hoped that we might collect facts covering various peoples, various ages, various civilizations. Search has been made through such records as are available in English in two ways. First, the literature on family and school education has been scrutinized; second, more than a thousand biographies or autobiographies have been examined.

We have excerpts exhibiting all that can be said to be surely known concerning the topic among the Greeks and the Romans. We have a fair degree of assurance that we have secured what knowledge there is of Egyptian, Chaldean, and Persian practice. A few scraps of evidence concerning certain savage and primitive peoples are at hand. Whatever the various encyclopedias offer concerning medieval European educational procedures has been noted. More than 1,000 biographies, including autobiographies, have been leafed through to note the pertinent early life experience in school and home of their subjects. The history and practice of various parochial and mission schools through the centuries after the dominance of the church in educational affairs became established, so far as it was found available in English, has been examined.

In all the sources, facts as to the specific rewards or punishments given and the effect thereof upon the person or persons receiving it have been sought. In the literature on family and school education, there is a paucity of such factual material. It is not possible to secure from it evidence adequate to appraise the

---

* Ella Woodyard is the author of this section.

effect of any reward or punishment upon children of any description. The evidence is adequate to show (1) that certain human groups have been very indulgent to their young, managing their training with a very small amount of corporal punishment and scolding; (2) that, until very recent times, European societies have relied very extensively upon the fear of punishment to prevent undesired behavior and also to cause desired behavior; and (3) that they have done so largely because of sheer custom, not to say superstition.

The best illustration of the first point is from the tribe in New Guinea with whom Margaret Mead lived. Punishments were used to teach babies to keep hold of the mother in the water, to teach respect for property, and to teach certain canons of shame, but not to enforce obedience, self-restraint, or labor.

"One woman starts to gather up her beads. 'Come, Alupera,' she says to her three-year-old daughter. 'I don't want to.' The fat little girl wriggles and pouts. 'Yes, come, I must go home now. I have stayed here long enough making bead work. Come.' 'I don't want to.' 'Yes, come, father will be home from market and hungry after fishing all night.' 'I won't.' Alupera purses her lips in ugly defiance. 'But come, daughter of mine, we must go home now.' 'I won't. . . .' The child jerks from her mother's attempt to detain her and turning, slaps her mother roundly in the face. Every one laughs merrily. Her mother's sister adds: 'Alupera, thou shouldst go home now with thy mother,' whereupon the child slaps her also. The mother gives up the argument and begins working on her beads again. . . . Alupera begins eating a small green fruit, with a sly glance at her mother. 'Don't eat that, Alupera, it is bad.' Alupera defiantly sets her teeth in the rind. 'Don't eat it. Dost not hear me?' Her mother takes hold of the child's hand and tries to wrest it from her. Alupera begins to shriek furiously. The mother lets go with a hopeless shrug, and the child puts the fruit to her lips again." [Mead, '30, p. 15f.]

"A man is chewing betel on his veranda. The platform shakes as a canoe collides with one of the piles. The man begins hastily gathering up the pepper leaves and betel nuts to hide them. . . . But he is not quick enough. A small head appears . . . and his six-year-old son Popoli climbs up dripping. . . . The child . . . whines out . . . 'A little betel?' The father throws him a nut. . . . 'Another,' the child's voice rises to a higher pitch. The father throws him a second nut, which the child grasps firmly . . . without acknowledgement. 'Some pepper leaf?' The father frowns. 'I have very little, Popoli.' 'Some pepper leaf.' The father tears off a piece of leaf and throws it to him. The child scowls at the small piece. 'This is too little. More! More! More!' His voice rises to a howl of rage. . . . The father's knife slips out of the bag and falls through a crack into the sea. 'Wilt get it, Popoli?' But the child only glares furiously, 'No I won't, thou, thou stingy one, thou hidest thy pepper leaf from me.' The child dives off the veranda and swims away." [Mead, '30, p. 20f.]

[The children] "eat when they like, play when they like, sleep when they see fit. They use no respect language . . . and are allowed more license in the use of obscenity than are their elders. The veriest urchin can shout defiance and contempt at the oldest man in the village. Children are never required to give up anything to their parents: the choicest morsels of food are theirs by divine right. They can rally the devoted adults by a cry; bend and twist their parents to their will. They do no work. . . . The community demands nothing of them except respect for property and the avoidance due to shame." [Mead, '30, p. 47f.]

A widely known case is Japan. Although the reports of casual observers with sentimental leanings doubtless exaggerate Japanese indulgence to children, the general fact remains. The following quotations give a fair picture of the fact.

"Among poor and rich, children are given full fling. They pervade every room, they swarm romping in the gardens. . . . Toys are showered on them. Girls have a toy festival in March, boys in May. No one denies them anything. Then at a certain age an iron rule for boys supervenes and a rigid standard is set for girls. The boy hardens into the youth and keeps hard until, a man at last, he may soften into the blandness that he sees about him." [Clarke, J. I. C., '18, p. 44.]

"The Japanese fondness for children is seen not only at festival time. Parents seem always ready to provide their children with toys. . . . A still further reason for the impression that the Japanese are especially fond of their children is the slight amount of punishment and reprimand which they administer. The children seem to have nearly everything their own way. Playing on the streets, they are always in evidence and are given the right of way. . . . In Japan . . . the industrial organization of society is still such that the father is home a large part of the time. . . . It is a common thing to see the father caring for children." [Gulick, S. L., '03, p. 96.]

"In general they [the children's games] seem to be natural, sensible, and in every sense beneficial. Their immediate or remote effect, next to that of amusement, is either educational or hygienic. . . . The study of the subject leads one to respect more highly . . . the Japanese people for being such affectionate fathers and mothers." [Griffis, W. E., '03, p. 465.]

"I think my parents were so careful about my home education. Whenever I was naughty they never smacked me but they always brought a looking glass in front of my crying face. I hated to see my own face so ugly with tearmarks and I immediately began to laugh. Very often when I wanted to cry a little longer, I used to scream, 'Oh don't show me the glass for a few moments!' I was never scolded severely. They always told me, 'You are a very nice boy, but just at this moment some evil is trying to dwell in you. How pity the evil is making you a bad boy and giving some trouble to your dear parents,' and I began to feel sorry for them, and I used to cling to their necks and say 'The evil is gone long time ago. I am your favorite boy.' . . . It was my greatest comfort to confess to my mother before bed everything (good and bad, all) what I had done during the day. . . . When I confessed these things to my mother, she used to take me to the school next day, and she sincerely apologized to the teachers and schoolboys. My father treated me even tenderer than my mother." [Markimo, Yoshio, '12, p. 3.]

"In primary schools the boys can dress as they please. . . . The children generally look tolerably neat and clean. The pupils are disposed on the whole to be orderly and respectful toward their teachers; but the absence of home discipline and the easy-going disposition of Japanese teachers themselves cause the discipline of the youngest classes to appear somewhat lax. As they grow older the pressure of public opinion takes the place of any from the teachers. . . .

"There are few of either rewards or punishments in a primary school, though some award small prizes of books, slates, pencils, etc., sometimes to a whole class, sometimes to 10 or 12 picked children. . . . Few punishments are inflicted beyond a verbal admonition or complaint to the parent. . . . Corporal punishment is prohibited. It is, however, permissible to haul a boy roughly out of the ranks by one ear, and make him stand apart in disgrace." [Sharp, W. H., '06, p. 90f.]

"Foreign teachers generally give Japanese students an excellent character for behavior, and say that punishment is seldom required; but I had the misfortune to encounter away from their school some very unfavorable specimens of middle-school boys, who were noisy, disorderly in their conduct with the waitresses, and absolutely untruthful about the school. . . . The recognized punishments are admonition, detention, suspension, expulsion." [Sharp, W. H., '06, p. 127f.]

No competent student of the history of education will dispute the second point, but the following may be useful to illustrate it:

The Greeks regularly permitted nurses to punish little children with the sandal; the guardian slave to punish older boys with the rattan or strap. [Gulick, C. B., *Life of Ancient Greeks,* 1902.] Whippings and noise were the characteristics of the Roman school. [Davis, W. S., *A Day in Old Rome,* 1925.] In the constitutions for monastic schools "there is scarcely any childish transgression even of the most pardonable and natural character, for which the rod is not definitely invoked." [Coulton, G. G., *Student Life: In the Middle Ages,* 1913.] The Prince Consort writes in his journal when about six years old, "I cried at my lesson to-day because I could not find a verb, and the Rath pinched me to show me what a verb was." Sir Jonah Barrington relates that in one of the best schools of the time he was "flogged for not minding my emphasis in recitation. . . . Castigation was regularly administered every Monday morning, to give me by anticipation a sample of what the repetition day might produce." [Barrington, J., *Personal Sketches of his Own Times,* 1827.]

The following case may have been extreme, but such a case could not have occurred at all unless the leaders in education had great confidence in punishment:

"The brutal, indecent, and humiliating indignity of flogging being at this time prevalent, of course we came in for our share. The instrument of castigation was a number of thin willow saplings, tough and pliable, tied together at one end for the convenience of handling, and the other spread out for the purpose of covering the widest possible space. The number of strokes varied according to the degree of transgression. The ill-concealed satisfaction that ruffian felt in his hangman's task caused me to regard him with abhorrence."

(Then he tells how the usher undertook to flog his younger brother, just up from a four weeks' illness, for inability to answer in oral examination. The brother ran to John to cling to him for protection. John exclaimed "What? Flog anyone in his condition of health? You dare not." The usher sent for the porter to hold the boy while he flogged him. The porter dragged the boys apart and the usher began preparation for the beating, stripping the boy to his loins. John, unable to endure it, clutched a heavy slate and hurled it at the usher, who fell as though shot. The boys ran from the room and that night ran away from school, home.) [Condensed from Brougham, J., *Life Stories and Poems of,* 1881.]

The evidence that the reliance upon punishment was due to custom rather than reason is the absence of any defense of it except in retort to criticism and the nature of the defenses, which to this day consist chiefly of repetitions of proverbial lore such as,

"Spare the rod and spoil the child." There is an often quoted report of a certain Swabian schoolmaster who had recorded the 1,394,021 punishments administered by him during fifty-one years, but there is no report of any schoolmaster giving even thirteen reasons for the reliance upon punishment as a panacea.

Our search through 1,068 biographies resulted in 191 reported instances of a reward or a punishment. In the case of eighty-eight of these there was some testimony concerning its effect. As shown in Table 15 below, the testimony taken at its face value shows the reward to have been almost universally beneficial (29 to 1), whereas the punishments did harm over twice as often as good.

TABLE 15

TESTIMONY CONCERNING THE EFFECTS OF REWARDS AND PUNISHMENTS

	To the right action	From the wrong action	To the wrong action	From the right action	No result stated or readily inferable	Total
English cases						
Effect of punishment	6	3	19	11	32	71
Effect of reward	17	1	1	0	8	27
American cases						
Effect of punishment	3	5	6	5	44	63
Effect of reward	0	11	0	0	19	30

In making this tabulation the criteria for allocation into categories were as follows:

Punishments. (1) "To the right action," if there was a definite statement that, as a result of punishment for "sins of omission or commission," the desired conduct ensued.

(2) "From the wrong action," if there was a clear indication that, as a result of such punishment, the undesired act was not repeated.

(3) "To the wrong action," if the statement was made or clearly implied that the punishment served to make the child (a) determined to pursue his conduct, (b) rebellious to the discipline, or (c) deceitful to continue his conduct but escape consequences.

(4) "From the right action," if the statements bore as their most probable implication the fact that, though no specific wrong action ensued, yet the child was repelled from, rather than attracted to, the desired conduct.

(5) "No result stated or readily inferable," if the anecdote was merely related as an experience of the subject without any suggestion of consequences either good or bad.

Rewards. (1) "To the right action," if there was a definite statement that, as a result of the reward for a specific act, the conduct was gladly repeated by the child (usually to the extent of the setting-up of a habit).

(2) "From the wrong action," if the indication was plain that, as a result of such reward, the child was later kept from yielding to the temptation to perform the act which he knew to be disapproved.

(3) "To the wrong action." The original criterion set up here was that a child was led by a reward to deceit or hypocrisy for the sake of obtaining unmerited rewards. No case meeting this criterion was found.

(4) "From the right action." In one case the child after a reward, feeling that it was insufficient, determined not to perform that right act again.

(5) "No result stated or readily inferable," if the anecdote was merely related as an experience of the subject without suggestion of consequent effect upon him. (The most common cases under this heading are statements that prizes were won, or that a person won the approval of his teachers, or the like.)

We report a fair sampling of the eighty-eight records in the case of boys in Appendix V. It would be risky to decide just what the eighty-eight records do prove, but they certainly do not prove that punishment of a given behavior can be relied on to diminish that behavior or stimulate its opposite.

Rewards and Punishments in Business and Industry *

There can be little doubt that employers have shifted during the past fifty years from emphasis on punishments for idleness, bad work, and infractions of rules to rewards for industry, competence, and coöperation with the management. It is also the fact that the various schemes for so-called "incentive" wages which experts have devised unanimously feature rewards. They usually have some basal minimum standard and definite additions for

* Irving Lorge is the author of this section.

this, that, and the other desirable behavior. What happens to the worker when he fails to attain the minimum standard is not advertised. Sometimes nothing adverse happens, as when a maker of a good suggestion is specifically rewarded, but no loss or opprobrium is incurred by the persons who make none. Sometimes the humane and intelligent procedure is followed of supplying necessary training. Sometimes probably there are scoldings and threats; and sometimes, doubtless, demotion to a lower job or dismissal.

The rewards in these schemes are oftenest money payments, but fame through publicity is common, and vacations are fairly common as rewards for regularity and promptness in coming to work. The qualities and acts which are rewarded are naturally those which increase the success of the business as measured by profit, in reality or in the employer's opinion.

We hoped to find in the reports of the workings of plans for piecework plus bonus, differential piece rates, bonuses for time saved, length of service bonuses, attendance bonuses, and the like, evidence concerning the efficacy of various rewards upon quantity and quality of work so as to compare them with one another and with punishments. But the reports which we have examined are far from clear on such matters.

The plan of incentives is often correlated with the setting of standards, the improvement of methods of work, and changes in training or supervision, or both. The gains shown in quantity and quality of work may be due to these concomitants.

The plan of incentives may be ostensibly a system of rewards for achievements above a certain minimum and yet permit substantial elements of punishments, for example, in threats of demotion or discharge by foremen or supervisors.

The plan may be one of promises and rewards so far as the top levels of management are concerned, but yet operate upon the individual worker by threats and punishments. In group-incentive plans in which a department or gang receives bonuses for the achievements of the group, the potency of the plan depends upon what the members of the group do to themselves and to each other as a consequence of it. They may praise each other for good work which helps to ensure the attainment of the bonus. They may punish each other for idleness or bad work. The latter is probably the more frequent. We may hope that experience will teach such groups to reward the good, and, when the bad does occur, to punish it in such wise that the wrongdoer then and there replaces the bad by the good behavior, but we can hardly expect it.*

What is a reward for A in intention, and on the company's books, and to the employee's mind for a time, may become psychologically a punishment for not-A. Thus if a month free from tardiness is rewarded by a certain bonus, and a worker earns this for, say, January to July, he may then, when he fails to receive it in August, consider that deprivation as a punishment for tardiness.

These and other difficulties prevent us from making any definitive statement and adducing evidence in support of it. But it is our impression that more and better work is done when the worker thinks of the 'right' activity as producing such and such a bonus or privilege than when he thinks of the 'wrong' activity (or the absence of the 'right' activity) as producing such and such a fine or deprivation. The management must think so, for their arrangement and presentation of plans are such as to encourage workers to think of everything possible as a reward up for A rather than a deprivation down for not-A.

Certain facts suggest that the amount of the reward for regularity or promptness of attendance at work is of relatively little importance, the main thing being to get favorable attention to it. For example, according to a writer in *System*, one company paid $25 to each employee who completed a year with no absences, no tardiness, and no excuses from work. Two won it in 1928 and eight in 1929. Another company paid each employee $1.50 every ten calendar days if there had been no absence, no lateness of more

---

* The confidence expressed by some experts in individual management that a group of workers will take good care of its own interests is somewhat surprising. The following statement, for example, seems rather naïve: "The relative contribution of the individual workers in the group is automatically regulated by the influence which the shirking worker exercises upon the earnings of the group. In other words the individual himself will see to it that his co-worker performs his share." [*System*, June, 1928, vol. 1, p. 73.] A psychologist would expect that the members of such a group would, if left without a boss, often trust too much to luck, indulge in recriminations, try to shift blame unfairly, be misled by petty demagoguery, bully weak members, and waste time in discussion. The explanation of the smooth operation usually reported is probably that each gang does have a boss. "The men will select a leader if none is provided for them officially." [Balderston, '30, p. 12.]

than ten minutes, and not more than one lateness of any sort, in the working days of the period. This would give an employee $54 a year and still permit thirty-six tardinesses. Even with eighteen absences and thirty-six tardinesses, an employee would receive $27. But there is no evidence that the improvement made was greater in the second case. The average number of tardinesses per employee dropped 4.1 (from 10.3 times in '28 to 6.2 times in '29) in the first company.

There is a tendency for defects in the quality of factory work to be charged against the training rather than the worker, and to try to cure them by further training as well as or instead of by punishments. ". . . all error notices are classified and returned to the departments concerned, together with a suggestive form notice signed jointly by the supervisor of the error division and the superintendent of training and education. This notice suggests that these returned error notices should be used in two ways, namely—to be recorded against the individual; and to be used for individual or group educational instruction." [*System,* vol. 2, p. 25.] "Study the kind of errors made and their causes and you are almost certain to find them due to faulty training." [*System,* vol. 1, p. 618.] The writer, however, almost in the same breath states that "No incentive plan should be used which does not carry a penalty for errors, this penalty to be deducted from bonus earned."

Chapter 11

PRACTICAL APPLICATIONS

THE value of any experience or activity—value for knowledge, skill, character, or any other quality or ability—depends upon what the after-effects of its various parts are and especially upon which of its tendencies have satisfying after-effects. Mere neutral repetition is a wasteful form of education. The effective provision of experiences must consider the learner's wants and make desirable parts of his activity satisfying.

The effective fact is in all cases the magnitude of the satisfaction the learner has, not that of the reward we give. But we have often to trust to the general correspondence between the two, since often we lack the time or the facilities (or both) to keep account of the former. In what follows, the words *satisfaction* and *reward* will be used according as the force in the subject's mind or the means used to arouse that force is to be predominant in thought.

In thus rewarding certain features of his behavior, we should be economical. So far as concerns the effect of a reward upon the particular connection whose satisfying after-effect the reward is, all that is necessary is enough to set off the confirming reaction, and moderate rewards attached to all desirable connections are actually superior to large rewards given less uniformly. Thus, four occurrences all followed by the minimum reward that will set off the confirming reaction are enormously more effective than one occurrence with a reward four times as great.

So far as concerns the effect of a reward upon larger units of activity (say the work of a minute or an hour), what is necessary is rewards large enough or frequent enough (1) to effect the attachment to connections that are 'successful,' 'right,' or 'useful for the work,' of enough satisfyingness to set off the confirming reaction; and (2) to make the interest in the activity in general strong enough to prevent other competing interests from causing the person to abandon or neglect it. A child in school or a worker in a factory needs enough satisfaction direct or *via* expectation to make the activity tolerable in spite of competing appeals and to secure the confirming reaction where it is appropriate. More than that is a luxury, except as a help in maintaining interest and satisfaction at success in still larger units of activity. It is a very desirable luxury, and—other things being equal—the more enjoyable work and learning are made, the better. But so far as learning and productivity are concerned, additions of rewards beyond a certain amount act under a law of sharply diminishing returns.

Experiments to be reported elsewhere show that intellect is notably resistant and resilient, so that if a person does continue work so unfit for him that he succeeds in less than one task out of ten, he will not lose much in power to succeed with the occasional tasks that are within his powers. Work that is too hard for a pupil is very bad, but it is not as bad as it might be.

These experiments consisted in doing long series of tasks, 5, 7.5, or 10 sec. being allowed for each. In some series the tasks were fairly easy so that the person would succeed with about one out of three; in other series the tasks were so hard that he would succeed with about one out of six, or one out of ten, or even one out of only fifteen. The tasks included:

Finding a rhyme, as for *fetid, general, cosine*
Completing a word with a specified number of letters, as
    fand . . . ., . . *uda* ., *me.di.a.* .
Making a word out of its disarranged letters, as *acdemnu*
Finding an opposite for a word, as for *plastic, charlatan, natant*
Making a true equation out of its disarranged elements, as, 1/7
    1/6 1/3 7/12 2/3 x x $\div$ $=$

At the beginning and end of each series there were test sets of tasks, one set of approximately the same difficulty as another. From the achievement in these test sets it is possible to compute the degree to which a person loses in alertness and efficiency from a spell of work with very few successes. These spells of work varied from eight and one-third minutes to nearly an hour. In some experiments one or two test tasks were also inserted in the course of the long spells of work with many and with few successes.

On the whole, the subjects (educated adults) showed little decline in achievement as a result of the great changes in the ratio of frustrations to successes. The work with few successes was unpleasant, and under ordinary circumstances they would doubtless tend to abandon or postpone it, but when they were required to continue it they could do so at nearly their maximum efficiency.*

Since, under certain circumstances, the occurrence of a connection with punishment leaves it stronger than before, there is obviously grave danger from practice in error even though the errors are pointed out to the learner. In our experiments the tendency to repeat what one had done was often stronger than the tendency to remember that it was wrong, and this may well occur in practice.

In general, punishment compares very unfavorably with reward in dependability. Unless it is a means of inducing the person to shift then and there to a right connection which is then and there rewarded, it may involve waste or worse. In particular (1) the attainment of active rather than passive learning at the cost of practice in error may often be a bad bargain. Refusal to supply information on the ground that the learner will be more profited by discovering the facts by himself runs the risk not only of excessive time-cost but also of strengthening of wrong habits. The learner's self-punishment when he makes a mistake may sometimes be no better than the punishment in our experiments. (2) The almost universal tolerance of imperfect learning in the early treatment of a topic, leaving it to be improved by the gradual elimination of errors in later treatments, is probably unsound, and certainly risky. What removes the errors in later treatments is the rewarding of the right connections, and such rewarding might better be put to work earlier. (3) The widespread limitation of guidance in oral and written composition, handwriting, drawing, and the like to designating errors is a sign of weakness in the techniques of teaching. With sufficient investigation and ingenuity, education should devise methods which would systematically make good work satisfying or at least replace bad habits by good ones.

The Practical Uses of Punishments

As was noted in Chapter 6, society makes habitual use of pain, ignominy, ridicule, or other consequences which attach fear, shame, or repulsion to ideas of, impulses to, the punished behavior.

* Details will be found in an article by E. L. Thorndike and Ella Woodyard entitled "The Influence of the Relative Frequency of Successes and Frustrations upon Intellectual Achievement," *Jour. Ed. Psych.*, 1934, vol. xxv, pp. 241-250.

The practical uses of these procedures deserves fuller treatment than can be given here. We shall neglect entirely the effects on the punisher, and treat very inadequately the effects on the person punished beyond the particular behavior punished, though both are of great importance. We shall also not develop the detailed consequences of any of the facts and principles discussed.

These attachments of fear, shame, and the like, to certain tendencies have a natural origin in the instinctive tendencies of man. To respond to a blow by a blow, to respond to the seizure of what is in one's hands or nest or sphere of control by grabbing it back, to respond to a person who interferes with one's progress by shoving him away—these are unlearned punitive tendencies. Such are to be found in the animal kingdom long before man. They occur in even the most kindly relations, that of mother and mothered. "Whom he loveth, he chasteneth" applies to human, canine, and feline parents as well as to the Hebrew and Christian gods.

In so far as they spring from man's original nature, they are natural social consequences just as falls, scratches, and bumps are natural physical consequences. Just as the latter are fairly well adapted to guide conduct in a world of trees, bushes, and rocks, so the former are fairly well adapted to family life in the wild.

Such instinctive punishments by parents, playmates, and other community members are, however, only a small fraction of the elaborate system of scoldings, blame, scorn, ridicule, ostracism, pains, and deprivations which have been developed from them by acquired customs. The family, the schools, government, and the church have all shared in inventing and popularizing new punishments. And behavior whatsoever that annoyed any person in authority was likely to be treated by him as a punishable offense. To the punishments given by men were added those which gods and demons might be expected to give. A hell after death was invented to supply more, and offenses against the gods increased the need for punishments in this world and the next. With and supporting all this was the dogma, accepted as axiomatic, that he who does wrong should be made to suffer. The doctrine also prevailed that the memory of past, and expectation of future, suffering would prevent the recurrence of the offense.

This doctrine had and has a substantial basis in fact. In proportion as virtue is unrewarded by the social system, pleasant vices can be diminished only by some unpleasant consequences. Fear and shame are potent. Workers do work partly because of fear of losing their jobs. Men do avoid breaking the laws partly because of fear of being put in jail. Children do study their lessons partly for fear of being laughed at by other pupils, or scorned at home for failure to be promoted. Many of our habitual moralities have roots in the fear of punishments. Certainly even the best of men act in part in fear of the punishments which their own consciences may inflict.

Let the reader consider why he does call the railway conductor who has forgotten to take his ticket, and present it to him. Is it not in part because he has a fear that possibly his neighbor in the train may have observed that he did not pay his fare or because of a sense of shame at taking something for nothing even from a large corporation or because of a dread that if he doesn't pay he may sometime feel uncomfortable and guilty in conscience or even because of a shadow of suspicion that the conductor may be testing his honesty deliberately?

In the factual discussion of Chapter 8, it appeared that "Any form of expectation of an annoying after-effect tends to evoke the particular behavior which experience has attached to it." The punishments with which we are concerned will by this principle often have a preventive value.

In the important cases where these punishments are used to secure a certain positive behavior by punishing anything other than it, they may have the effect of rewarding that positive behavior. It may be the satisfyingness of security from fear and shame that makes a workman do his work, a soldier maintain his post, a student attend to his lesson. In all cases where the choice is between two alternatives, what originated as an expectation of annoying consequences due to a punishment of behavior A may easily shift to a sense of comfort after behavior B. The relief from, or absence of, the annoying consequence or the expectation of it may cause as real, though not as intense, a satisfaction as success, praise, or sensory pleasure.

The conventional system of punishments is, however, beset by difficulties and dangers.

(1) It tends to work best where it is least needed, and least well where it is most needed. Individuals who are sensitive to

moral issues and to the feelings of others and who will probably in any case approximate what is right and proper, are influenced markedly by punishments. Those more callous and base in nature, who are not easily stimulated by nobler means, are not easily improved by punishments.

(2) The punishments sometimes do not prevent or lessen the punished behavior but only make the person more miserable, frightened, and ashamed. The fear and shame occur, but they do not prevent recurrence. He continues to sin, but he is more remorseful and unhappy.

(3) The essential service of the punishments is to thwart or repress certain impulses by adding counterbalancing negative impulses. This conflict of impulses is supposed by most psychiatrists to be an unhealthy and irritating state of affairs.

(4) A person can weaken, or even nullify, the force of all save the purely physical pains and deprivations by choosing as the social group whose opinions he will value one that is to any degree liberal, unorthodox, eccentric, low, or vicious. This is very commonly done. Indeed the action of the law of effect requires that individuals favor and select a social milieu in which they are comfortable. So traders are not much annoyed by the scorn of communistic idealists. Politicians are not punished by the attacks of reformers. Many college boys feel little dissatisfaction at being disesteemed by their professors. They would be much more disturbed if they were accused by their cronies of "being like the profs." A crook lives in a crook's world.

(5) There is danger of arousing more fear or shame than is needed to counteract some pleasant minor sin, and so of dulling the person's sensitiveness to punishment. It is easy to scold violently, give harsh sentences, or exact cruel deprivations—much easier than to provide adequate and steady satisfactions for well-doers. In certain schools of the not so remote past there was so much and so heavy punishment that a little more or less did not seem to matter, and many pupils probably gave up their attempts to avoid it.

(6) There is danger of cruel atrocities which no reasonable or humane society should tolerate. This has happened so often in schools, in the treatment of slaves and child laborers, in armies, and in religious persecutions that it must be reckoned as an almost necessary feature of the punitive system.

(7) What little evidence is available suggests that the influence of customary punishments as actually administered has been inferior to that of customary rewards. The relevant facts are presented in Chapter 10, pp. 135 to 144.

Improvements in the Administration of Punishments

Psychology suggests five ways of improving the results from punishments.

The first is to try to make sure in each case that the punishment belongs to the behavior in question. If it cannot be its direct after-effect, means should be taken to recall the occurrence and to make clear and emphatic connection in the punished person's mind between the impulse to that behavior and the expectation of the punishment.

The second is to forestall the punishment in cases where the want which led to the offense can be satisfied innocently. A large fraction of punishments is used to counteract the otherwise satisfying consequences of certain behavior. Some of this behavior is really innocent and desirable and should not be punished at all. It was for example sheer folly to make children of five to ten sit still for hours in school and to punish them if they fidgeted. Some of it can be obviated by the provision of an innocent outlet. So children who steal jam may in some cases be cured by providing sufficient sweets in the diet, and athletic clubs may prevent hooliganism.

The third is to shift the emphasis from the discomfort of A to the relief, security, and comfort of not-A, when it is prudent to do so, as it usually is.

The fourth is to search for ingenious ways of using the sure and almost fool-proof methods of arousing the confirming reaction by attaching relevant satisfiers to the desired connections, in place of punishments for wrong connections. There are now homes in which the ratio of rewards to punishments for children from birth to fifteen years or later has been as high as 20 to 1, perhaps 50 to 1, with apparently excellent results. The motivation to learning in the primary grades of schools has changed in a half-century from pain to pleasure, to the great advantage of all concerned. If weakness and sentimentality can be avoided and sufficient ingenuity can be exercised, the management of men in all lines by the selection of their good tendencies rather than the repression of bad ones is a hopeful prospect.

The fifth is to arrange in a scientific, or at least a reasonable, manner the punishments which, even after the fullest use of rewards, will still remain as important means of human control. Much of the use of punishments in the past has been doctrinaire, haphazard, fantastic, and perverted.

Human use of both rewards and punishments remains in many respects at an irrational, instinctive level. Men usually do nothing until they are annoyed and then use retaliatory measures against the annoyer. The better way is to work scientifically to improve our state, no matter how good it is, to prevent troubles from occurring at all, and to do both by rewarding behavior that is rational, scientific, inventive, decent, healthy, and law-abiding. When rewards are given, our distribution of them too often befits chimpanzees in a state of nature rather than intelligent men in the civilization of 1930. People reward with pity and money a beggar with a running sore, but not an overworked mother. They reward with approval physical prowess and gorgeous display, but not their real benefactors. They reward with power, popularity rather than ability.

Intrinsic and Extrinsic Interests

Educational theorists have emphasized the merits of intrinsic rather than extrinsic satisfactions and rewards. The distinction is not altogether clear, but roughly the former are those which are due to the activity itself as engaged in by the person in question, whereas the latter are added to it, and would not be present unless brought into action by forces outside the activity and the actor— the material to be learned and the learner. The two extremes may be illustrated by a ten-year-old child reading a story for pleasure and reading the Bible for money. The classic expression of the advantages of intrinsic interests is that of Dewey, especially in his *Interest and Effort in Education.*

In certain respects, intrinsic interests do possess greater merit. In so far as the task of education (or business, or government, or religion) is to develop or strengthen certain interests as more or less permanent features of a person's make-up, the more intrinsic the interest can be, the less dependent upon outside aids and circumstances, the better. Even when the task is to develop an interest purely as a temporary means to get something else learned or done, intrinsic interests are somewhat stronger and more dependable.

But their advantages in this respect have been exaggerated in the educational theories of the last half-century. If an educated adult for any reason is induced by any force, no matter how external, to want to learn a certain thing, no matter how remote learning it is from his other, deeper, and more 'real' needs, he can learn it, provided of course that it is within his powers. He can learn it nearly or quite as well if his desire to learn it is due entirely to the desire for money or fame as if his desire is for the knowledge itself (provided the work does not last more than an hour, and probably even if it does). How far the same holds true of persons younger, or less trained, or both, cannot be safely affirmed, but the probability is that the differences are only such as are covered in the next paragraph.

What prevents the learner from learning anything that he has the ability to learn and wants to learn, is not a lack of appeal to intrinsic interests which are caused by and in harmony with his deeper and more characteristic wants, but rather a weakening of the want to learn it or a failure to withstand the competition of other wants, such as to play, to rest, to make progress in some cherished enterprise, to follow the lure of some seductive stimulus from without or idea from within.

The word *do* may be used in place of *learn* in the last two paragraphs for the facts and principles are general. An Einstein can (and probably does) sharpen pencils to write his equations as well as ponder on the equations themselves. If, by sharpening pencils diligently an hour a day for a month, he could earn enough money to support some cherished research project, he could (and probably would) be diligent at that occupation despite its intrinsic foreignness to his 'real needs.'

If by a miracle the learning and work which the world now gets done by social forces acting upon individuals from outside (by laws, customs, wages, profits, persuasion, approval, etc., etc.) could be done from intrinsic interest, each person's inner choices harmonizing perfectly with his allotted duties in an automatic paradise, the world would, as suggested, be much happier; but it is not likely that either the work or the learning would get done in one-tenth the time now taken, or in a quarter of it, or in a third of it.* Some saving there would be; its amount the reader may estimate for himself from the facts of Chapter 9. Man can learn and do what he wants to learn and do whether he likes it or not. How well he likes it does matter, but on the whole as a minor factor.

* As usual, we assume that other things than the intrinsicness of the interests are kept equal. The same persons do the same work as now. There is to be no readjustment to fit varying abilities and no change from wanting not to do the work to wanting to do it, but only a miraculous transformation of the causation of the desire.

PART II

CHANGES IN WANTS, INTERESTS AND ATTITUDES

Chapter 12

INTRODUCTION TO PART II

THERE can be no doubt that men and animals change their wants, attitudes, and interests in the sense that the situation which once evoked certain ones comes to evoke others. Tendencies to respond by like, dislike, attention, neglect, fear, and affection change as surely as knowledge or skill. There can be no doubt that deliberate training can produce such changes. But how it does so and what limitations there are to its efficacy are questions which can be answered only doubtfully and incompletely. The great bulk of the experimental work on changes by training has been restricted to knowledge, intellectual abilities, and acts of motor skill. Some psychologists would expect just the same general principles which are true for learning ideas and movements to apply to changing wants, interests, and attitudes. But some would probably not; and there are certainly notable differences in the particular practical procedures which psychologists have used to teach the multiplication tables or typewriting and those which they would use to teach love of country, physical courage, an interest in Greek art, disgust at sentimental drivel, or good humor under misfortune.

In fact, the current recommendations concerning the training of wants, interests, and attitudes do not emphasize the principles of repetition and reward which have been found fundamental for intellectual and motor learning, but advocate principles or practices which may be grouped roughly under these headings: imitation, association, the formation of conditioned reflexes, and negative adaptation.

Imitation. It is asserted that a person acquires the emotional attitude which his family or group display toward a situation by a sort of direct contagion. I need not give quotations or illustrations since the reader will probably have met many.

Association or Contiguity. It is asserted that the want or interest or attitude evoked by situation X will attach itself to whatever occurs in association with X. If the child likes the person who teaches him algebra, he will learn to like algebra. If he is frightened by his nurse while playing with a snake, he may become afraid of snakes.

The Formation of Conditioned Reflexes. The doctrine here is a more definite statement of one case of the many that are possible under the vague caption of *association*. It is that if X evokes the want or interest or attitude R, and if Y occurs and X is added to it to form X+Y evoking R, then, after a sufficient number of such occurrences, Y alone will evoke R.

Negative Adaptation. It is asserted (especially in the case of dislike, fear, repugnance, aversion, and the like) that the mere repetition of the situation will result in a weakening of the attitude toward indifference. In popular lore concerning human nature and education we find an extension of this doctrine to the effect that repetition will not only weaken these attitudes toward indifference but transform them into positive liking.

There are important cases of changes in the propensities evoked by situations which are due to the fact that the intellectual apprehension of the situation is changed. The olive which at first is merely bitter becomes primarily pungent and only secondarily bitter. The oyster which is at first predominantly slimy becomes predominantly succulent. The foreigner who is queer and contemptible to the ignorant is attractive and estimable to those who know his history and achievements. A large fraction of the successful practices in changing emotional propensities is based on this fact. The training does not try to change the connections leading from the situation to the emotion directly, but by means of intellectual intermediaries. It is carried on by the methods used in intellectual and motor training.

There are also important changes in the propensities evoked by situations which are due to the fact that the motor response to the situation is changed. The person is taught to act *as if* he felt brave and calm and optimistic. Just how the performance of certain acts in response to a situation modifies the feelings one has toward it, need not now be considered; nor how pervasive and penetrating the results of such training are. Our present concern is to note that the responses used are responses of movement or conduct and that the principles applicable are those of training in action.

Our experiments contribute little or nothing directly concerning the modification of wants, interests, and attitudes by way of intellectual apprehension or motor responses, nor concerning the alleged potency of imitation. But we have tried to settle the questions as to whether the principles of learning by repetition and reward which apply in the spheres of intellect and action apply also to wants, interests, and attitudes.)

In these experiments we have used esthetic wants and gratifications, for two reasons: (1) that our facilities did not permit the use of 'real' fears, loves, hates, sorrows, and the like; and (2) that, even if they had permitted this, the prudent course seemed to be to explore the field first in the case where abundant material could be gathered in a reasonable time. Any conclusions could, if necessary, be checked with the more violent propensities.

We have also made experiments to advance knowledge of the influence of association, including the special case of the conditioned reflex phenomenon, and of negative adaptation through repetition. In these experiments we have used both 'real' and esthetic propensities.

Chapter 13

CHANGING WANTS, INTERESTS, AND ATTITUDES:
THE INFLUENCE OF OCCURRENCE PLUS A
POSSIBLE REWARD; THE INFLUENCE
OF CONTIGUITY

LEARNING in the spheres of intellect and action is caused largely by repetition and reward. Connections are strengthened by inducing them to occur and by attaching satisfying after-effects to them. In seeking to discover how far this applies also to connections between situations and emotions, desires, or propensities, it is of relatively little importance to study the influence of occurrence pure and simple. We do not much care how the efficacy is divided between mere occurrence and after-effect. The elaborate arrangements used in *The Fundamentals of Learning* to attain this end are therefore dispensed with here. We have, however, devised one set of experiments in which satisfying after-effects are relatively infrequent and unimpressive and another set in which they appear regularly and in amounts which would surely give them potency in the case of ideational or motor connections. The former are described in this chapter, together with experiments arranged to supply data concerning the power of mere contiguity to attach attitudes to situations.

The general plan of these experiments was to present a certain object to certain persons among objects which would often be liked and to other persons among objects which would often be disliked and to determine whether such presentation increased the liking for the object in the former case and decreased the liking for it in the latter case. The ostensible reason for the presentation was, in some cases, to obtain comparative ratings of the esthetic excellence of certain objects in the former case, and of their esthetic inferiority in the latter. In other cases it was to obtain data on recognition memory. Couplets, lines of verse or prose, single words, pictures of buildings, Christmas cards, and pieces of colored and patterned paper were used. Specimens A . . . N were presented along with likable objects to persons 1 to x and along with disliked objects to persons 1^1 to x^1. Specimens $a \ldots n$ were presented along with likable objects to persons 1^1 to x^1 and along with disliked objects to persons 1 to x. Then all the persons (1 to x and 1^1 to x^1) were asked to examine specimens A . . . N and $a \ldots n$ and state, in the case of each, whether they liked it, liked it especially, disliked it, disliked it especially, or felt no clear liking or dislike for it.

In some cases there was not only contiguity of the "neutrals" with the liked (or disliked) objects, but also an added provocation or inducement to take the attitude of liking (or disliking) to the neutrals in the form of such statements as that "these couplets were written mostly by famous poets," or that "these couplets were mostly written in haste in an experiment in psychology by students devoid of literary gifts, as you will realize when you read them."

Samples of the materials and instructions in the case of experiment 41 will define the procedure.

Experiment 41

"You will receive sheets containing twenty sets each consisting of four couplets, mostly by famous poets. Read the four couplets of set 1; mark the couplet you think is the best 1 and the one you think is next best 2. If you think you know who was the author of any couplet, write his name in the margin. Do the same for set 2, set 3, set 4, and so on. As soon as you finish, write your name at the top of each sheet and bring the sheets to me."

'Neutrals' with 'Goods'

1. A. ...It was that fatal and perfidious bark,
   Built in th' eclipse, and rigg'd with curses dark.

   B. ...Around his form his loose long robe was thrown,
   His hand uplifted made the people groan.

   C. ...Remote from man, with God he passed his days;
   Prayer all his business, all his pleasure praise.

   D. ...A solitary shriek, the bubbling cry
   Of some strong swimmer in his agony.

2. A. ...For those whom God to ruin has designed,
   He fits for fate, and first destroys their mind.

B. ...All nature is but art, unknown to thee;
   All chance, direction which thou canst not see.

C. ...And, see, soft unfolding those portals of gold,
   The King all arrayed in his beauty behold!

D. ...These are my realms, no limits to their sway.
   At last I am monarch of all I survey.

3. A. ...If then to all men happiness was meant
   Why could it not to all men have been sent?

B. ...Our vows are heard betimes! and Heaven takes care
   To grant before we can conclude the prayer.

C. ...As if misfortune made the throne her seat,
   And none could be unhappy but the great.

D. ...The love of praise, howe'er concealed by art,
   Reigns more or less, and glows in ev'ry heart.

A day later they spent about twenty minutes in choosing the worst and next to worst from each of twenty other sets of couplets, like those shown below, in accordance with the instructions printed below. This was part of ninety minutes of examination of objects presented with conditions favoring dislike.

"You will receive four sheets containing twenty sets each consisting of four couplets mostly written in haste in an experiment in psychology by students relatively devoid of literary gifts, as you will realize when you read them. Read the four couplets of set 1 and mark the couplet which you think is the worst 4. Mark the couplet which you think is next to the worst 3. Do the same with set 2, set 3, set 4, etc. As soon as you finish, write your name at the top of each sheet and bring the sheets to me."

'Neutrals' with 'Bads'

1. A. ...A man condemned to sorrow and to woe
   The fires of life in him no longer glow.

B. ...There are no slaves and men at last are free
   To work or play or sleep in liberty.

C. ...But still he only saw and did not share;
   And, damned of seeing, was of comfort bare.

D. ...I must confess that I view with alarm
   Genius so great and resistant to charm.

2. A. ...What she has done no tears can wash away:
No words impassioned can his curses stay.

B. ...A man whose life is blasted by a crime
Still loves his wealth and clings to every dime.

C. ...Nothing at all does this dull record show
Of his life up above or his life down below.

D. ...They live lives small. They stumble in great halls,
Fate holds and hinders them when duty calls.

3. A. ...Here one may dwell and dream amidst the breeze:
Here one may loll and idle at his ease.

B. ...Old scenes of glory, times long cast behind,
Unfurled with battle flag and brought to mind.

C. ...Above, below, on land, on sea, is found
Praise that forever will sound and resound.

D. ...Spirits of freedom know no craven fear
Though refuge be absent and danger be near.

Two days later the subjects of Group A were given rating sheets containing the forty couplets which had been presented in either sort of surroundings and requested to "Write LL before each that you like especially, L before each that you like, D before each that you dislike, and DD before each that you dislike especially. You are not now judging these couplets as to literary excellence, but simply expressing your personal feeling about each. If you have no clear feeling of like or dislike, write nothing before the couplet."

Group B (consisting of eight other educated adults) had the same history except that the couplets presented to Group A under conditions favoring liking were presented to Group B under conditions favoring dislike, and vice versa.

The frequencies of likes and dislikes were as follows:

	LL	L	Indif	D	DD
After presentation among 'good' couplets	47	91	82	73	27
After presentation among 'bad' couplets.	22	80	87	94	37

In order to obtain a convenient single measure of the difference we may make the justifiable, and entirely impartial, assumption that the scale from LL to DD is continuous, and let the interval of it covered by Indif be represented as from $+0.5$ to -0.5. Then the median attitude after presentation among 'goods' was $+0.23$, whereas the median attitude after presentation among 'bads' was —0.17. If we assume further that

$$LL = \text{from } +2.5 \text{ to } +1.5$$
$$L = \text{from } +1.5 \text{ to } +0.5$$
$$D = \text{from } -0.5 \text{ to } -1.5$$
$$DD = \text{from } -1.5 \text{ to } -2.5$$

we may compute the corresponding averages. They are +0.18 and —0.14. The difference is then 0.40 by medians and 0.32 by averages.

In experiments 45 and 49, described in Appendix VI, similar results were obtained. From all three the experimental conditions provocative of like (or dislike) may be estimated to cause a difference of about 0.41 (0.43 by medians, 0.39 by averages).

In experiment 53 the same sets of 'good,' 'bad,' and 'neutral' couplets were used in the same way as in the experiments hitherto described, except that mere contiguity plus what it inevitably suggested was used. The same 'neutrals' were read by one group with 'goods' and by another group with 'bads,' but nothing was said about the one set having been written mostly by famous writers or about the other set having been written by students hastily in an experiment. Nor were the subjects told to choose in the one set the two they liked most from each four, nor to choose in the other the two they disliked most. They were simply required to read eighty couplets (not now divided into sets), then to reread them until told to stop, and finally to do the same with eighty other couplets.

After they had thus read twenty 'neutrals' scattered amongst sixty 'goods' and twenty other 'neutrals' scattered amongst sixty 'bads,' they were asked to listen to a long series of couplets (eighty in all) and record two facts after each. The first fact was their personal liking or dislike for the couplet; the second was whether it was or was not one of the couplets which they had previously read. Of this series of eighty, forty were the 'neutrals' of the earlier sets and forty were totally new couplets.

Group A consisted of thirty adults or adolescents over seventeen who had 'neutral' couplets A to N along with 'good' couplets and 'neutral' couplets a to n along with 'bad' couplets. Group B consisted of thirty adults who had A to N along with 'bad' couplets and a to n along with 'good.' *

* The couplets were read to Group B.

The subjects of Group A were later asked to report any failures to express their own personal feelings. There were only four persons who had so failed, and three of these only very rarely (in 1, 5, and 10 percent of the cases by their reports). The fourth person said that she really disliked all of the couplets but forced herself to rate some as only probable dislike or indifference. The records of these four show nothing demonstrative of any difference from the other twenty-six in respect of the influence of contiguity, and we retain them in the computations.

The expressions of liking and dislike were as shown in Table 16.

TABLE 16

The influence of contiguity. Frequencies of expressions of liking and dislike after experience in contiguity with "good" or with "bad" couplets

Contiguity	LL	L	Indif	D	DD
With 'good' couplets A—N	182	107	120	110	81
With 'good' couplets a—n	124	161	212	65	38
With 'good' couplets, all	306	268	332	175	119
With 'bad' couplets A—N	116	155	224	67	38
With 'bad' couplets a—n	194	123	101	89	93
With 'bad' couplets, all	310	278	325	156	131

The medians are +0.42 and +0.46 after contiguity with 'good' and 'bad' respectively; the averages are +0.39 and +0.40. Mere contiguity with 'goods' was impotent to increase liking; and the mere contiguity with 'bads' was impotent to increase dislike. The results of experiments 41, 45, and 49 were due to the special inducements to take the attitude of liking (or dislike).

Experiments 42, 46, 50, and 54 were strictly comparable to experiments 41, 45, 49, and 53 respectively except that single lines were used instead of couplets. When the subjects were encouraged to like the 'neutral' lines among the 'goods' and to be satisfied by such liking (and similarly for dislike of the 'neutrals' among 'bads') there was an indubitable influence from the association, producing an average difference of 0.18. But when mere contiguity was the only force, there was no difference between association with 'good' lines and association with 'bad' lines. These experiments and their results are described in Appendix VI.

We have made two experiments on liking and dislike for words, experienced previously in contiguity with liked and with disliked words respectively. Neither measures the influence of mere contiguity, though one does almost that. In experiment 55, the inducement to take an attitude of liking (or of dislike) and be satisfied by doing so was like that used in experiments 41 and 42 with the couplets and lines. Sheets containing eighty 'neutrals' among 240 'goods' and sheets containing eighty 'neutrals' among 240 'bads' were used. The first twenty words of each were as follows:

1. serene	1. belch ....
2. tranquil	2. wart ....
3. aglow	3. mawkish .....
4. allowable	4. Austria ....
5. madonna	5. asthma ....
6. bobolink	6. croak ....
7. dawn	7. artery ....
8. India	8. brat ....
9. adrift	9. apse ....
10. lilac	10. hog ....
11. Andes	11. assuage ......
12. antic	12. bosky ....
13. silvery	13. nasal ....
14. serenade	14. fag ....
15. laurel	15. defunct ....
16. habitat	16. tribunal ......
17. Alpine	17. lobster ....
18. slumber	18. veteran ....
19. ting	19. cackle ....
20. Geneva	20. carboy ....

The instructions were:

For the 'Neutrals' with 'Goods.' "I shall read you a long list of words which have been rated high for pleasantness of sound by a group of persons of good taste in literature and music. As I read each word, write N after it if you disagree, that is, if you do *not* like the sound of the word. Do not be timid about doing so. Your record in this experiment will not be used to determine your earnings."

For the 'Neutrals' with 'Bads.' "I shall read you a long list of words which have been rated low for pleasantness of sound by a group of persons of good taste in literature and music. As I read each word, write N after it if you disagree, that is, if you *do* like the sound of the word. Do not be timid about doing so. Your record in this experiment will not be used to determine your earnings."

The inducement to like the 'neutrals' among the 'goods' and to dislike the 'neutrals' among the 'bads' was probably not nearly so strong as in the case of lines written by famous poets and by students of psychology, respectively. The prestige of "a group of persons of good taste" is not great, and anybody may feel fairly satisfied to differ from it in the unstandardized matter of taste as to euphony in words.*

An expression of liking for each of the 160 'neutrals' was obtained by the use of a list of 320 words containing them and 160 other words. As each word was read by the experimenter, the subject recorded his liking or dislike and his judgment as to whether the word was among the 640 previously read. The eighty 'neutrals' experienced with 'goods' and the eighty 'neutrals' experienced with 'bads' were known from other investigations to be intrinsically equally likable, so that any difference found in the experiment will be due to its special conditions.

The results were:

	LL	L	Indif	D	DD
After experiences favorable to liking	500	421	566	493	420
After experiences favorable to dislike	423	427	485	481	584

Let us assume, as in the case of the couplets and lines, that the scale from LL to DD is continuous and treat LL as equal to the interval from $+2.5$ to $+1.5$, L as equal to the interval from $+1.5$ to $+0.5$, Indif as equal to the interval from $+0.5$ to -0.5, D as equal to the interval from -0.5 to -1.5, and DD as equal to the interval from -1.5 to -2.5. Then the median attitudes after the experiences provocative of liking and of dislike are respectively $+0.01$ and -0.22. The corresponding averages are $+0.04$ and -0.16. The difference (of 0.23 or 0.20) has a probable error of about 0.03 (more for the 0.23, but less for the 0.20). The difference is about one twelfth of the difference between the average attitude toward *Acadia, Hermione, Hiawatha,* and *valentine* on the one hand and that toward *ache, waddle, ogre,* and *cankerworm* on the other ($+1.17$ and -1.07 respectively. The median attitudes were $+1.60$ and -1.55).

* A more potent inducement might have been to describe the lists as words chosen for euphony and cacophony by a committee consisting of Galsworthy, Benet, and Edna St. Vincent Millay. Unwillingness to deceive subjects and the probability that shrewd subjects would not believe the statement prevented us from doing this.

In our second experiment (experiment 43) the inducement to like (or dislike) the 'neutral' words was only what was due to their being read in lines each containing two 'neutrals' and two 'goods' (or 'bads') and being treated in accordance with the following instructions:

With 'goods':

"You will receive two sheets containing eighty sets, each consisting of four words. Read the four words of line 1, and write 1 before that word of the four which you like best in the sense that you think you would prefer to read it or say it twenty times than to read or say any of the other three twenty times. Write 2 before the word you like next best. Then do the same with the four words of line 2, then with those of line 3, and so on. As soon as you finish, write your name at the top of the sheets and bring them to me."

With 'bads':

"You will receive two sheets containing eighty sets, each consisting of four words. Read the four words of line 1 and write 4 before the word you dislike most in the sense that you would prefer to read or hear any other of the words twenty times than read or hear it twenty times. Write 3 before the word you dislike next most of the four. Then do the same with the four words of line 2, then with the words of line 3, and so on. As soon as you finish, sign and bring the sheets to me."

The words used as 'goods,' 'bads,' and 'neutrals' were not the same as in experiment 55. The following are random samples of them.

'Good' words were *allegiance, ambrosia, ancestral, American, asphodel, amber, alchemy, alleviate, altar, ardent, adorable, Alpine, adore, always, appanage, ability, ancient, arena, angelic,* and *ancestor.* 'Bad' words were *abduct, amatory, ague, asphyxiate, abdomen, asexual, anarch, abscess, aha, asthma, ascetic, apse, adjudge, avid, accomplice, abortion, amours, ant, arch-duke,* and *arid.* 'Neutral' words were *alliance, anvil, angular, avow, almanac, anomaly, allowable, annotate, awaken, aorta, antelope, adrift, affiliate, Aragon, Austria, anterior, artery, arose, algæ, alpaca.*

Half of the 'neutrals' were presented to one group of eight persons along with 'goods' and to another group of eight persons along with 'bads.' The other half of the 'neutrals' reversed this arrangement. The subjects were educated adults.

There is no observable influence of the difference in contiguity.

The median attitude toward the 'neutrals' after presentation with 'goods' is +0.14; that after presentation with 'bads' is +0.13. The corresponding averages are +0.20 and +0.19.* The frequencies of LL, L, Indif, D, and DD respectively were as follows:

	LL	L	Indif	D	DD
After experience with 'goods'.....	195	602	1358	322	83
After experience with 'bads'......	200	584	1361	341	74

This failure of contiguity with 'goods' (or 'bads') to produce liking adds to the evidence that mere contiguity is not potent.

Experiments 44, 48, 52, and 56 were similar experiments with pictures, Christmas cards, and specimens of colored paper. The inducements to like the 'neutrals' which were examined along with the 'goods' were the suggestion made by the 'goods' and the following directions:

"You will receive sheets, each containing four pictures or Christmas cards or samples of paper or other objects. Nearly all of them have been noted to have artistic merit by a jury of presumably competent persons. Select the one you like best and write its letter as directed on the record sheet. Then select the one you like next best and write its letter as directed."

In the case of 'neutrals' examined along with 'bads,' "to be ugly, or at least not pleasant" took the place of "to have artistic merit"; "dislike most" and "dislike next most" took the place of "like best" and "like next best."

In the later expressions of likings concerning the neutrals, copies of these were seen one at a time and the LL, L, DD, and D were used with the same meanings: *Sure you like, Think you like, Sure you dislike, Think you dislike.*

The results are presented in Appendix VI. The average difference between the attitude after presentation with 'goods' and the attitude after presentation with 'bads' was +0.12 or +0.13 according as averages or medians were used in the computation.

When the same examination of cards and later expressions of likes and dislikes were made under the guise of a recognition-memory experiment, with no suggestion that certain sets were liked by experts, there was no difference.

The simplest explanation of all the results of this chapter is the very radical one that mere contiguity to liked (or disliked) situa-

* Using the values for LL, L, Indif, D, and DD noted on p. 167.

tions does little or nothing, but that if liking (or dislike) is induced to occur as a response to a situation, its occurrence strengthens the connection, at least if the subject is satisfied with it as a fit and proper response to the situation in question.

This seems to be also a true and adequate explanation. In the experiments when nothing was done save to present 'neutrals' with 'goods' or with 'bads,' nothing happened as a result of the association. In the experiments in which suggestions were made that those presented with 'goods' were to be esteemed and liked and that those presented with 'bads' were to be disesteemed and disliked, they did gain in liking and disliking respectively.*

* It should be noted that many, perhaps all, of the cases used as evidence by advocates of the potency of mere association in time have strong elements of provocation toward the assumption of the attitude in addition to the temporal association. The mothers and nurses whose screams frighten children who are about to pat or grasp a snake commonly do all they can to provoke fear of snakes. Indeed their intent in screaming is not to cause a fear of the scream which then by association attaches itself to the snake. Their intent is to cause a fear of the snake directly, as by a warning cry. And perhaps their screams do serve as warning cries. The parents who feed infants spinach with smiles and honeyed words, eating some of it themselves and smacking their lips, do so not only with the hope that thereby the child's liking for the smile will indirectly shift to the spinach, but still more with the hope that the child will then and there directly the first time like the spinach better than he otherwise would.

Chapter 14

CHANGING WANTS, INTERESTS, AND ATTITUDES: THE INFLUENCE OF OCCURRENCE PLUS EMPHATIC REWARD

EMPHATIC is perhaps too strong a word for the rewards whose influence is to be reported in this chapter. The satisfyingness of the after-effect was in every case that of finding one's feeling or attitude in agreement with, and justified by, that of some person or persons accepted more or less as competent in the matter of taste at issue. We did not make the experiments ostensibly training in appreciation, with after-effects of "Right" and "Wrong," "Experts share your feeling" and "Experts have the opposite feeling," or the like. We feared that if this was done the subjects of the experiments would report intellectualistic judgments, telling what they thought it would be commendable to feel, rather than genuine personal feelings. In all of the experiments but one, we took special precautions to camouflage the fact that any change in any attitude was being measured, or, indeed, was occurring at all.

Some of our experiments were with subjects taken one at a time, some with groups. The general plan was to present a series of sights or sounds (pictures, words, short poems, or parts of poems or paragraphs), asking him to express his own personal feeling of liking, indifference, or dislike, not his opinion about the esteem in which people do or should hold the specimen in question. Concerning many of his responses no after-effect was supplied by the experimenter, but expressions of liking for some specimens were rewarded, as by saying "Yes! I like that too" or "Yes! that is a very fine bit" or "Yes! An exquisite design," and the like, and expressions of dislike for some specimens were rewarded (as by saying "Only stupid people like that," or "A pompous word," or "A silly jingle," or the like). In the individual experiments no response was ever punished. That is, the experimenter's comments never opposed the subject's expressed feeling. In the group experi-

ments the subjects expressed their feelings in writing. The responses to many of the pictures, words, and so on were provided with no after-effect by the experiment, but comments like the above were made to some. In a few cases these would be in opposition to the subject's feeling, but favorable comments were in the great majority of cases attached to specimens which were generally liked, and unfavorable comments to specimens generally disliked.

In all experiments, the selection of specimens was not at random, nor was the attachment of comments always by general merit or demerit, but certain qualities in the specimens were also favored or disfavored. In a series of Christmas cards, for example, landscapes, abstract designs, and gold were favored, whereas pictures of persons or events and the absence of gold were disfavored in two ways. The cards characterized by the former were better in other ways than those characterized by the latter, and favorable comments were often attached to the former and unfavorable comments to the latter. As a consequence we have frequency of occurrence and reward both operating to favor landscapes, abstract designs, and gold.

The measurement of their combined influence was made in two ways: (1) by having some specimens responded to both before and after the training, and (2) by having some specimens responded to after the training which were new to the subject, but which were equivalent in essential respects to some that had been responded to before the training.

In the group experiments, the subjects had no notion that they were being trained or taught. There were no breaks between the expressions used to measure attitudes early and late and those used to change them. In one of the individual experiments, the subjects could infer that the experiment gave a record of changes in their taste.

Group Experiment 61

The four types of material used were Christmas cards, poetry, colored papers, and pictures of buildings.

Two different groups participated in the experiment. One was a group of twenty-one college undergraduates; the other was a group of twenty-five Teachers College candidates for a higher degree. The Teachers College group, however, was not trained with the buildings series.

Each series consisted of a pre-training test, a training series, a post-training test, and a repetition of the pre-training test. In the pre-training test, the subjects worked under the following directions:

"You are to record your likes and dislikes for a series of Christmas cards, a series of pieces of colored paper, a series of short selections of poetry and prose, and a series of pictures of buildings or scenery. You will look at the card, or piece of paper, or selection, and if you are sure you like it, write 1 after its number on the record sheet. If you think you like it but are not sure, write 2. If you are sure that you dislike it, write 9. If you think that you dislike it but are not sure, write 8. If you have no feeling at all either of like or dislike make a dash (—) after the number. Always write some number or make a dash to show that you have examined the specimen. In every case, express your own personal feelings. We do not wish to know whether you think that the card or poem, etc., deserves liking, but whether you yourself like it.

"The material concerning which you are to record your likes and dislikes is as follows:

Christmas cards,	numbers	1-20
Christmas cards,	numbers	21-40
Christmas cards,	numbers	41-65
Colored papers,	numbers	1-20
Poems, etc.,	numbers	1-20
Poems, etc.,	numbers	21-35
Buildings, etc.,	numbers	1-30

"You will be given some one set to start with by the experimenter. Take the pack of cards from the envelope, look at the one on the top of the pack, record your liking or dislike, put the card face down at your right. Continue till all are done. If any number is missing, notify the examiner. Then put them in the envelope and return it to the experimenter, who will supply you with another set. When you have completed all, give the experimenter your record sheets. Be sure they are signed. Then await further instructions."

Each subject finished the rating of all the pre-training tests before the training series was begun.

The training was done under the following directions:

Part II. You are to record likes and dislikes just as before. The only difference is that, after you have recorded your like or dislike and put the card face down at your right, you may read what you see written on its back, if you care to know whether you agree with the general likes and dislikes of a group of artists, critics, and persons of general cultivation. Do not ever turn the card over again to look at its face, and, of course, do not ever look at the back of any card until after you have recorded your like or dislike. Also do not spend time beyond one quick reading of what is written on the back. Do not stop to think about any card after you have recorded your like or dislike. When *low* is written there, it means that the group dislike it or like it little. *High* means liking. Other comments which may be of interest are given sometimes. Sometimes nothing is reported, either because there is no clear feeling toward the card, sentence, etc., or because the card is a new one where we have as yet no information.

"Bear in mind that you are always to record your own personal like or dislike, not your opinion about whether the card or selection ought to be liked."

The training series for Christmas cards consisted of cards 66-400, 335 in all; for the colored papers, of strips 101-200, 100 in all; for the buildings post-cards, of cards 31-140, 110 in all; and for the poetry selections, of cards 36-200, 165 in all. The post-training test for each of the functions was given in such a way that the subject never realized that it was a test, since it was given in continuity after the subject had finished all the training. In the post-training test occurred cards which were other than those used in the pre-training series. The cards were, however, matched card for card by judgment of experts to be equivalent in favor or disparagement value.

Part III, a repetition of Part I, was given ostensibly as a means of determining the constancy and reliability of expressions of liking and dislike. It also served to camouflage the post-training test in the minds of any subjects who considered the main series as a form of training of some sort whose results were to be tested.

Results with Christmas Cards

The qualities in the Christmas cards favored in the training series were simplicity, good spacing, landscapes, abstract designs, and gold as against ornateness, crowdedness, persons, pictorial quality, and lack of gold. Favored cards usually carried on the back a written comment "high." A few cards had other comments such as "simple and honest," "high by many," "liked by many," and "an interesting design." Disparaged cards usually carried the written comment "low," but a few carried comments such as "too miscellaneous," "too crowded," and "disliked by many." Cards that were neither favored nor disparaged usually carried no comment, though an occasional comment like "some do and some don't," "half and half," or "divergent opinions" was used.

The cards of the pre-training and post-training test series were rated by two judges, whereby each card was given a value of 1 to 5 for each of the criterion variables: simplicity 1 as against ornateness 5; open spacing 1 as against crowdedness 5; landscape 1 as against persons 5; abstract design 1 as against pictorial quality 5; and gold 1 as against its lack 5. Each card was given a score equal to the sum of the five ratings. The pre-training test consisted of twenty-one cards rich in the qualities favored in training, with an average *per judge* rating of 13.0; of thirteen cards like those left without comment in training, with an average *per judge* rating of 17.4; and of twenty-two cards rich in the qualities disparaged in training, with an average *per judge* rating of 20.5. The post-training test consisted of twenty-one favored, thirteen indeterminate, and twenty-two disparaged cards matched card for card with those of the pre-training test, with average *per judge* ratings of 13.2, 17.7, and 20.5 respectively. Each series had interpolated in it nine other cards to fill it out to sixty-five.

The change attributable to the training by comments which rewarded when coincident with the subject's opinion, and which punished when in opposition to the subject's opinion, can be measured by determining the shifts in liking from the pre-training to the post-training series. They were as follows in the case of the subjects of Group I for the twenty-one cards rich in favored qualities:

	1	2	Indif	8	9
For 21 pre-training cards.......	112	76	29	68	156
For 21 post-training equivalents..	189	90	19	50	93
Difference (post — pre)	77	14	—10	—18	—63

If the rating 1 is considered to be a step from $+2.5$ to $+1.5$, 2 the step from $+1.5$ to $+0.5$, Indif the step from $+0.5$ to -0.5, 8 the step from -0.5 to -1.5, and 9 the step from -1.5 to -2.5, the median shift can be computed. The favored cards change from a median rating of -0.55 on the pre-training test to $+1.15$ on the matched post-training test. Disparaged cards changed from $+0.68$ to -1.18. Cards neither favored nor disparaged shifted from $+0.61$ to -0.84.

Group II shifted for favored cards from $+0.04$ to $+1.20$ and for disparaged cards from $+0.28$ to -0.89. Cards neither favored nor disparaged shifted from -0.65 to -0.87.

Combining the medians for the two groups with equal weight, we have a shift up of 1.47 for favored cards, a shift down of 1.52 for disparaged cards, and a shift down of 0.84 for cards neither favored nor disparaged. Using averages, the corresponding numbers are 0.72 up for favored, 0.60 down for disfavored and 0.26 down for the others.* The probable errors of the 0.72 and 0.60 are about 0.05. The facts in detail appear in Table 17.

The occurrence of a liking (or dislike), plus the confirmation it received from the comments found on the back of the cards, is then very potent in making certain qualities liked (or disliked) even when they appear in entirely different cards. How much of the change is due to occurrence and how much to reward is left undetermined.

Results with Poetry

In the poetry series, selections which were restrained, thoughtful, and original or subtle, varied, irregular in metrical form, and frivolous in content were favored. There was disparagement of selections which were pompous, sentimental, commonplace, singsong in meter, and pious. Selections which were concerned with war and fighting, death, and Christmas were also disparaged. Five judges † rated each selection in the pre-training and post-training series in accord with the following directions:

"Please rate the enclosed specimens for restraint versus pomposity on a scale of 1 to 5, 1 being very restrained and 5, very pompous. Enter this in column I. Rate each specimen also for thoughtfulness vs. sentimentality on a scale of 1 to 5, 1 for very thoughtful, 5, very sentimental, in column II. In column III rate specimens for originality vs. commonplaceness, 1 to 5, 1 for original. In column IV rate for subtle and irregular and varied metrical forms vs. singsongness, very singsong being at the 5 end. In column V rate for frivolous (1) vs. pious (5). Will you also note in the columns marked W, D, and X a check for the specimen if it contains anything about war and fighting (W), death (D), and Christmas (X), respectively?"

---

* This general shift down may be due to becoming bored by Christmas cards, or to the growth of a higher standard for liking as a result of the negative comments, or to both causes. The likings for cards characterized by the favored qualities increased notably in spite of it.

† K., S., E., L., and W.

TABLE 17

The frequency with which cards were rated 1 (surely liked), 2 (probably liked), Indif (indifferent), 8 (probably disliked), and 9 (surely disliked), before and after training with 335 Christmas cards in which judgments coincident with the criterion were rewarded, and in which judgments in opposition to the criterion were punished: Groups I and II

THE KIND OF CARD WHICH IN TRAINING WAS	NO. OF CARDS	INITIAL PRE-TRAINING TEST: EXPRESSIONS OF LIKE AND DISLIKE							FINAL MATCHED POST-TRAINING TEST: EXPRESSIONS OF LIKE AND DISLIKE						
		1	2	Indif	8	9	Mdn*	Av	1	2	Indif	8	9	Mdn*	Av
GROUP I (n = 21)															
Favored	21	112	76	29	68	156	−0.55	−0.18	189	90	19	50	93	+1.15	+0.53
Left indeterminate	13	85	58	15	39	76	+0.61	+0.14	62	54	4	48	105	−0.84	−0.29
Disparaged	22	143	107	25	81	106	+0.68	+0.22	87	74	7	92	202	−1.18	−0.54
GROUP II (n = 25)															
Favored	21	135	110	38	83	159	+0.04	−0.04	216	153	11	66	79	+1.19	+0.69
Left indeterminate	13	57	78	18	64	108	−0.65	−0.27	61	65	6	83	110	−0.87	−0.36
Disparaged	22	128	136	49	111	126	+0.28	+0.05	99	108	10	148	185	−0.89	−0.39

*The medians were computed on the assumption that 1 is a step from +2.5 to +1.5, 2 from +1.5 to +0.5; Indif from +0.5 to −0.5, 8 from −0.5 to −1.5, and 9 from −1.5 to −2.5.

The sum of the ratings on the five variables was used as a score per selection. In this manner twelve selections in the pre-training test of the kind favored in the training were equated to twelve selections in the post-training test. The average *per judge* rating of the favored selections test was 15.6 in both pre- and post-training. Similarly, twelve selections of the kind disparaged in the training were matched in the pre- and post-training test with average *per judge* ratings of 19.6 and 19.7 respectively. In the favored series, war, death, and Christmas were mentioned in two instances in each test; in the disparaged series, war, death, and Christmas were mentioned twenty-five times in the pre-training test and thirty-two times in the post-training. The material for the poetry series was less extensive than that for the Christmas card series, so that a mediocre selection could not be made. Just as in the Christmas card series, favored selections had the comment "high" and disparaged selections the comment "low." When these comments agreed with the subject's ratings, they presumably often gave satisfaction, and when they were opposed to the subject's judgment they presumably often annoyed him. The measure of the effect of training is obtained by determining the shift from pre- to post-training test. Table 18 presents the data for both groups.

Though there were but 165 selections in the training series, both groups change in the direction favored by the rewards. Group I changed on favored specimens from +0.70 to +1.40 and Group II from +0.59 to +0.86. Disparaged cards are liked less after training. The shift in Group I is from —0.24 to —1.23 and in Group II from +0.47 to —0.79.

Results with Colored Papers

The third series (of colored paper strips) was made up of envelope linings. The comments on the back favored dignity, simplicity, restraint, and gold, and disparaged cheapness, ornateness, gaudiness, and lack of gold. Judges rated the strips of the pre-training and post-training test on each of the four variables on a scale from 1 to 5, favored variables being given 1 and disparaged 5. In this manner six strips were equated in each test for favored attributes with average *per judge* ratings of 9.3 and 9.2 in the pre-training and post-training tests, respectively. Seven strips were matched for disparaged attributes with average *per*

TABLE 18

The frequency with which selections were rated 1 (surely liked), 2 (probably liked), Indif (indifferent), 8 (probably disliked), 9 (surely disliked), before and after training with 165 poetry selections in which judgments coincident with the criterion were rewarded, and in which judgments in opposition to the criterion were punished: Groups I and II

THE KIND OF SELECTION WHICH IN TRAINING WAS	NO. OF SELECTIONS	INITIAL PRE-TRAINING TEST RATING							FINAL MATCHED POST-TRAINING TEST RATING						
		1	2	Indif	8	9	Mdn*	Av	1	2	Indif	8	9	Mdn*	Av
GROUP I (n = 21)															
Favored	12	77	61	18	32	64	+0.70	+0.22	121	48	11	19	53	+1.40	+0.65
Disparaged	12	76	36	19	52	69	−0.24	−0.01	62	32	8	33	117	−1.23	−0.44
GROUP II (n = 25)															
Favored	12	92	64	44	43	57	+0.59	+0.30	105	70	28	49	48	+0.86	+0.45
Disparaged	12	79	70	30	48	73	+0.47	+0.11	58	56	22	49	115	−0.79	−0.36

*The medians are computed as in Table 17.

judge ratings of 18.3 and 18.5 for pre-training and post-training tests respectively.

The specimens rich in favored qualities showed the following results:

	1	2	Indif	8	9	Mdn	Av
Gr. I. Pre-training	56	29	14	17	10	+1.26	+0.83
Gr. I. Post-training ...	69	32	2	9	14	+1.59	+1.06
Gr. II. Pre-training	59	30	17	14	30	+0.97	+0.49
Gr. II. Post-training ...	63	43	8	19	17	+1.22	+0.77

The specimens rich in disparaged qualities showed the following results:

	1	2	Indif	8	9	Mdn	Av
Gr. I. Pre-training	14	24	4	17	88	−1.66	−1.12
Gr. I. Post-training	12	9	21	18	106	−1.81	−1.56
Gr. II. Pre-training	31	28	12	33	71	−1.00	−0.57
Gr. II. Post-training ...	24	29	5	50	67	−1.09	−0.71

The four shifts of medians are thus +0.33, +0.25, −0.15, and −0.09. The shifts of averages are +0.23, +0.28, −0.34, and −0.14. The changes are small, as is natural from so short a training series, but they are all in the direction expected from the after-effects. The general fact is reliably determined.*

Results from Pictures of Buildings

Group I also rated a series of pictures of buildings in which tallness, alone-ness, whiteness or grayness, and water were favored, and shortness, being with others, color, and irrelevant balloons and airplanes were disparaged. The criterion also favored bridges. The pre-training test consisted of six cards of the sort favored in training and six of the sort disparaged in training, which were matched card for card to the post-training test with average *per judge* ratings of 10 and 10 for favored cards and of 14.8 and 14.8 for disparaged cards. Regrettably, through an oversight, the favored cards in the post-training series contained many

*For Group I the standard error of the difference between the averages of pre- and post-training series was 0.14 for favored cards, and 0.15 for disparaged cards. The differences of 0.43 and 0.45 are four and a half times their probable errors. For Group II, the standard error of the difference between averages is 0.12 for favored cards and 0.13 for disparaged cards. The difference of 0.15 is nearly twice its probable error; that of 0.47, over five times its probable error. The average shift of 0.25 is over seven times its probable error.

irrelevant details such as moon, clouds, and signs, so that the matching was far from perfect.

The group changed on favored cards from 70, 24, 7, 13, and 12 to 42, 33, 4, 20, and 27 in the frequencies of ratings 1, 2, Indif, 8, and 9 in pre- and post-training test respectively. The median changed from +1.6 to +0.8. The average changed from +1.0 to +0.3. Disparaged cards changed from 34, 32, 9, 24, and 27 to 19, 24, 4, 34, and 35, a median shift from +0.6 to —1.0. The average changed from +0.2 to —0.3. The net result was thus doubtful.

On the whole, experiment 61 proves the potency of occurrence plus a satisfying after-effect to strengthen the connection between a situation and a response of liking or dislike, provided the subjects' expressions represented genuine likes and dislikes.

As a means of discovering how far the subjects fulfilled the requirement that genuine personal attitudes be expressed, not ratings for esthetic merit, some of them, a random sample, were asked to reply to the following questions:

1. Did you always express your real likings and dislikes, not your notions of what you ought to like and dislike? ....

2. If you did not always do so, in what percentage of the cases do you think you failed to do so? ....

3. Certain of the specimens were rated a second time to secure measures of reliability. In what percentage of these second ratings do you think you failed to express your real likings and dislikes? ....

4. Were you aware during the experiment of any changes in your likes and dislikes? .... If so, what were these changes? ....

The median percentage of failures reported for the main series was 2; for the second ratings of the specimens rated twice it was 5. The corresponding averages were 5 and 7. Of thirty-two individuals, not a single one gave any indications that he had surmised that certain qualities were favored or disfavored by the comments irrespective of the general merit of the specimen. Only seven gave any indications that they were influenced to express notions contrary to their real feelings and in the direction of conformity to what the comments commended, and these indications referred almost exclusively to the specimens reported on twice. It is therefore almost certain that the changes in the expressions of liking and dislike were due in large measure to direct strengthenings of the connections between situations and attitudes, not to ideas about esthetics inferred from the comments.

The results of experiments 64, 65, 66, and 67, which are described in Appendix VII, provide evidence to the same effect.

Individual Experiment 62

Experiment 62 used likes and dislikes for Christmas cards as the attitudes to be changed and high school students as the persons. They were tested and trained individually. The training consisted of approving comments in some of the cases when their attitudes were consistent with the composite judgment of a group of adult students of art. Any other authority would have served as well, but we wished to change appreciations in an esthetically approved direction.

The general plan of the experiment was to record the attitudes of the individual toward each of forty cards and to train him with a group of 160 different Christmas cards. He was rewarded by approval, etc., when his likes and dislikes coincided with the art students' judgments of like and dislike. Finally his attitudes toward forty entirely different cards were recorded. All of the testing and training was done by the same person, Miss Mabel Wilcox.

The cards comprising the test and training series were selected from a larger series of 540 Christmas cards. The 540 Christmas cards were rated by each of twelve competent art students on a five-point scale under the following instructions: "You will look at each Christmas card. If you are sure you like it, record 1. If you think you like it, but are not sure, record 2. If you are not sure whether you like it or dislike it, record Indif. If you think you dislike it, but are not sure, record 8. If you are sure you dislike it, record 9." Each card was then given a weight by summing the ratings of the twelve judges. These sums ranged from 17 to 108, where the low scores represent liking and the high scores dislike. The best-liked 56 cards, ranging in sums from 17 to 49, were called 'good'; the least-liked 56 cards, ranging from 99 to 108, were called 'poor'; and the middle 128 cards, ranging in sums from 78 to 90, were called 'mediocre.' From these three groups of cards two test series and the training series were developed. Each test series contained ten 'good,' eleven 'mediocre,' and ten 'poor' cards which were matched card for card by composite ratings and by similarity. Each test series was filled out to forty by the inclusion of seven random 'mediocre' cards. The test series was scrambled by chance. The average value of the ten 'good' cards in the initial test was 37.5 and in the matched final test was 37.5. The ten 'mediocre' cards averaged 85.6 in the initial and 85.8 in the final, and the average for the 'poor' cards was 102.5 in the initial and 101.9 in the final. The training series comprised 160 cards, of which thirty-six were 'good' cards, thirty-six were 'poor' cards, and the remainder were 'mediocre.' The 'good' and 'poor' cards were distributed so that nine of each occurred randomly in each forty of the training series.

Twenty high school students participated in the experiment. Each subject was given the following directions:

"This is an experiment in appreciation. You are to tell your likes and dislikes for a series of Christmas cards. You will look at the Christmas card and if you are sure you like it you are to say 1. If you think you like it you are to say 2. If you are not sure if you like it or dislike it, say 5. If you think you dislike it but are not sure, say 8. If you are sure you dislike it say 9. Remember 1 means you surely like it; 2 means you think you like it but are not sure; 5 means you neither like it nor dislike it; 8 means you think you dislike it but are not sure; 9 means you surely dislike it.

"Always say something for each card. In every case express your own personal feelings. We do not wish to know whether you think the card deserves to be liked or disliked, but whether you do yourself like it or dislike it.

"Sometimes after you have said 1 or 2 or 5 or 8 or 9, I will let you know whether you agree in general with a group of very competent artists and people of general good taste. As soon as you have told me how you like any one card, immediately move to the next unless I make a comment, in which case move to the next card immediately after the comment is made. Do not stop to think about any card after you have told me whether you like it or dislike it. Bear in mind that you are always to record your own personal like or dislike, not your opinion whether the card or selection ought to be liked."

After the instructions had been given, the experimenter then gave the initial test, cards 1-40. The training series, cards 41-80, 81-120, 121-160, and 161-200 were then administered four times. Whenever the subject said "1" for a 'good' card, the experimenter rewarded him with a comment such as "A very attractive picture" or "Good feeling, attractive to artists" or "I like it, I don't know why" or "Beautiful in its classical simplicity." Whenever the subject said "9" for a 'poor' card, he was rewarded with a comment such as "A mess, artistically" or "People of taste consider it poor" or "I dislike it intensely" or "I hope I never receive an atrocity like it." If the subject responded with any number other than "1" for a 'good' card or "9" for a 'poor' card, no comment was made. Neither was comment made for any of the remaining cards in the series.

After the training series had been administered four times, the matched final test, cards 201-240, was given, and then the initial test again, cards 1-40. The experiment was so paced that subjects completed the entire experiment in a single session of about an hour.

The efficacy of the training can be measured by determining the difference in the number of cards in the test series that were rated 1, 2, 5, 8, or 9 initially or finally in each group of 'good,' 'bad,' and 'mediocre' cards. The facts are presented in Tables 19, 20, and 21.

If we treat liking as + and dislike as − and consider that judgments 1, 2, 5, 8, and 9 cover equal intervals from +2.5 to +1.5, from +1.5 to +0.5, from +0.5 to −0.5, from −0.5 to −1.5, and from −1.5 to −2.5, respectively, we may compute medians. Changes in these medians will indicate the changes in attitude. The medians and changes are as follows:

	'Good'	'Mediocre'	'Bad'
Initial test	+0.53	+0.78	+1.25
Final test	+1.53	+0.57	+0.59
Repetition of initial test after training	+1.34	+0.67	+0.54
Change from initial to final test	+1.00	−0.21	−0.66
Change from initial test to the repetition of it after training	+0.81	−0.11	−0.71

Even in so short a training there is unquestionable change in the subject's judgments. There is unquestionable change in their likings, unless they inferred from the rewards that certain qualities were estimable, recognized those qualities in the final test, and reported that they liked them though they did not (and conversely for disesteemed qualities). Some influence from such inferences there doubtless is, but only a very able analyst would

TABLE 19

The frequency with which each subject rated the ten cards of the 'good' series 1, 2, 5, 8, or 9 on the initial test before training, on the final matched test after training, and on the repetition of the initial test after training; 5 = indifferent

Rating	A	B	C	D	E	F	G	H	I	J	K	L	M	N	O	P	Q	R	S	T	Total
Initial rating																					
1	1	2	2	3	3	2	4	4	5			7		10	8	3	1	4		1	63
2		2	2	2	3	5	2			3	3	2	3			4	2	4	3	1	38
5		4	3	2	3	2	1	2				1			1			1	2	2	24
8	2	2	1	1	2		3	2	3	3	3		3			1	3	1	2	4	26
9	7	1	2	2	1	1		4	5	4	4		6		1	2	4		5	2	49
																					+0.53*
Final rating																					
1	6	5	3	3	2	6	7	3	6	7	6	7	9	10	5	3		7	7	1	103
2	1	2	4	2	5	1	3	2	1	1		1	1	1	2	4	1			2	33
5	1	1	3	2	1			1			1				2	2	1	1	3	3	24
8	2	1			1	1		1			3	2					5	2		3	22
9		1		3	1			3	2	2					1	1	3			1	18
																					+1.53*
Repetition of initial after training																					
1	3	4	4	3	4	6	6	3	6	7	4	6	7	10	5	4		6	4	1	93
2	1	3	4	1	3	3	3	3	1	1		4	2		4	4		3	4		44
5	2	2	1	3	1		1	2	1		4		1			1		1	2	2	23
8	4		1		1			2		2	2						3			7	23
9		1		3	1	1			2	2					1	1	7				17
																					+1.34*

*Medians.

TABLE 20

The frequency with which each subject rated the eleven cards of the 'mediocre' series 1, 2, 5, 8, or 9 on the initial test before training, on the final matched test after training, and on the repetition of the initial test after training; 5 = indifferent

	Rating	A	B	C	D	E	F	G	H	I	J	K	L	M	N	O	P	Q	R	S	T	Total
Initial rating	1	2	2	2	..	1	5	8	1	5	8	4	6	1	6	5	5	1	4	5	..	71
	2	3	1	5	1	4	..	2	3	1	..	1	4	6	3	3	3	1	4	..	5	54
	5	2	5	4	7	5	1	1	4	2	..	4	..	..	2	1	1	4	2	5	3	55
	8	3	2	3	2	1	1	..	2	3	2	2	2	2	..	2	2	4	1	3	2	25
	9	1	..	1	1	..	..	..	1	..	2	2	1	2	..	2	..	1	..	1	1	15
																						+0.78*
Final rating	1	..	3	1	..	3	4	5	4	7	1	4	3	3	7	2	4	2	2	..	..	54
	2	1	2	2	1	5	4	6	2	1	2	3	3	7	2	3	4	5	..	5	5	60
	5	6	5	8	1	2	2	..	2	2	1	2	..	1	2	5	3	..	3	6	6	62
	8	3	1	..	5	..	..	..	2	3	3	2	5	..	..	..	..	3	4	..	..	27
	9	1	..	..	4	1	1	..	2	4	4	..	..	..	..	1	..	..	2	..	..	17
																						+0.57*
Repetition of initial after training	1	..	5	2	..	2	5	5	3	6	..	1	3	7	7	1	2	1	4	..	..	58
	2	3	2	1	..	6	3	6	2	2	5	4	1	2	2	4	5	3	2	6	6	63
	5	2	4	6	1	2	2	..	3	..	3	3	..	2	2	3	3	5	2	5	5	46
	8	3	3	2	7	1	1	..	2	3	2	2	7	..	..	1	1	..	3	..	..	35
	9	3	..	2	3	..	1	..	1	2	3	1	..	..	..	2	..	..	2	..	..	18
																						+0.67*

*Medians.

TABLE 21

The frequency with which each subject rated the ten cards of the 'poor' series 1, 2, 5, 8, or 9 on the initial test before training, on the final test after training, and on the repetition of the initial test after training; 5 = indifferent

	Rating	A	B	C	D	E	F	G	H	I	J	K	L	M	N	O	P	Q	R	S	T	Total
Initial rating	1	3	3	5	2	6	5	4	5	5	6	6	2	6	5	1	6	3	8	6	3	87
	2	·	2	5	2	2	4	4	2	2	·	3	4	2	1	2	3	3	2	3	5	51
	5	2	4	·	3	1	1	2	1	2	1	·	1	1	2	2	·	7	·	1	·	31
	8	4	1	·	3	1	·	·	1	1	3	·	3	·	·	·	·	·	·	·	2	13
	9	1	·	·	·	1	·	·	1	3	3	1	3	1	2	5	1	·	·	·	·	18
																						+1.25*
Final rating	1	·	·	·	·	5	4	6	6	3	1	5	·	6	1	·	7	·	·	6	7	58
	2	1	2	·	·	4	4	4	1	3	2	2	3	3	2	·	1	5	4	4	3	46
	5	1	4	·	·	·	2	·	2	3	·	2	·	1	2	1	2	5	2	·	·	33
	8	4	1	3	3	1	·	·	1	1	·	·	7	·	1	1	·	·	2	·	·	27
	9	4	3	6	7	·	·	·	·	·	7	1	·	·	4	8	·	·	2	·	·	36
																						+0.59*
Repetition of initial after training	1	·	·	·	·	5	4	3	6	3	·	7	·	7	1	·	7	·	3	3	6	53
	2	1	2	2	·	3	5	7	1	2	·	2	2	3	3	1	3	·	3	5	4	49
	5	1	4	7	2	1	1	·	2	3	·	1	·	·	3	·	·	3	3	2	·	31
	8	5	1	·	8	·	·	·	1	2	1	·	8	·	1	·	·	6	3	·	·	30
	9	3	3	·	·	1	·	·	·	·	9	·	·	·	2	9	·	1	1	·	·	37
																						+0.54*

* Medians.

be able to make the inferences correctly. And only a person very zealous to win the esteem of an unknown experimenter would repeatedly disobey instructions and say that he liked what he did not and that he disliked what he really liked. The probability that the ability, the craving, the disobedience, and the dishonesty should all be found together in any large percentage of high school students is to my mind very small.

The number of rewards which each of the twenty subjects had in each round of the training series is reported in Table 40 of Appendix VIII. There was wide variation (from 4 to 33 in the first round and from 6 to 171 in all four rounds together).

Two of the subjects (Q and T) had at the start such bad taste that in the first round of training they had only four judgments of 1 and 9 in agreement with the consensus. Receiving so few rewards in the first round, they naturally would do little better in the second except by some happy accidents. In fact they did worse, totaling five instead of eight. In rounds 3 and 4 they totaled three and three. They naturally showed no improvement in the final test over the initial. If their records had been omitted, the average gains reported would have been higher.

Experiment 63 was like experiment 62 in all respects except that the twenty subjects were all educated adults aged forty to seventy, and that the initial or pre-training test and the matched final or post-training test were interchanged for ten of the subjects.

The frequencies of the expressions of liking and disliking before and after the training were as shown below (1 = sure liking, 2 = probable liking, 5 = indifference, 8 = probable dislike, 9 = sure dislike; counted as +2.5 to +1.5, +1.5 to +0.5, +0.5 to −0.5, −0.5 to −1.5, and −1.5 to −2.5, respectively).

There is thus a general shift toward less liking, as shown by the eleven mediocre cards and by the totals. The median for all cards shifts from +0.35 to −0.71 from initial to matched final. The training overcomes this tendency in the case of the 'good' cards and adds to it in the case of the 'bad' cards. For 'good' and 'bad' cards combined, the change in the direction of the training is 0.73 (using medians) or 0.46 (using averages) from initial to matched final. From initial test to the repetition of the initial test at the end of training it is 0.64 (using medians) or 0.44 (using averages).

	1	2	5	8	9	Mdn	Av
Ten 'good' cards:							
Initial	80	38	42	17	23	+0.97	+0.69
Matched final	70	67	20	17	26	+1.05	+0.69
Repetition of initial at							
end	66	56	30	24	24	+0.89	+0.58
Eleven 'mediocre' cards:							
Initial	50	63	48	33	26	+0.55	+0.36
Matched final	18	35	47	25	95	—0.90	—0.66
Repetition of initial at							
end	15	35	46	34	90	—0.91	—0.68
Ten 'bad' cards:							
Initial	22	36	49	26	67	—0.36	—0.40
Matched final	10	10	17	33	130	—1.73	—1.32
Repetition of initial at							
end	7	6	22	37	128	—1.72	—1.37

We have made a number of other experiments of the same general nature as these, both with individuals and with groups. They are reported in Appendix VII.

The results of our experiments support the conclusion that a person can be taught new attitudes and tastes as surely, though not as easily, as he can be taught facts or skills. The basic principles of learning by repetition and reward seem to operate with wants, interests, and attitudes as they do with ideas and movements.

Consideration of the acquisition of likes, dislikes, fears, hates, and sympathies in childhood or in adult years will, in general, support the same conclusion. There is, however, one apparently puzzling set of facts, the continuance of nostalgia, nervous irritation, worry, envy, fear, shame, and disgust as responses. If reward strengthens connections leading to emotional responses, one would expect that a situation leading sometimes to nostalgia and sometimes to cheerful contentment would increasingly lead to the latter, that a situation leading sometimes to worry and sometimes to peace would increasingly lead to the latter, that a child who was sometimes terrified by a thunder-storm and at others enjoyed it would increasingly enjoy it. How can envy, fear, and shame, which make us miserable, avoid being vanquished by good-will, courage, and self-confident pride, which are self-rewarding? Why do not the pleasant interests and attitudes displace the unpleasant?

The answer to this apparent puzzle is probably to be found in the following facts: (1) The pleasant response sometimes does not occur or occurs too infrequently. Since punishment does not directly weaken connections and is useful only in so far as it causes the person to make some other response which is rewarded, or at least tolerated, a situation such as a thunder-storm or the sight of the happiness of others may forever arouse panic, fear, or gnawing envy.

If the situation has a very strong connection with some attitude by original nature or long habit, even the deliberate efforts of a parent, teacher, priest, or psychiatrist may be unable to substitute a different and happier attitude often enough to displace the other. Much less can the ordinary course of life be expected to do so.

(2) The unpleasant response may have secondary consequences which are satisfying. The child who is miserable with fear may be rejoicing in the affectionate care which his misery evokes from his mother. The wife who is miserable with worry may be luxuriating in the attention which her husband gives her. What annoys one segment or level of a person may gratify some other segment or level.

These two exceptions are really cases of the general rule, which is that the satisfying wants, interests, and attitudes *do* vanquish their opposites where they compete as responses to the same situation. Most people do come to think well of themselves rather than suffer from a perpetual sense of guilt and shame. Most people come to enjoy the spectacle of the fortunate without much envy and that of the unfortunate without much anguish. Most of us can be glad to get home and yet not suffer nostalgia when away.

Chapter 15

THE INFLUENCE OF ASSOCIATIVE SHIFTING: CONDITIONED REFLEXES

WE have seen in Chapter 13 that mere temporal association or contiguity probably has little or no power to link an interest or attitude or other emotional response to a situation. If S_1 is made contiguous with S_2 which has the power to evoke R_x, S_1 does not thereby gain notably in power to evoke R_x. To increase that power, R_x must be made *as a response to* S_1.

R_x may be linked to S_1 effectively in two ways.* The first is by contriving that S_1 include R_x among its responses and rewarding $S_1 \rightarrow R_x$ when it occurs. This is learning by simple connecting and selecting (repetition and reward), illustrated in the case of interests and attitudes by the experiments of Chapter 14 and Appendix VII.

When it is impossible or very difficult to contrive that S_1 shall evoke R_x directly, we have recourse to learning by associative shifting, wherein we find some situation (call it S_2) that does evoke R_x and change $S_2 \rightarrow R_x$ over to $S_1 \rightarrow R_x$ (by additions until we have $S_2 + S_1 \rightarrow R_x$, and later subtractions until we have $S_1 \rightarrow R_x$). Thus suppose that the aim is to link the attitude of liking to Uncle Jonas, who is not intrinsically able to arouse it in his nephew, aged five. We first present Jonas dressed as Santa Claus doing amusing tricks and bearing gifts, and interest is aroused. The Santa Claus disguise is taken off gradually, without destroying the liking. Uncle Jonas stops performing his tricks and still retains his nephew's liking. He is divested of the gifts and still retains it, the originally unattractive Uncle Jonas being now able alone to arouse the response originally aroused only by S_2. Rewards for the $S_1 \rightarrow R_x$ when it is obtained as a result of the shift may be used to maintain and strengthen it.

When the response is a reflex and when the shifting is made in

---

* R_x may also be linked to S_1 by sheer frequency of connection by contriving that S_1 evoke R_x many times and evoke anything other than R_x never or rarely. But this is a wasteful method.

a certain way (by presenting S_1 for a time and then continuing it with the addition of S_2 with certain special arrangements and conditions), the general case of associative shifting becomes the well-known special case of the so-called conditioned reflex.

Changing a person's attitudes and interests by associative shifting is important especially because attitudes and interests are usually not "available," summonable at will, or arousable by command, description, the presentation of a model, or easy stimulation *ab extra*. Associative shifting can then, as was suggested earlier, be used where learning by simple connecting and selecting is not feasible. As a possibility, the method is omnipotent in the sense that any response of which a person is capable may thus be connected with any situation to which he is sensitive. It is theoretically possible to make a person afraid of the sunshine or flowers, or courageous in the face of a jumping tiger, provided (1) there is at the outset anything of which he is afraid and there is anything which arouses courage in him and provided (2) the shifted connections can be kept satisfying and made strong enough to overcome instinctive or acquired opposition. The last twofold proviso greatly restricts the actual achievements of associative shifting, as of any modification of wants, attitudes, and interests.

As a sample, we may take the case of timidity and fear. The child responds to the jumping, barking dog + being held calmly by the mother + hearing her soothing words, by the absence of fear. This response may continue when the soothing words are withdrawn, when the mother holds only his hand, when the mother is simply present, and finally when the jumping, barking dog is no wise alleviated. The facts that the jumping, barking dog does not bite or knock down or otherwise do any intimate harm, and that it gradually comes to possess interesting features and to reward courageous behavior by entertaining sport may play important parts, of course. If, however, original nature and past experience have established a very strong tendency to fear of the situation, all the accessories we supply may only counteract it or distract attention from it, and when the counteracting accessories are withdrawn, the fear may return. Or, if the more courageous behavior receives no reward as one accessory after another is removed, it may remain so weak that being bitten or knocked down a few times may undo our work and reinstate the original fear.

Changes of attitudes by associative shifting will be easy in proportion as the shifted connection meets little opposition and has satisfying after-effects. Thus it is easy to shift hate or scorn to Mormons, Germans, Jews, beer-drinkers, or prohibitionists when it is fashionable to do so. Man enjoys hate that is convenient, and he likes to gain self-respect by scorning others. But shifting love from oneself to one's neighbors, shifting impartial objectivity from arithmetical or scientific to political and personal problems, and shifting calmness from healthful, happy liberty to pain, attack, and calamity are so difficult and rare that such shifts are expected only of saints or pathological personalities.

General observation will convince any impartial observer that the improvement of attitudes and interests and wants by associative shifting, including the special techniques used in forming conditioned reflexes, is a slow and arduous process in school-children and adults. But many social reformers and workers for child welfare, and some psychologists, seem to believe that the case is otherwise with very young children, and that the world may find its educational salvation through radical modifications of wants, attitudes, and interests in infancy. In the report of the Hoover Research Committee on Social Trends,* the following is asserted:

"But the fundamental personalities of children are pretty well formed by the time they go to school. Between birth and the age of six, the year when the child is generally first exposed to the influence of formal education, he comes in contact chiefly with the other members of the family group and is permanently affected by them. They are the stimuli to which he responds, many times each day and every day in the year. Such a repetition and limitation of stimuli cannot but leave on the infant's plastic nature a reaction pattern involving affection, fear and rage, the development of the ego, quickness of response, feelings of inferiority, inhibitions, etc." [W. F. Ogburn, vol. 1, p. 697.] [The general introduction approves this doctrine, in these words:] "Mental and social qualities are particularly susceptible to influences of the cultural environments. In early childhood in the family environment the more firmly imbedded traits of personality are fixed, particularly the basis for mental health or disorders." [p. xxv.]

Experimental studies of associative shifting of attitudes and interests have been very few. The best known is that of Watson

* *Recent Social Trends in the United States* (McGraw-Hill Book Company, Inc.).

and Rayner ['20] concerning the shift of fear, as shown by startle, crying, and avoidance, from the sound made by striking on a steel bar with a hammer, to the appearance and approach of a white rat, a rabbit, and a dog. The one subject studied was a child of eleven months who is reported to have been phlegmatic and fearless hitherto, and in particular to have shown no fear at the white rat, rabbit, or dog in a test at nine months.

After eight joint stimulations by the sight of the rat and the clang of the bar, each of which evoked evidences of fear,[*] the rat was presented alone. "The instant the rat was shown the baby began to cry. Almost instantly he turned sharply to the left, fell over on left side, raised himself on all fours and began to crawl away so rapidly that he was caught with difficulty before reaching the edge of the table."

Five days later the rat alone again aroused whimpering, falling, and turning away, or moving away on all fours. The rabbit alone, dog alone, and a fur coat alone on this same day aroused similar responses.

Two explanations of these results are possible. One is that they illustrate a general fact—that emotional reactions are easily shifted from S_2 to S_1 by a few occurrences in response to $S_1 + S_2$. The other is that they illustrate a very special case rather than a general fact.[†]

By the first explanation babies should be as easily taught to fear a hairbrush or thermometer as a rat. Also babies should be as easily taught to enjoy S_1 by presenting it along with S_3, which arouses enjoyment, as to fear S_1 by presenting it along with S_2, the fearsome clang of the hammer on the steel rod.

However the Watson-Rayner case is explained, everybody must admit that the general facts concerning the shifts or "conditioning" of emotional reactions may best be discovered by using

[*] In the first five the baby "jumped" or "started" three times, "fell over" five times, and "whimpered" once. In the last three it "started" once, "puckered face" once, "whimpered" twice, "cried" once, "fell over" once, and "withdrew body" once.

[†] This explanation might argue that the human infant at or near the age when it begins locomotion is disposed to manifest fear responses at strange objects which approach it, especially such as wriggle or contort themselves, and to the unexpected touch of fur, so that these situations are much more likely to evoke fear than, say, motionless flowers. Regardless of the merits of this argument, the shift of fear reactions from animal plus clang to animal alone might still not represent the general fact.

as the S_1 each of several situations none of which can be suspected of any special, inherited attachments and by using with half of them some S_3 which arouses a pleasant reaction.

We have done this, in experiment 68, with fifteen babies of about the age of the one subject studied by Watson and Rayner and with results which demonstrate that their case was a special case and was definitely misleading concerning the probability of "leaving on the infant's plastic nature a reaction pattern involving affection, fear and rage, the development of the ego, the quickness of response, feelings of inferiority, inhibitions, etc.," by any such quick and easy process of "conditioning." On the contrary, the influence of joint stimulation is so slight that we cannot demonstrate even its existence.

The work was done by Dr. Bregman, whose report appears in the *Journal of Genetic Psychology*, No. 45, pp. 169ff. A bell behind the baby's back caused startle. Instead of the white rat, the objects St 1, St 2, St 3, St 4, St 5, and St 6 were presented. Instead of the clang of the hammer on the steel bar, an electric bell rung behind the baby's back was used, which caused fear or startle. A rattle and the melody played by a little music-box were used, which caused relief, contentment, and interest.

A careful record was kept of the baby's behavior when each 'neutral' stimulus (St 1 to St 6) was presented alone, when the bell was sounded alone, when the rattle was presented alone, when the joint stimulations were made of bell + St 1, bell + St 2, bell + St 3, rattle or melody + St 4, rattle or melody + St 5, rattle or melody + St 6, and when, after a certain number of joint presentations, St 1, St 2, St 3, St 4, St 5, and St 6 were presented alone.

At the end of the first cycle of joint presentations, the responses to St 1, St 2, and St 3 showed no more shift toward fear or startle than the responses to St 4, St 5, and St 6. At the end of the second cycle of joint presentations for the thirteen babies that completed two cycles, there is a little less shift toward contentment and interest for the former. When the differences between the responses before and after the joint stimulation are rated on a scale running from "Change toward fear" to "Change toward increased interest with diminution of fear" the median falls in the "No change" category for both St 1, St 2, and St 3 and St 4, St 5, and St 6, at the end of the first cycle. At the end of the second cycle the median for St 1, St 2, and St 3 falls at the end of the "Increased interest" category nearest the "No change" category, while the median for St 4, St 5, and St 6 falls in the "Increased interest" category. For the two children who completed three cycles, there is also a little greater change toward interest and contentment in the case of St 4, St 5, and St 6.

Dr. Bregman's work then shows a very slight and unreliable shift toward the responses made to the associated situations. Her results are like what parents usually get who try to shift attitudes toward fear of matches, knives, bottles, dangerous spots, and the like or toward tolerance and affection for uncles, aunts, physicians, cod-liver oil, green vegetables, keeping on mittens, and the like. Progress is slow.

There are occasional sudden and dramatic shifts from a few associations (often only one), as when a child who is frightened and hurt shortly after being seated with a stranger in a railway car seat is extremely averse to being seated with any stranger in such a seat for months thereafter, or as when a child who has received a fright in a bus rebels violently against entering it again. But these are extremely rare. An observing parent would hardly find one per child per year. They are also specialized. They are deserving of study, especially of impartial study such as they do not commonly receive. But they are not typical of the great bulk of associative shifting. To use them as explanations of changes in attitudes and interests in general or as the foundation of a theory of education is in every way unjustifiable. Indeed, it is perverse.

Before leaving this topic, mention should be made of the careful experiments of Harold Jones ['31], who found a greater effect than Bregman did. He used a bell as the supposedly neutral stimulus and an electric shock delivered through a grid in the mat on which the infant sat as the primary excitant of startle. The sound alone did become more startling than it was before the joint stimulation.

I hope some one will repeat the Jones experiments with other stimuli than the bell and parallel them by experiments to shift smiling, laughing, or other reactions showing pleasant interest. The use of unfamiliar sounds as the secondary stimulus and startle as the response is undesirable in experiments on the general problem for two reasons. First, little children are prone to respond to strange sounds by startle, so that the connection is very sensitive and ready to act. It is one of the least instructive cases that could be chosen. Second, there is more to be gained from showing how to 'condition' courage or other desirable attitudes. In practice a policy of protecting babies, children, or adults from various unfortunate attachments of fear is inferior to a policy of developing courage toward situations which require it.

In actual educational work associative shifting, including the special form of it found when reflexes are attached to situations that would not otherwise evoke them, is chiefly useful as a technique to put a certain response in connection with a certain situation. Satisfying accompaniments or after-effects of the connection when it is obtained are usually relied upon to establish and preserve it. In some cases, of course, the response itself brings its own reward. For example, any activity which has as its consequence the voluptuous sensations of sex may easily form strong connections with any stimulus. To a less degree the same occurs with bodily play, manipulation, laughter, chewing, and other behavior which is its own reward. But in most of the cases in which civilized industrial society desires to shift attachments, some external force is required to provide satisfiers, or the shifted connections will not withstand competition, interference, and decay.

Chapter 16 *

CHANGES IN THE UNPLEASANTNESS OF A STIMULUS DUE TO ITS REPETITION

COMMON experience furnishes fairly frequent cases of diminished dislike when what is, or at least seems to be, the same situation, is repeated again and again. So, in the Arctic, Stefansson lost his disgust at decayed fish. So infants or savages lose their irritation at wearing clothes. So the misery of stage-fright abates in the preacher or lawyer. So the lack of coffee, alcohol, tobacco, and the like, at first almost unendurable, may become almost or quite unnoticed.

One doctrine to account for such facts is that there is, under certain conditions, a fundamental and universal tendency for a stimulus causing unpleasantness to cause less and less of it in the person who experiences the stimulus repeatedly. A possible extension of such a doctrine is that enough repetition changes the person's response from dislike through indifference to liking. The belief in something like this is fairly common. A possible correlative doctrine is that there is, under certain conditions, a fundamental and universal tendency for a stimulus causing pleasant feeling to cause less and less of it with repeated occurrences. A composite doctrine, of attractive simplicity, is that the feeling tone or emotional attitude toward any oft repeated stimulus has a fundamental and universal tendency toward indifference.

We have carried out experiments designed to increase knowledge concerning the extent of the decrease of dislike with repetition and concerning its causes.

Experiments 69 to 71

A volunteer group interested in the psychology of learning undertook to repeat several disagreeable activities daily. Of this group, ten undertook to take a distasteful food once or twice daily, rating their feelings of utter dislike. Five of these ten took a teaspoonful of olive oil twice daily, three took a similar amount

* Irving Lorge is the author of the greater part of this chapter.

198

TABLE 22

The rating on a scale of unpleasantness from 0 to −100 for each of a
series of repeated takings of obnoxious food; eleven volunteer subjects;
by day, by session, and by subject

SUBJECT AND FOOD *

DAY	SESSION	Lo 00	Ke 00	Wo 00	Du 00	Fo 00	Bl CLO	Tu CLO	Ja CLO	Ca RL	Ga RL
1	1	−25	−35	−60	−35	−22	−20	−12	−15	−20	−8
	2	−30	−35	−70	−25	−11	...	−15	−15	−15	−9
2	3	−20	−33	−30	−17	−13	−15	−12	−12	−18	−9
	4	−20	−27	−20	−17	−9	...	−12	−12	−15	−10
3	5	−25	−25	−20	−10	−7	−10	−11	−12	−15	−10
	6	−25	−15	−10	−10†	−6	...	−14	−12	−12	−9
4	7	−20	−15	−10	...	−6	−7	−10	−8	−10	−11
	8	−25	−15	−10	...	−6	...	−10	−8	−10	−12
5	9	−30	−15	−10	...	−5	−7	−9	−8	−8	−10
	10	−30	−15	−10	...	−8	...	−9	−8	−8	−9
6	11	−25	−10	−5	...	−9	−7	−10	−6	−5	−11
	12	−25	−30	−20	...	−7	...	−9	−6	−5	−10
7	13	−20	−10	−10	...	−6	−5	−11	−6	−3	−8
	14	−15	−10	−5	...	−8	...	−8	−6	−3	−8
8	15	−15	−10	−10	...	−6	−5	−9	−3	−3	−7
	16	−20	−10	−10	...	−6	...	−9	−3	−3	−8
9	17	−20	−20	−25	...	−5	−5	−7	−3	−3	−8
	18	−25	−15	−20	...	−9	...	−9	−3	−3	−7
10	19	−25	−20	−15	...	−10	−5	−10	−3	−3	−7
	20	−25	−20	−10	...	−11	...	−8	0	0	−7
11	21	−25	−25	−5	...	−11	−5	−7	0	0	−7
	22	−25	−20	−10	...	−12	...	−5	0	0	−7
12	23	−20	−15	−5	...	−10	−3	−8	0	0	−4
	24	−25	−15	−10	...	−10	...	−8	0	0	−5
13	25	−20	−20	−10	...	−13	−3	−8	0	0	−5
	26	−25	−15	−15	...	−14	...	...	0	0	−7
14	27	−25	−15	−10	...	...	−2	−8	0	0	−5
	28	−25	−20	−5	...	...	...	−8	0	0	−5

* OO = olive oil, CLO = cod-liver oil, RL = raw liver.
† Abandoned experiment after nausea.

of cod-liver oil once or twice a day, and two chewed and ate
almost half a cubic inch of raw liver daily. The ratings show that
with repeated ingestion the initial dislike was, on the whole,
abated during the course of the experiment. Two subjects reached
indifference (Ja and Ca). Three (Lo, Ke, and Fo) did not change

demonstrably in attitude. The ratings for the first fourteen days (or for the duration of the experiment) are presented in Table 22.

Seven persons gave up some pleasant habit, such as smoking, coffee, sugar in coffee, or desserts. Of these seven who found initial deprivation unpleasing, six disliked it less at the end of the experiment and one reported no change.

Nine persons found physical discomfort in walking, early rising, brushing teeth more frequently than was their habit, wearing special bits in their mouths, or carrying weights suspended at their necks. Of these nine, five tended to dislike the task less with repetition and four did not change their initial attitude.

The results from these volunteer subjects show that initial dislike tends to indifference with repeated performance. The experiments were not controlled, nor can there be assurance that the results are unbiased by desire to turn in a *good* report.

Experiments 72, 73, 74, and 75

Paid subjects were required to perform various tasks which seemed likely to be displeasing to many. Four such situations were presented to each of twenty-nine educated adults twice daily for seven days and once on one day. The tasks were handling a snake, drinking cod-liver oil, completing couplets before an audience, and standing on the toes of one foot before an audience.

The snake to be handled was a common garter-snake twenty inches long and one and a half inches in circumference. This snake was in a cage in the experimental room in which another, but much larger, garter was also housed. In a second cage was a four-and-a-half-foot black water-snake. The subjects came into the experimental room four or five at a time. Each subject was handed the smaller garter-snake by the experimenter and required to hold it for ten seconds.

The cod-liver oil was "Squibb's Cod-Liver Oil" which had been exposed to air to remove the protective action of the carbonic acid gas, so that, in addition to the oiliness, considerable fishiness in odor and taste was present. Each subject was given, at the beginning of the experiment, a set of measuring spoons varying from a quarter-teaspoon to a tablespoon. The unvarying dose was a quarter-teaspoonful. The subject was allowed to drink water after taking the dose.

The couplets to be completed were presented on cards to the

subject. Each person had to complete at each session each of four couplets in fifteen seconds before an audience.

Standing on the toes of one foot necessitated standing with no other support and with hands outstretched for thirty seconds.

These four situations are hereafter referred to as *snake, oil, poetry,* and *toes* respectively.

Twenty-nine educated adults participated in the experiments. Of this group, nineteen were older than forty years and ten were younger than twenty-five years. Each subject was offered each of the four situations twice daily—in the morning from 11:15 to 12:15 and in the afternoon from 3:45 to 5:00 on each experimental day from May 29 to June 7 with the exception that on June 7 the situations were offered but once, from 3 P.M. to 4 P.M.*

Before each session on the first day, the experimenter announced:

"You will be offered four different tasks which you are to do. You may, however, avoid doing any task or tasks by payment of thirty cents for each task you do not want to do."

From day 2 to the end of the experiment the same announcement was made except that the deduction was fifteen cents.

Immediately after each task was performed, the subject rated the task on the basis of the scale of pleasantness—unpleasantness shown below. Each rating was made on a separate card, so that the subject knew his previous ratings only by memory. The scale of the ratings, while crude, nevertheless allowed for genuine differentiation of attitude.

Rating Scale

You will be asked to perform certain tasks of different degrees of pleasantness. After you have performed each task you will be asked to rate its pleasantness for you on a scale from +100 to —100. Certain points on the scale have been described. The descriptions are suggestive. You may use intermediate ratings to represent your feelings clearly.

—100   so unbearable that you would prefer death to repetition
       or continuance
 —90
 —80
 —70
 —60

* No experiments were performed on Saturday or Sunday, June 3-4.

—50 as unpleasant as a violent headache or toothache, or listening to a bore

—40

—30

—20 —25: as unpleasant as a moderate burn, or a scornful comment about you

—10 as unpleasant as a glare in the eyes, or a slight frost-bite

±0 utterly indifferent, like putting on your shoes

+10 as pleasant as a cool wind on a sultry day

+20

+30 +25 as pleasant as sleeping when fatigued, or a casual approval about you

+40

+50 as pleasant as eating your favorite food, or enjoying your best friend, or drinking your favorite drink

+60

+70

+80

+90

+100 so pleasant that nothing could be more enjoyable

For each task, the median and the quartile points of the distribution of ratings for each session were computed. These values for *snake* are presented in Table 23 and Figure 5.

The group as a whole learn to dislike the unpleasant task less with repetition of the task. The upper quarter of the group as measured by the upper quartile go from slight dislike to slight liking. The median measure changed from considerable dislike to a positive value close to indifference. The lower quartile shows a marked change from a considerable feeling of unpleasantness at the beginning to only a slight dislike at the end of the experiment.

The scores of the six persons who considered the task least unpleasant at the beginning of the experiment changed but little toward the positive end of the scale. The scores of the seven who found the task most obnoxious at the beginning almost reach indifference at the end of the experiment. The facts appear in Table 24.*

* In Tables 23 and 24, and in all the computations, we have included Subject 22, who paid the fines day after day rather than touch the snake, recording her attitude as —100 throughout. This is on the assumption that if she *had* held the snake she would have reported —100 throughout. It is probable that, if she had held it, she would have lost some of her repugnance toward doing so, as did Subject 20, who would not touch it until the sixth session. So also Subject 20 would probably have reduced her dislike more than she did if she had begun the handling in session 1 instead of session 6. If Subject 22 would have,

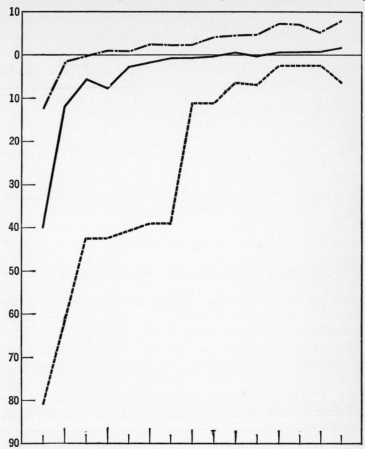

FIGURE 5.—The median (solid line), the upper quartile (dot-dash line) and the lower quartile (dash line) of the ratings on a scale of pleasantness—unpleasantness for the situation of handling snakes, by sessions.

The task of *snake*, however, is not one of mere repetition of an act. It is the repetition of a task plus after-effects of saving money, of self-satisfaction, of possible prestige influence with the experimenter and witnesses, and of personalizing the relations with the snake.*

as is conceivable, shifted from repugnance to indifference or actual liking faster than the lower quartile, our changes in Table 23 and Figure 5 are too small. But this is extremely unlikely.

* Many subjects gave the snake a name. Naming the snake made the task less abhorrent for those persons.

TABLE 23

The median, upper quartile, and lower quartile of the ratings on a scale of pleasantness-unpleasantness in the situation of handling a snake; twenty-nine subjects by day and session

Day	Session	Upper quartile	Median	Lower quartile
1	1	−11.8	−39.2	−89.2
	2	−1.7	−12.0	−61.9
2*	3	−0.3	−5.8	−42.5
	4	+0.8	−7.5	−42.5
3	5	+0.8	−2.5	−21.2
	6	+2.4	−1.7	−39.3
4	7	+2.1	−0.6	−39.3
	8	+2.2	−0.7	−11.2
5	9	+4.3	−0.2	−11.2
	10	+4.7	+0.2	−6.2
6	11	+4.7	0.0	−6.9
	12	+7.1	+0.6	−2.4
7	13	+7.1	+0.6	−2.4
	14	+5.3	+0.6	−2.4
8	15	+8.1	+1.6	−6.2

* Subject 25 was absent from all sessions on day 2.

No situation can be fully freed of such after-effects as self-assurance, prestige, or personalization. The nearest approach to such a pure situation is in the ingestion of cod-liver oil. The after-effect of saving money is always present in this experiment, but additional displeasing physical after-effects are present also. Nausea and physical disgust are concomitants of repeated taking of oil. The upper quartile and the median change but little during the course of the experiment. Both measures hover close to the zero of the scale, the indifference point. The lower quartile changes toward less dislike during the course of the experiment. The seven persons disliking *oil* least show little change during the course of the fifteen trials, but the seven disliking *oil* most changed their attitude significantly in favor of less dislike, tending toward indifference. Figure 6 shows the changes for the *oil* experiment. Tables 34 and 35 in Appendix VIII give further details.

The task of standing on the toes of one foot is rated in part for attitude, and in part for the skill that is learned. All measures show improvement toward the liking end of the scale. The seven who liked the task most at initial trial tended, in general, toward

TABLE 24

The scores of the six individuals who rated the task *snake* highest on initial presentation, and the scores of the seven individuals who rated the task *snake* lowest on initial presentation, by session and by individuals

INDIVIDUAL	DAY 1		DAY 2		DAY 3		DAY 4		DAY 5		DAY 6		DAY 7		DAY 8
	1	2	3	4	5	6	7	8	9	10	11	12	13	14	15
HIGHEST GROUP															
29	10	10	10	10	30	30	20	20	30	30	10	15	0	30	10
21	5	5	-10	5	-1	5	0	5	5	5	5	5	5	5	10
26	1	2	2	2	2	5	5	5	5	5	5	5	15	15	15
15	0	0	0	0	0	0	0	0	0	0	0	0	0	0	0
2	0	0	0	0	0	0	0	0	0	0	0	0	0	0	0
25*	0	0	.	.	0	0	0	0	0	0	0	0	0	0	0
LOWEST GROUP															
22†	-100	-100	-100	-100	-100	-100	-100	-100	-100	-100	-100	-100	-100	-100	-100
20‡	-100	-100	-100	-95	-95	-95	-90	-90	-90	-90	-90	-90	-75	-75	-50
12	-100	-100	-90	-70	-50	-50	-40	-40	-50	-50	-40	-30	-35	-40	-25
16	-100	-100	-75	-100	-50	-40	-50	-50	-25	-25	-25	-25	-25	-25	-10
8	-100	-25	0	0	0	0	0	0	0	0	0	0	0	0	0
24	-100	-40	-40	-40	-20	50	60	40	-10	50	0	10	30	0	30
14	-90	-80	-20	-20	-10	-40	-40	-10	-10	0	5	0	10	5	10

* Subject 25 was absent from all sessions on day 2.

† Subject 22 never handled the snake, paying sixty cents on day 1 to avoid the task, and fifteen cents for every session thereafter.

‡ Subject 20 did not handle the snake until session 6, paying thirty cents to avoid each of sessions 1 and 2, and fifteen cents each to avoid sessions 3, 4, and 5.

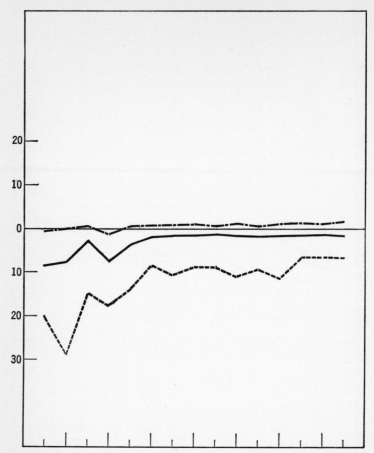

FIGURE 6.—The median (solid line), the upper quartile (dot-dash line), and the lower quartile (dash line) of ratings on a scale of pleasantness—unpleasantness for the situation of taking cod-liver oil: by sessions.

indifference, whereas the seven disliking it most tended to like it more and more as the experiment progressed. Figure 7 shows the changes. Tables 36 and 37 in Appendix VIII give further details.

The task of completing couplets before an audience shows little change. The changes that occurred tended toward indifference. The seven liking the task changed from enjoyment toward indifference; the seven disliking it most changed from mild dislike toward indifference. Figure 8 shows the changes. Tables 38 and 39 in Appendix VIII give further details.

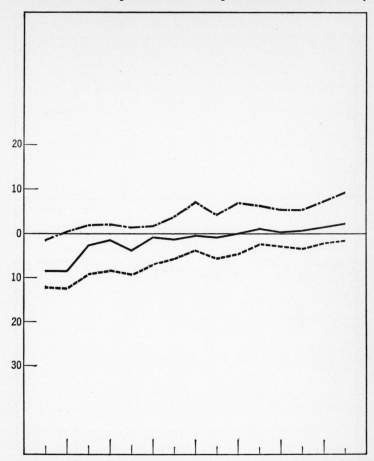

FIGURE 7.—The medium (solid line), the upper quartile (dot-dash line), and the lower quartile (dash line) of ratings on a scale of pleasantness—unpleasantness for the situation of standing on the toes of one foot: by sessions.

Our experiments provide evidence of progress from dislike to indifference (*snake* and *oil*), of progress from dislike through indifference to liking (*toes*), and of regression from liking toward indifference (*poetry*). They contain no clear case of regression from liking to dislike, but such could probably be found by suitable choices of persons and stimuli. They show that the phenomena of change in attitude or feeling which occur when a situation is repeated are certainly too complex to be explained by any one or two general laws. Common experience in general confirms this.

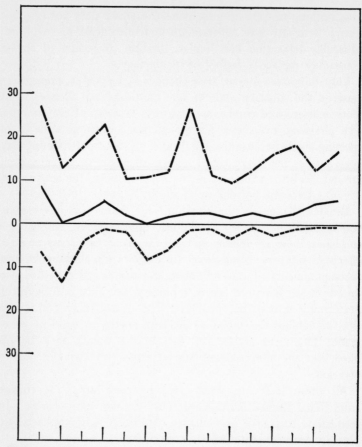

FIGURE 8.—The median (solid line), the upper quartile (dot-dash line), and the lower quartile (dash line) of ratings on a scale of pleasantness—unpleasantness for the situation of completing couplets before an audience: by sessions.

Our experiments show further that such changes may be and usually are influenced by factors other than the mere repetition of the same situation.

The situation may change. In standing on tiptoe with arms outstretched, the skill acquired may alter the act of balancing and reduce the strain.

If the same situation is repeated, intermediate responses to which the dislike is in whole or in part due may change. Dread due to a strong belief that something terrible will happen weakens if the belief weakens, and the belief weakens when time after time nothing terrible does happen. The snake does not bite, feel slimy, or in any way substantiate undefined fears or revulsions. Muscular relaxation may replace tension. A feeling of competence may replace a feeling of inadequacy.

Very important among such changes in responses intermediate between the situation and the like or dislike are changes in attentiveness to and emphasis on various features of the situation. The physician overcomes his repugnance at tasting urine or inspecting stools because the significance of the experience for diagnosis pushes the conventional aspects of nastiness into the background. So little a thing as giving a pet-name to the snake made it easier for some persons to handle it.

Besides changes in the situation and changes in intermediate responses, including responses of selection, rejection, and changed emphasis, there are influences from the accompaniments or after-effects of whatever connections are parts of the situation or close accompaniments of it. Very often the disliked situation is produced or accompanied by a voluntary act. The after-effect of performing it may be satisfying. The person may feel exultation at holding the snake, or making poetry as good as others made. The taste of decayed fish in the mouth may be disliked, but the alleviation of hunger from swallowing it may be pleasant.

All these facts also hold true, by and large, for changes from liking toward indifference. The situation may change.* Intermediate responses may change. Attention may emphasize unpleasant features. After-effects may be bad.

It is possible that such facts are adequate to account for the phenomena of changes in likes and dislikes which have been ascribed to general fundamental influences of repetition *per se*. It may be that the occurrence of a connection between a certain situation and dislike (or liking) tends in and of itself to strengthen the tendency for that situation to evoke precisely that dislike (or liking), not a less degree of it. This possibility is given added probability by the fact that our experiments and the common observations deal with dislikes of situations which many persons do like and which therefore probably have likable features. What

---

* Novelty and surprise which are features of the situation as experienced *must* weaken with repetition, but these are perhaps better considered as not residing in the situation, but in the person.

would happen in experiments with electric shocks, needle-pricks, crushing weights, sneers, and the like is uncertain.

Moreover, there is probably a large body of evidence available, if we should seek it, showing cases where the more the person did the disliked thing, the more he disliked it. There are children who have taken cod-liver oil a hundred times with no less distaste the hundredth time and who ceased to do so the moment parental pressure or the sense of duty relaxed. There are workers who have climbed out of bed at the sound of the alarm-clock thousands of times with no diminution of their dislike. There is similar evidence of failures of pleasant events to lose their pleasantness: of gourmands who love the oft-eaten turtle soup no less, of golfers who love the game the thousandth day better than ever, of lovers, hunters, fighters, misers, poets, gamblers, and unnumbered others in whom familiarity breeds no contempt. Still another sort of evidence should be considered—that from persons who will not tolerate extensive repetitions of the unpleasant situation because such repetitions as they have experienced have not diminished its virulence.

The whole matter needs much more study and experimentation than we have been able to devote to it. In the meantime the following working opinions seem reasonable: (1) A course of action or experience that is unpleasant but otherwise desirable may wisely be repeated in the hope that its unpleasantness will diminish; but this cannot be guaranteed as a universal tendency. Observations and experiments will gradually establish what can and what cannot be expected in various sorts of experiences, how many trials should be made with no effect before abandoning the attempt in any case, what aids to mere repetition are profitable, etc. (2) If a number of normal persons find the experience enjoyable or at least indifferent, this increases the probability that repetition may alleviate dislike. (3) Dislikes due to unnecessary or erroneous attachments to the experience or to parts of it are relatively easy to abolish. (4) Satisfying consequences of the experience may be used to counteract its unpleasantness. (5) It is healthier to search for specific causes of whatever decreases are found than to attribute them to a dubious general tendency to "negative adaptation," "affective habituation," or the like, though the existence of such a general tendency is not disproved.

There is another aspect of the possible influence of repetition upon emotional attitudes which should be mentioned, though almost nothing is known about it. This is the influence of repetition of an experience which at the start is neither liked nor disliked. There are certain facts suggesting that in certain cases repetition changes indifference into liking. Certain cherished habits, ranging widely from food preferences to religious rites, seem to be cherished only because they are habits.

It is the writer's opinion that forces other than mere repetition are responsible for these changes. In particular, (1) the satisfying accompaniments which established the habits in the beginning may have left traces of pleasantness attached to it; (2) doing the customary may be pleasant relatively as an avoidance of, or relief from, the strain of choosing a new course of action and carrying it out; (3) it is unpleasant to be thwarted or checked in any activity once entered upon; (4) the customary is likely to seem fit and proper, so that doing it produces a mild but dependable satisfaction; (5) the customary often has a sense of security associated with it. The whole matter should, however, be investigated.

The opposite doctrine, that repetition in and of itself changes indifference to dislike, is hardly credible save by certain intellectuals who themselves have an exceptional craving for mental activity and novelty, which they unscientifically impute to human minds at large. Under certain circumstances, repetition does, of course, cause dislike *via* boredom or irritation; and even the most torpid minds require occasional fillips of novelty and surprise. But the general rule is that to keep one's habits is, other things being equal, pleasanter than to change them.

Chapter 17

DIFFICULTIES IN THE EDUCATION OF WANTS, INTERESTS, AND ATTITUDES

WE have found that the same forces of repetition and reward, occurrence and confirming reaction, which cause the strengthening of connections leading to ideas and acts also cause the strengthening of connections leading to wants, interests, and attitudes. The essentials of training of the emotional and appetitive activities is then to induce the person to make the desired response and to reward it.

Such training is often difficult to carry out for the reason that the desired response (of affection, kindly feeling, courage, calmness, enjoyment, desire, and the like) is usually much less 'available' than ideas and acts are. It cannot so easily be summoned by the learner at will or aroused in him by stimulation from without. It is easy to put names or numbers or items of fact in connection with seeing a tiger, seeing a snake, seeing an insane man, and seeing a cubic equation, if these situations are at hand. But it is very hard to make a person feel courage as he faces the tiger, affection as he turns to the snake, shift to sympathy for the insane man, and then to excited curiosity at the cubic equation. We have no convenient means to evoke these responses or to dismiss them, nor has the person. The situations to which the educator wishes to connect courage, affection, sympathy, and so on as responses are also likely to have already other responses firmly connected with them, and these often are opposed to those desired by the educator. But this is only an accentuation of a difficulty which is often met in connecting ideas or acts with situations.

The practices used in education, government, and business to connect desirable emotional and appetitive responses with the situations of life usually rely on associative shifting or other indirect methods. To get R_d as a response to S_1, S_2 which does evoke R_d is used, then $S_1 + S_2$, and finally S_1 alone; or various activities are encouraged which make R_d or something like it likely to occur in response to something like S_1. Ideas that are helpful are provided. Procedures which discourage connections from S_1 to the opposite of R_d are employed. The training may be elaborate, intricate, and prolonged. A recital of the training by which an ingenious kindergartner replaces shyness by a moderate sociability, or by which an army officer tries to ensure that young men will enjoy sticking bayonets into the bellies of other young men, would require several pages. The psychology of it would, however, in the main be covered by the facts and principles of Chapters 12 to 16.

Some of the practices of religious and other cults rely on more direct means. In particular, certain wants, interests, or attitudes are linked to certain ideas, slogans, postures, ceremonies, or the like, which are available—summonable at will. Then the person is taught to summon the desired feeling by summoning the idea, slogan, or posture. Trustworthy information about the nature and operation of such clues by which a person may make himself courageous, calm, confident, ashamed, humble, remorseful, happy, and the like at will, is scanty, hard to find, and disturbed by supernatural explanations. But the religious life is real, and one of the most real things about it is the power certain persons have of being happy in pain, secure in danger, confident in failure, and the like.

The phenomenon is not restricted to religion. Many forms of mental healing seem to be serviceable by giving their patients access to the attitude of calm and security and thus secondarily bettering their health in divers respects. A famous business man is said to have been able to summon a fit of rage when he liked and to have done so as a routine means of impressing persons in business that their cut in price, delay in shipment, or what not was outrageous. The reader perhaps has some slogan or device which at least helps him to be calm, to be polite, to be attentive, or to go to sleep.

Where there is availability or summonableness of emotions, desires, and so on by way of clues of any sort, a sound practice requires that the desirable connections be not only put in action but also rewarded. The religious life provides this in the approval of God, witnessed by his representatives. In secular life the approval of the society which one esteems, witnessed by one's own conscience, will serve the same purpose.

The practices of religion, mysticism, mental healing, and other extra-scientific treatments of wants, interests, and attitudes probably contain much chaff along with the wheat. In particular the attainment of emotions by denial of reality or withdrawal from it may be a very bad bargain. The attainment of peace or calm by dismissing personal responsibility may be as vicious as obtaining it by alcohol or opium.

One promising method for evoking a want, interest, or attitude is to act as if one already possessed it. Let the nervous person take long, deep breaths and relax his muscles, let the coward advance upon his foe, let the shy one look every man in the eye. Make the child kneel before the altar, salute the flag, feed the stray dog, and take care of his baby sister. In so far as the state of feeling is, as supposed by the James-Lange theory, a product of the bodily states which 'express' it, the assumption of the appropriate bodily states will produce it. And even if that theory is wholly or partly false, the intimate association of the feeling and its bodily expression makes it probable that either will tend to evoke the other.

This method does not however promise so much in reality as it seems to promise in words. Many features of the emotional and appetitive life may have no distinguishable specialized bodily correlates outside of the neurones. Even if every want, interest, and attitude did have a peculiar bodily expression or correlate outside the neurones, many of these would be unknown. Of those which are known, many are not summonable by any known means. Of those bodily conditions which are summonable, some can be summoned only by rather elaborate techniques which may require special ability or training. As a result, we often do not know what to tell a person to do in order to feel so and so; and if we should tell him to perform certain acts—e.g., to secrete a little adrenalin or stop the spasm of his coronary artery—he could not do it.

This method does have the great merit that the acts are often beneficial, whether or not they evoke the desired feelings. If properly directed, they produce socially desirable behavior, in any case. They also usually tend to inhibit certain undesirable feelings.

Whether we employ associative shifting, the action of potent clues, or acting *as if* one had the want or interest or attitude, there is likely to be a certain incompleteness about the desires or emotions which are evoked. They are likely to be less rich, vivid, and thrilling, less corporeal, less absorbing, in a word, less emotional. A person may learn to hate false logic or misleading advertisements, but not quite as he hates his mother-in-law. He may learn to enjoy good painting, but not quite as he enjoys flowers. He may learn to be calm in conflict, but the calmness is not the rich enfolding calmness which he feels when the conflict is over, the victory won, and repose well earned.

These imperfections are not of great importance. The thrills of elation and the pangs of depression are really relatively unimportant features of the emotions in question. The exciting quality, common to both, is of very little importance. It seems to wane as we grow, to be less in healthy and capable minds than in sick and foolish ones. It has no known uses except perhaps to serve as a signal that some bodily action is needed and is being prepared for by the autonomic system. These signals are often very misleading in the circumstances of civilized life, and prudent persons largely disregard them. The violent thrills of hate for the mother-in-law, for example, must not be assuaged by beating her. It would certainly be folly to tear to pieces the book containing false logic.

The thrills and pangs include more than mere excitement and seem important features of life to many persons, who will object to any education of the feelings which reduces their rich vitality. However, any losses in subjective satisfaction that are involved in reducing the thrills are more or less balanced by the reduction in the pangs. The quarrels between the romanticist, the young, the enthusiasts, and other devotees of an intense emotional life and the classicists, the old, the temperate, and other devotees of restraint, balance, and "nothing too much" suggest that there is at least no great loss from calming the tempests of feeling.

Even when the learned attitude is almost bereft of genuine emotional content and nearly indistinguishable from a purely matter-of-fact habit, the learning may be of very great social value. If a mother loves her child enough to take the best of care of it and satisfy fully its cravings for affection, if a citizen loves his country enough to suffer rather than be a burden to it and to serve its interests well and gladly, if a scholar loves the truth enough to do all the work he can in its service, the love is adequate socially; whether it has a suitable quota of passionate feeling is largely irrelevant for social ends. If, in addition, the persons enjoy their feelings toward child, country, and truth and the useful behavior to which they lead, nobody should greatly lament their emotional poverty.

The establishment of a certain want, interest, or attitude as the response to a certain situation may be facilitated or resisted by original or acquired tendencies. Thus it is easier to strengthen the connection leading from being alone in a strange place in the dark to fear than that leading from it to laughter. It is easier to teach a smoker who wants a smoke after each meal to want one also just before going to bed, than to teach him to want to chew the cigarette after breakfast instead of smoking it, or to want to stand in a corner facing the wall after each meal instead of smoking. Especially important cases concern the attitudes which are so annoying or so satisfying that any after-effect which can be added will hardly suffice to make the total produce or prevent the confirming reaction.

In the formation of intellectual connections such difficulties are rare. By original nature men are indifferent to what words shall mean what things, what names shall mean what persons, when events shall have happened, and the like. And their acquired habits, having been established by repetition and reward are alterable thereby.

The disconnecting of certain wants, interests, and attitudes from *all* situations offers another set of difficulties. There may be a certain more or less permanent quality of an organism which demands that a certain want, say, for food or sex activity or sleep, must be felt. If the person is taught not to feel hungry at the sight of food, at the smell of food, or at the onset of contractions of the stomach, the want may still show itself somewhere, perhaps whenever he wakes up, or whenever he moves about, or irregularly. There may be some inner springs, say of hate, which must flow, so that if the person is taught to love his enemies, all men, and all animals, he will suffer from spells of hating the trees or stars or furniture.

The existence of such wants and desires that can only be directed, not repressed, is not absolutely proved. The amount of hunger or sex passion or hate or pride or affection or craving for excitement that is irrepressible is surely much less in most men than the amount that actually appears. The extreme doctrine that the amount is a constant which cannot be increased or lessened, but only turned from one channel to another, is fantastic. But the general fact remains that repression—that is, the prevention of attachment to any situations whatever—is often extremely difficult and perhaps impossible. Where it is possible, it may be highly inadvisable, since the repression may cost much more than it is worth and may indirectly damage mental and physical health. As between a person who feared nothing, hated nobody, and felt envy of no man living or dead and a person who feared earthquakes and public ignominy, hated sneaks and bullies, and envied heroes of the past, psychologists and psychiatrists would prefer the latter. Even he would be viewed with some alarm as a prig of too abnormal a character to be quite safe. It therefore seems desirable to provide useful, or at least harmless, outlets for many of the desires and emotions which human beings have as a heritage in the genes.

In spite of difficulties in making wants, interests, and attitudes available as controlled responses, in shifting them without losing their essential features, and in overcoming resistances met in trying to put them in desirable connections, the education of the feelings should be much more effective than it has been. Parents, teachers, social workers, and rulers have no difficulties that they did not have before, and they are better off to the extent that they need not waste time in dubious practices. We now know that the fundamental forces which can change desires and emotions, directing them into desirable channels, are the same as change ideas and actions. A human being learns to react to the situations of life by such and such wants, interests, and attitudes, as he learns to react to them by such and such percepts, ideas, and movements. In both cases, the task of education is to cause the desired connection to occur and to attach the confirming reaction to it.

Appendix I

THE INFLUENCE OF FAVORITISM FOR NUMBERS IN EXPERIMENT I

There is no adequate evidence of reversal from trial to trial for any person in experiment 1; and since this is also inherently improbable, it may be dismissed. The favoritisms in which we are interested are those within the 200 responses to each set of forty words. The count of occurrences of 1, 2, 3, 4, 5, and 6 in any such 200 will, however, exaggerate the amount of favoritism, because the influence of chance error due to the small size of the sample will combine with the influence of favoritism. The favoritism computed from two successive series will probably give nearer the true influence of favoritism in each.

The frequencies of choice of the numbers 1 to 6 by each subject in twelve lots, each of 400 consecutive choices, or in a representative sampling of the twelve lots, have been counted. The percentage of repetitions to be expected of any person in any two trials, apart from occurrences and after-effects, is reported in column I of Table 25.* The other columns of Table 25 report the difference between this and the actual percentages in the trial after one first occurrence (rewarded), one first occurrence (punished), two occurrences (consecutive, both rewarded), two occurrences (consecutive, both punished), two occurrences (non-consecutive, both rewarded), and two occurrences (non-consecutive, both punished).

* This percentage is the average of the percentages of the twelve lots of 400 each, or of so many of them as were counted. Its probable error is about 0.4 percent when all twelve lots were used and is never over 10.7 percent

TABLE 25

The strengthening due to one or two rewarded or punished occurrences
of a connection; in permilles

SUB-JECT	REPETITION DUE TO CHANCE AND NUMBER FAVORITISM	EXCESSES OVER EXPECTATION BY CHANCE AND NUMBER FAVORITISM					
		FIRST OCCURRENCES		CONSECUTIVE DOUBLES		NON-CONSECUTIVE DOUBLES	
		Rew.	Pun.	Rew.	Pun.	Rew.	Pun.
1	200	191	109	333	260	500	144
2	174	154	33	487	128	382	52
3	170	205	27	537	110	497	—18
4	189	236	—3	659	49	629	—35
5	185	113	10	501	145	215	101
6	196	386	7	667	10	518	4
7	210	229	30	640	166	457	102
8	199	286	31	634	122	690	21
9	175	298	64	742	106	671	86
10	185	210	71	582	199	690	300
11	174	288	20	604	118	634	226
12	208	293	35	617	156	581	154
13	180	438	39	749	161	820	153
14	180	278	25	755	211	534	—117
15	180	79	50	432	93	320	—19
16	174	192	45	688	127	281	122
17	177	445	4	781	105	723	240
18	182	150	42	610	188	524	118
19	205	105	14	499	—24	170	45
20	189	271	111	685	231	686	103
21	183	231	48	710	171	544	—40
22	190	416	52	519	134	710	310
23	220	97	33	495	144	380	169
24	180	345	8	724	140	820	120
Mdn	185	230	33	625	142	562	103
Av	188	248	38	610	135	541	98

Appendix II

LEARNING VALUED MATERIAL VERSUS LEARNING USELESS AND HARMFUL MATERIAL

Experiments 11 to 16 with celebrities and nonentities were of the same general sort as experiments 7 to 10. Their end results are presented in Table 26 so far as concerns those who reported that

TABLE 26

LEARNING THE BIRTH YEARS OF CELEBRITIES AND NONENTITIES

Experiments 11 to 16; subjects reporting equal effort (95% to 120%)

EXPERIMENT	n	RATIO CELEB/NONENT		DIFF. IN RATIOS
		Separate	Mixed	
11	5	1.9	1.9	0
12	5	1.6	1.6	0
13	21	1.8	2.6	0.8
14	8	...	3.3	...
15	9	1.6	3.2	1.6
16	5	0.9	1.8	0.9
Median, assuming that the ratio for 14 would be near 1.6		1.6	2.3	0.85

they used equal effort for the two sorts of material. The subjects in experiments 10, 11, 13, and 16 were educated adults. Those in 14 and 15 were male college students.

In experiments 11 and 12 the subjects were left to their own impulses as regards the amount of effort, nothing being said about the matter by the experimenter until the close of experiment 12, when the subject reported his relative effort from memory. In experiments 13, 14, 15, and 16 the subjects were pledged beforehand to try equally hard in the two cases. Even when pledged to try equally hard and reminded of the pledge from time to time in the course of the experiments, the subjects are in some cases unable to do so, if we may trust their reports.

The facts for the subjects who reported only 90 percent as much effort or less are presented in Table 27, which includes also

TABLE 27

LEARNING THE BIRTH YEARS OF CELEBRITIES AND NONENTITIES

Experiments 11 to 16; all subjects

EXPERIMENT		CELEBRITIES	NONENTITIES	NUMBER OF REPETITIONS	REPORTED PERCENT WHICH EFFORT WITH NONENTITIES WAS OF EFFORT WITH CELEBRITIES	NUMBER OF SUBJECTS	RATIO CELEB/NONENT For separate	RATIO CELEB/NONENT For mixed
11	Separate	40	40	2	95-120	5	1.9	1.9
	Mixed	40	40	2	90 or less	18	2.2	1.9
12	Separate	40	40	6	95-120	5	1.6	1.6
	Mixed	40	40	6	90 or less	14	1.5	2.1
13	Separate	40	40	4	95-120	21	1.8	2.6
	Mixed	40	40	4	90 or less	2	2.5	2.3
14	Separate	40	40	3	95-120	8	...	3.3
	Mixed	..	..	..	80-90	9	...	3.8
					75 or less	10	...	3.1
15	Separate	20	20	3	95-120	9	1.6	3.2
	Mixed	..	..	..	80-90	11	2.3	3.4
					75 or less	7	1.7	2.4
16	Separate	20	20	3	95-120	5	0.9	1.8
	Mixed	..	..	..	80-90	7	1.2	2.6
					75 or less	7	1.9	4.9

the facts of Table 26 for comparison.* The Celeb/Nonent ratios are higher than for those reporting equal effort, but not much higher (about 1.8 instead of 1.6 for the separate sets and about 2.6 instead of 2.3 for the mixed sets). It may be that the memory of having tried less hard is illusory, due to the awareness of having remembered only about a third as many. For our general problem we need not decide. Those who do try equally hard cannot learn the valueless and uninteresting facts as well as the valuable and interesting ones. The others cannot try as hard to learn them even though they promise to do so.

The advantage for celebrities over nonentities was nearly one and a half times as great when the two sorts of connections were mixed in series of twenty as when all twenty were of the same sort. The median Celeb/Nonent ratio was 3.0 ± 0.1 for the mixed arrangement and 2.0 ± 0.1 for the separated arrangement in experiments 7, 8, 9, and 10. In experiments 26 to 29, it was 3.6 ± 0.3 for the mixed arrangement and 2.5 ± 0.3 for the separated arrangement. In experiments 11 to 16, it was 2.3 for the mixed and 1.6 for the separated. The ratio of the ratios is thus 1.50, 1.44, and 1.47 in the three sets of data.

Experiment 17

Two lists each of sixty names of famous persons with the year of birth of each were prepared, one limited to those born 1700 to 1799, the other to those born 1800 to 1899. Two other lists were prepared comparable in all respects save that the names were of persons of no importance and that the dates were chosen so as to be different from but equal in difficulty to the dates for the famous.

Twenty-four educated adults spent fifty minutes in the study of each list, all on one afternoon, the order being Famous I, Nonentities I, Nonentities II, Famous II. They were instructed as follows (1) before the list of famous names:

"I shall give each of you a list of names of famous writers, painters, musicians, statesmen, scientists or philosophers with the year of birth of each. You will have fifty minutes to learn the year in which each was born. In the test at the end of fifty

---

* In Table 26 no correction is made for previous knowledge of the dates for celebrities. The correction is inconsiderable. In tests without training these subjects of experiments 11 to 15 had only twenty-four right out of 6,060, or about four per thousand.

minutes, the names will be presented in a changed order. When I say 'Go,' turn the sheet over and learn the birth-dates for as many as you can until I say 'Stop.' When I say 'Stop,' turn the sheet face down again. The letters M, P, S, Sp and W mean 'Musician,' 'Painter,' 'Statesman,' 'Scientist,' or 'Philosopher,' and 'Writer.' But pay no attention to them. You will be neither told nor asked anything about them."

(2) before the list of nonentities:

"I shall give each of you a list of cobblers, farmers, tailors and other persons of no importance with the year of birth of each. You will have fifty minutes to learn the year in which each was born. In the test at the end of fifty minutes, the names will be presented in a changed order. When I say 'Go,' turn the sheet over and learn the birth-dates for as many as you can until I say 'Stop.' When I say 'Stop,' turn the sheet face down again."

As soon as the fifty minutes was completed, the study sheet was replaced by a test sheet containing the names in a changed order, and each subject wrote a date for each name. The subjects were working for money and understood that they would be paid according to the number of dates that they learned. The results appear in Table 28.

The average number correct was 31.3 for F I, 27.8 for N I, 31.0 for N II, and 40.3 for F II, averaging 35.8 for the famous and 29.4 for the nonentities. The Celeb/Nonent ratio is then 1.22. Three persons had all sixty correct in F II, so that the 1.22 is a bit below the probable true value. Seventeen of the twenty-four subjects learned more dates for the famous, five learned fewer, and two learned the same number. The median Celeb/Nonent ratio was 1.20 (between 90 C and 76 N and 101 C and 83 N).

From other experiments with comparable subjects we know that the number of birth years of the famous known in advance of the experiment would be about four per thousand. Out of 6,060 responses in tests of knowledge of the dates for celebrities in subjects having no training, only twenty-four were correct. So we may correct the 1.22 and 1.20 to 1.215 and 1.195. We may then set the Celeb/Nonent ratio in the experiment as 1.2. Its probable error is about 0.06.

In the previous experiment the ratios were 1.6 (experiments 11 to 16) and 2.0 (experiments 7 to 10). It decreased from 2.3

to 1.6 and from 3.0 to 2.0 with the change from series of celebrities and nonentities mixed to series all of one sort or the other.

The disadvantage of the uninteresting and valueless in these experiments cannot be due to a general and cumulative action of the mind. If such were its cause, the inferiority of learning about nonentities should be less in separate than in mixed series and the inferiority should be as great or greater in long series with fifty minutes of study than in short series heard for about a tenth that time and then tested and dismissed. It can hardly be due to any one inevitable cause, since the Celeb/Nonent ratio differs so greatly for 'mixed' and for 'separate.' The experiments reported in the next section will help to explain its real causation.

TABLE 28

Number of birth-dates learned in fifty minutes (test immediately thereafter); experiment 17; twenty-four adult students

Subject	1 Famous I	2 Nonentities I	3 Nonentities II	4 Famous II
1	40	31	45	50
2	18	18	23	40
3	46	35	48	55
4	28	8	15	30
5	30	17	12	33
6	32	14	21	24
7	19	10	6	23
8	31	25	20	38
9	59	47	58	60
10	16	38	53	60
11	41	32	39	49
12	34	27	14	28
13	57	54	54	58
14	49	51	58	57
15	38	23	41	60
16	7	15	14	22
17	10	28	19	34
18	16	18	18	14
19	43	34	44	51
20	36	46	44	49
21	19	24	28	39
22	10	18	13	21
23	37	30	30	27
24	34	25	22	46
Av	31.3	27.8	31.0	40.3

Experiments with Right and Wrong Dates and Meanings

Experiments 22 to 25 were like experiments 18 to 21 in all respects. Thirty-two educated adults learned 989 of the correct dates and 961 of the wrong dates, 753 of the correct meanings and 447 of the wrong meanings. Correcting as above, we have 978 and 961 for useful and harmful dates, and 705 and 447 for useful and harmful meanings. The superiority for the useful meanings is found in twenty-eight of the thirty-two persons. In this second experiment the useful/harmful ratio is thus 1.02 for dates and 1.58 for meanings. Combining the two groups, we have 1.03 for dates and 1.58 for meanings.

In the case of thirty-one of the subjects of experiments 22 to 25, we have answers to the following questions:

Name ....
1. Did you try equally hard to learn the right dates and the wrong dates? ....
2. If not, how did your effort rate in the two cases? Calling the amount of effort for the right dates 10, was the amount of effort for the wrong dates about 9 or about 11 or about 8 or about 12 or about 7 or about 13? ....
3. Did you try equally hard to learn the right meanings for the words and the wrong meanings? ....
4. If not, how did your effort rate in the two cases? Calling the amount of effort for the right meanings 10, was the amount of effort for the wrong meanings about 9 or about 11 or about 8 or about 12 or about 7 or about 13? ....

Twenty-one answered "Yes" to question 1; one reported that he tried 20 percent harder; two reported percentages of 90; four reported percentages of 80; and three reported percentages of 70. Nineteen answered "Yes" to question 3; one reported that he tried 10 percent harder; four reported percentages of 90, two reported percentages of 80, four reported percentages of 75 or 70, and one reported a percentage of 40.

The useful/harmful ratio for the dates was 1.03 for the twenty-two reporting equal or greater attention to the wrong, and 0.99 for the ten reporting less. The useful/harmful ratio for the meanings was 1.73 for the twenty reporting equal or greater attention to the wrong, and 1.32 for the eleven reporting less.

Experiments 30 to 33 were like experiments 18 to 21 except that (1) only forty were studied instead of eighty, (2) the learning of the wrong dates and wrong meanings preceded the learning of the right dates and meanings, and (3) the same famous persons and words were not used with wrong and also with right meanings. Thirty educated adults or adolescents over seventeen (the same as participated in experiments 26 to 29) were the subjects. Bonuses were to be given according to the amounts learned. One subject who reported greater effort to learn the right dates and meanings was excluded. Some of the others reported differences, but these were equally divided between greater effort on the right and greater effort on the wrong.

The twenty-nine subjects learned 429 of the correct dates and 369 of the wrong dates. Correcting as in experiment 18, we have 424 and 365. The useful/harmful ratio is thus 1.15.

In the case of both the right and wrong meanings, especially the latter, the learning of this group was much inferior to that of the two groups in the earlier experiment. There were many scores of 0 right out of 20. Leaving out of the computations the records of eight individuals who reported less effort on the wrong meanings, we have 228 and 75 as the number of words given.* Correcting as in the earlier experiments, we have 211 and 75, giving a useful/harmful ratio of 2.81.

These same thirty subjects were also given (in experiment 34) two mixed lists each consisting of ten words with right meanings and ten words with wrong. Using the twenty-two persons who tried equally hard, we have 92 and 51. The correct responses were 100 and 53. Correcting as above, the useful/harmful ratio is 1.74.

The results for all groups agree in showing that connections of wrong dates with the names of famous persons are strengthened nearly as much as connections having right dates. The average of the useful/harmful ratios (1.04, 1.02, and 1.15) is 1.07 and has high reliability. The results for right and wrong meanings of words agree in showing a substantial superiority for the right meanings but disagree as to its amount. The ratios (1.57, 1.58, and 2.81) are not suitable for averaging, since the third is computed from records showing much less learning for both right and wrong meanings. But the useful/harmful ratio may be taken as 1.58 or higher.

---

* It would have made no appreciable difference if the records of these eight individuals had been left in. The useful/harmful ratio for them was 2.90, about the same as for the others.

In connection with experiments 26 to 34, a comprehensive test of the right dates of celebrities and the dates of nonentities, 160 in all, was given, the order of the names being random, seventy-two hours after the learning of the forty celebrities and forty nonentities in separate lists of twenty each, and forty-eight hours after the learning of four mixed lists. After allowance for the probable number of dates known before the experiment, the number correct was four times as great for celebrities as for nonentities when in separate lists (48 and 12) and three times as great when in mixed lists (51 and 18).

A comprehensive test of the right meanings of forty words and the wrong meanings of forty different words was given seven days after the wrong were first learned and five days after the right were first learned. This comprehensive test included also the right meanings of twenty words and the wrong meanings of twenty different words learned six days before. All the 120 words were mixed in a new order. After allowance for the probable number of words known before the experiment, the number correct was many times as great for the right meanings as for wrong (54 and 3 out of 880 when in separate lists, and 22 and 2 out of 440 when in mixed lists).

If the Celeb/Nonent and useful/harmful ratios are compared with those obtained in the tests made immediately after the learning, the useless and false seem to have suffered more from the lapse of time, and from the competing and interfering activities with which it was filled, than the useful and true. But the ratios obtained in the memory tests after several days are not strictly comparable with the others or among themselves. Indeed, the whole matter of comparing losses (or gains) is beset with dangers. Also the exactness of our allowances for pre-learning knowledge, which is of little consequence when it runs from 1 to 8 percent of the score corrected, becomes of considerable consequence when it rises to 25 or 30 percent of it.

All the relevant facts are presented in Table 29, including the scores uncorrected for knowledge possessed before the learning, the scores as corrected by the results from control groups who took the tests without the training, and the scores as corrected by double the amounts indicated as correct by our controls.

In all these tests the subject was instructed not to write any number or meaning unless he had some slight belief that it was the number or word belonging with the name or word. Since the chance of getting a correct date by chance is only one in a hundred (except when all the dates in a set of twenty were observed to be within a certain part of a century), since the chance of getting a correct word by chance is infinitesimal, and since the subjects in general had not over three wrongs per right, no correction for chance is required. If any were made, it would raise the ratios. So omitting it is a factor of safety in our conclusion that time weakens the useless and harmful connections more than the useful and true.

If the amounts remembered in the immediate test are the same for useful and for harmful, the actual observed further losses in the test after several days will measure the influence with which we are concerned. In right versus wrong dates, this condition is approximately met. Using our correction for pre-knowledge, we have the following records of learning:

Ex.   Right dates, 890 out of 2230 possible, falling 800 to   90
      Wrong dates, 859 out of 2240 possible, falling 835 to   24
Ex.   Right dates, 978 out of 2549 possible, falling 837 to 141
      Wrong dates, 961 out of 2560 possible, falling 901 to 60

Using double our correction for pre-knowledge, we have the same amounts of falling, resulting in 80 learned out of a possible 2,220 (as against 24 out of 2,240), and 131 learned out of a possible 2,538 (as against 60 out of a possible 2,560).

If the amounts remembered in the immediate tests are not the same for useful and harmful, etc., the best available procedure is to consider that each connection may vary from 0 strength to such a strength that it would surely be remembered for far longer than five days; to assume that among, say, the 2,230 or 2,220 initially unknown connections the variations in this after four hearings will be distributed in a continuous surface of frequency; to discover what the form of this is for the useful and for the harmful; and to compare these when superimposed so that the points on the scale dividing success from failure in each coincide.

I have done this for a combination of the results in experiments 20, 21, 24, 25, 30 and 33 with right and wrong meanings of words first learned in separate sets of twenty. The original data corrected for pre-knowledge by our controls and summed are, for right meanings (R) and wrong meanings (W) respectively:

TABLE 29

Data for comparing the superiority of useful to useless or harmful learning at the immediate close of the learning with the same superiority several days later

Experiment	Nature of material	1 Possible score	2 Actual score immediately after the learning	3 Actual score on retest one to five days later
26	Celeb separate:			
	Uncorrected	880	409	52
	Corrected	875	405	48
	Double correction	870	401	44
27	Nonent separate	880	197	12
28	Celeb mixed:			
	Uncorrected	880	476	55
	Corrected	876	472	51
	Double correction	872	468	47
28	Nonent mixed	880	185	18
18	Right dates:			
	Uncorrected	2240	900	100
	Corrected	2230	890	90
	Double correction	2220	880	80
19	Wrong dates	2240	859	24
22	Right dates:			
	Uncorrected	2560	989	153*
	Corrected	2549	978	142*
	Double correction	2538	967	131*
23	Wrong dates	2560	961	60*
20	Right meanings:			
	Uncorrected	2240	761	180
	Corrected	2200	721	140
	Double correction	2160	681	100
21	Wrong meanings	2240	459	20
24	Right meanings:			
	Uncorrected	2480	753	301*
	Corrected	2433	705	253*
	Double correction	2386	657	205*
25	Wrong meanings	2480	417	44*
30	Right meanings:			
	Uncorrected	880	228	71
	Corrected	863	211	54
	Double correction	846	194	37
33	Wrong meanings	880	75	3
34	Right meanings mixed:			
	Uncorrected	440	100	30
	Corrected	432	92	22
	Double correction	424	84	14
34	Wrong meanings mixed	440	53	2

* Only thirty-one of the thirty-two subjects were available for the retest. We have added 1/31 of the total for them to give an estimated total for thirty-two, comparable to the score following the learning.

(R) Possible, 5496; immediate, 1637; after 1 to 7 days, 447
(W) Possible, 5600; immediate, 951; after 1 to 7 days, 66

In percentages, these numbers become:

(R) Possible, 100.0; immediate, 29.8; after 1 to 7 days, 8.1 (8.14)
(W) Possible, 100.0; immediate, 17.0; after 1 to 7 days, 1.2 (1.18)

I assume that both surfaces are normal and of equal variability. Then the average strength of the R's is 0.425 S.D. above that of the W's at the time of the immediate tests, and 0.86 S.D. above it at the time of the test some days later. It should be noted that in one of the three experiments the R's had the advantage of being tested after five days, whereas the W's were tested after seven days. But this probably made little difference.

If the doubled correction is used, we have:

(R) Possible, 5,392; immediate, 1,532; after 1 to 7 days, 342
(W) Possible, 5,600; immediate, 951; after 1 to 7 days, 66

In percentages these numbers become:

(R) Possible, 100.0; immediate, 28.4; after 1 to 7 days, 6.3 (6.34)
(W) Possible, 100.0; immediate, 17.0; after 1 to 7 days, 1.2 (1.18)

Then the average strength of the R's is 0.385 S.D. above that of the W's at the time of the immediate test, and 0.73 S.D. above it at the time of the later test.

If this method is used for the material of each sort separately, the results are as shown in Table 30. A weighted average (using weights of 2 when $n = 440$, 3 when $n = 880$, and 5 when $n = 2,240$, 2,480, or 2,560) of the measures which show the greater superiority of the useful and true connections in the late test as compared with their superiority in the immediate test gives 0.32 S.D. for the corrected results and 0.22 S.D. for the results with double correction. The results for the right and wrong dates and meanings are in close agreement and give a weighted average of 0.45 S.D. (0.37 S.D. with double correction). The results for the celebrities and nonentities vary rather widely and average —0.25 (—0.39 with double correction). They are thus in marked opposition to the general trend.

TABLE 30

The influence of time upon useful versus useless or harmful connections

EXPERI- MENT	NATURE OF MATERIAL	SUPERIORITY IN LEARNING USEFUL AND CORRECT MATERIAL				DIFFERENCE BETWEEN SUPERIORITY IN IMMEDIATE TEST AND SUPERIORITY AFTER SEVERAL DAYS	
		In immediate test		*In memory after several days*			
		Cor- rected	Double correc- tion	Cor- rected	Double correc- tion	Cor- rected	Double correc- tion
26, 27	Celeb vs. Nonent	0.67	0.66	0.62	0.57	—0.05	—0.09
28	Celeb vs. Nonent	0.91	0.90	0.47	0.21	—0.44	—0.69
18, 19	Right vs. wrong dates	0.04	0.03	0.57	0.50	0.53	0.47
22, 23	Right vs. wrong dates	0.02	0.02	0.40	0.36	0.38	0.34
20, 21	Right vs. wrong meanings	0.36	0.34	0.84	0.69	0.48	0.35
24, 25	Right vs. wrong meanings	0.41	0.37	0.84	0.73	0.43	0.36
30, 33	Right vs. wrong meanings	0.68	0.63	1.02	0.84	0.34	0.21
34	Right vs. wrong meanings	0.38	0.32	0.97	0.77	0.59	0.45

On the whole we have evidence that, in ways as yet unknown, a learner can learn material that he cherishes and material that he regards as worthless so as to remember the former longer than the latter, even though at the immediate close of the learning the two are equally well remembered.

Appendix III

TESTS OF THE RESULTS OF READING 100,000 WORDS FROM THE BIBLE (EXODUS, JOSHUA, JUDGES, NEHEMIAH, AND DANIEL)

Matching Test on Joshua

In the space before each number on the left of the page write the number of the matching item in the column on the right side of the page. The same number may be used more than once.

.... 1. The minister of Moses	1. Achan
.... 2. The harlot of Jericho	2. Beth-horon
.... 3. A king of the Amorites	3. Ed
.... 4. The man who appropriated "the devoted thing"	4. Gibeon
.... 5. The home of the people who became "hewers of wood and drawers of water"	5. Gilgal
.... 6. A king who leagued with Adonizedek against Gibeon	6. Hebron
.... 7. The original book which relates the story of the slaughter of the Amorites	7. Jashar
.... 8. The Canaanite name for Jerusalem	8. Jebus
.... 9. The place where lots were cast for locating the last seven tribes	9. Jericho
....10. The first city of refuge	10. Joshua
....11. A city allotted to the children of Aaron	11. Kedesh
....12. The place of the encampment near Jericho	12. Makkedah
....13. The battle preceding which the rite of circumcision was practised	13. Merom
....14. The head of the delegation sent to investigate the building of the altar at the Jordan	14. Og
....15. The name of the altar built by the Reubenites and Gadites	15. Phinehas
....16. The battle in which a hailstorm aided the Israelites	16. Piram
....17. The burial place of the bones of Joseph	17. Rahab

232

....18. The cave wherein the five fleeing
       kings hid   18. Shechem
....19. The burial place of Joshua   19. Shiloh
....20. The waters near where the coalition
       of kings encamped to fight Israel   20. Timnath-serah

II

Relationship Test

Select names from the list on the right side of the page to make each statement true. The same name may be used more than once if desired. To save time the number of the name should be written, instead of the name itself.

1. Joshua was the son of................	1. Abinoam
2. Achan "	2. Ahisamach
3. Caleb "	3. Amram
4. Phinehas "	4. Anath
5. Shamgar "	5. Carmi
6. Ehud was the son of................	6. Colhozeh
7. Barak "	7. Ebed
8. Gideon "	8. Eleazar
9. Abimelech "	9. Eliashib
10. Gael "	10. Gera
11. Tola was the son of................	11. Gilead
12. Jephthah "	12. Hacaliah
13. Abdon "	13. Hillel
14. Nehemiah "	14. Hur
15. Zaccur "	15. Immer
16. Rephaiah was the son of................	16. Imri
17. Zerubbabel "	17. Jephunneh
18. Joiada "	18. Jerubbaal
19. Gershom "	19. Joash
20. Aaron "	20. Maaseiah
21. Bezalel was the son of................	21. Nun
22. Oholiab "	22. Moses
23. Meremoch "	23. Puah
24. Zadok "	24. Shealtiel
25. Shallun "	25. Uri
26. Azariah was the son of................	26. Urijah

III

Quotations Test

The following quotations are taken from the books you have read. On the dotted line write the number of the book as chosen from the list at the end of the test. The same number may be used more than once if desired.

1. Then the king went to his palace, and passed the night fasting; neither were instruments of music brought before him: and his sleep went from him. Then the king arose very early in the morning.
   ....

2. And it came to pass when the priests that bare the ark of the covenant of Jehovah were come up out of the midst of the Jordan, and the soles of the priests' feet were lifted up unto the dry ground, that the waters of the Jordan returned unto their place, and went all over its banks, as aforetime.
   ....

3. From heaven fought the stars,
   From their courses they fought against Sisera,
   The river Kishon swept them away,
   That ancient river, the river Kishon.
   ....

4. And Bezalel made the ark of acacia wood: two cubits and a half was the length of it and a cubit and a half the breadth of it, and a cubit and a half the height of it.
   ....

5. In those days also I saw the Jews that had married women of Ashdod, of Ammon, and of Moab: and their children spake half in the speech of Ashdod, and could not speak in the Jews' language, but according to the language of each people.
   ....

6. And I sent messengers unto them saying, I am doing a great work, so that I cannot come down: why should the work cease, whilst I leave it and come down to you?
   ....

7. And she said unto her father, Let this thing be done for me: let me alone two months, that I may go up and down upon the mountains and bewail my virginity, I and my fellows.
   ....

8. I thank thee, and praise thee, O thou God of my fathers, who hast given me wisdom and might, and hast made known unto me now what we desired of thee.
   ....

9. And he said unto them,
   Out of the eater came forth food,
   And out of the strong came forth sweetness,
   And they could not in three days declare the riddle.
   ....

10. The Tirshatha gave to the treasure a thousand drams of gold, fifty basins, five hundred and thirty priests' garments, and some of the chief of the fathers gave to the treasure of the work twenty thousand drams of gold.
    ....

11. And the bones of Joseph, which the children of Israel brought up out of Egypt, buried they in Shechem, in a parcel of ground which Jacob bought of the sons of Hamor, the father of Shechem, for a hundred pieces of silver; and it became the inheritance of the children of Joseph.

....

12. If thou buy a Hebrew servant, six years shall he serve; and in the seventh he shall go free for nothing. If he come in by himself, he shall go out by himself: if he be married, then his wife shall go out with him.

....

1. Daniel	4. Ezra	7. Judges	10. Nehemiah
2. Deuteronony	5. Genesis	8. Kings	11. Ruth
3. Exodus	6. Joshua	9. Leviticus	12. Samuel

IV

Information Test

Make a plus (+) sign before each of these statements that you think is true; and zero (o) before each of them that you think is false.

1. Moses was the father-in-law of Jethro.
2. The land assigned by Jehovah to Israel was to extend from the Mediterranean Sea to the Euphrates River.
3. The Judahites when they captured Adoni-bezek cut off his thumbs and great toes.
4. Daniel was the son of Ashpenaz.
5. Moses was sixty years old and Aaron sixty-three when they besought Pharaoh to free the Israelites.
6. The spies sent out by Joshua to reconnoiter Jericho lodged in the house of Achar, the harlot.
7. The ancient city of Luz was renamed Beth-el when it was captured by the Israelites.
8. Pharaoh pursued after the Israelites with several hundred chariots and overtook them at Pihahiroth.
9. Nehemiah learned from his brother Hamari of the sad plight of the Jewish remnant left in Palestine after the captivity.
10. In the early days of Nehemiah's work in Jerusalem Rephaiah of the family of Hur was ruler over a third part of the city.
11. When Moses stretched forth his hand over the waters of Egypt, frogs came up from the water and spread over the land.

12. The method of identifying the house of the family to be succored when Jericho was captured was to tie a scarlet thread in the window.
13. Caleb promised his daughter in marriage to the captor of Kirjath-arba.
14. Nehemiah was the cup-bearer of King Cyrus.
15. Three princes of the Midianites were captured in the battle which Gideon fought with 300 selected men.
16. Reuel was the father of Zipporah.
17. Moses' rod was turned into a serpent in his hand as a sign that the Almighty commissioned him to deliver the oppressed Israelites.
18. The passage by the Israelites under Joshua over the Jordan ford was made near Jericho.
19. Joshua was 110 years old at the time of his death.
20. Sisera was the king of Canaan who mightily oppressed the Israelites in the time of the prophetess Deborah.

21. Sanballat the Horonite abetted Gershem the Arabian against the remnant of the Israelites who had been carried into captivity.
22. Shadrach was the Babylonian name of Daniel.
23. Moses was not a circumcised Israelite.
24. The first Passover after the crossing of the Jordan was celebrated on the plains of Jericho.
25. The first of the judges mentioned by name was Othniel, a nephew of Caleb.

26. In rebuilding the wall of Jerusalem under Nehemiah, the priests worked at the valley gate.
27. Daniel, Shadrach, Meshach, and Abednego were thrown into an exceedingly hot fiery furnace for refusing to worship a golden image set up by the king.
28. The ark of bulrushes wherein Moses was hidden in the flags at the river's edge was daubed with terebinth.
29. The manna upon which the Israelites fed in the wilderness continued to be supplied to them until the first Passover after the crossing of the Jordan.
30. Ehud was slain by Eglon because he oppressed the Israelites.

31. Nehemiah refused to accept the perquisites of his office during the twelve years of his governorship of Judah.
32. Daniel was recommended by the queen to Belshazzar as the most skilled of all dream interpreters in the kingdom.
33. Gideon was enheartened to expect victory against the Midianites by the test of the fleece being wet when the ground was dry and vice versa.
34. In encompassing the walls of Jericho the armed men followed the priests bearing the ark.

35. Moses had the ark of the covenant made of satinwood overlaid with gold.
36. The four Hebrews who would not eat the king's meat were Daniel, Hananiah, Mishael, Azariah.
37. Belshazzar was so highly incensed at Daniel's interpretation of the handwriting on the wall that he put him in prison.
38. Moses met his future wife when she and her sisters came to water their father's sheep at a well in Midian.
39. Jehovah commanded Joshua to proclaim a curse upon the gold and silver and brass and iron taken at the capture of Jericho.
40. Nehemiah was commissioned by Darius to rebuild the walls of Jerusalem.
41. Six gates in the wall of Jerusalem are listed by name as being mended by the Jews working under Nehemiah.
42. When Darius the Persian captured Babylon, he organized the kingdom into 120 princedoms with three presidents, of whom the chief was Belteshazzar.
43. Six times Sanballat sent messages to Nehemiah asking for a meeting outside the city, but each time he refused to go.
44. Ibzan of Bethlehem was a judge of Israel succeeding Jephthah.
45. Gideon built an altar to commemorate the place where the angel of the Lord performed a miracle for him.
46. In the night time Gideon destroyed the altar of Baal located on his father's land and sacrificed a bullock to Jehovah instead.
47. In the rebuilding of the walls of Jerusalem the nobles of Tekoa were especially active.
48. Cyrus cast Daniel into the den of lions because of his disobedience to a decree of the king.
49. The inhabitants of Ai, to avoid the destruction which had come upon Jericho, tricked Joshua into making a league with them.
50. King Nebuchadnezzar commanded Arioch to put to death all the wise men of Babylon because of their failure to tell and interpret his dream.
51. When Daniel was cast into the den of lions the mouth of the den was stopped with a stone which was sealed both by the king's signet and by that of the lords who were Daniel's enemies.
52. In Daniel's dream during the first year of Belshazzar's reign the curious beast with ten horns burned the other three beasts with flames.
53. The preparations of Nehemiah for a valiant defense of Jerusalem sufficed to keep Sanballat from attacking it.

54. The feast of the Passover was instituted to celebrate the crossing of the Red Sea dry-shod.

55. When the plague of blood was sent upon the Egyptians, not only the rivers but all the water in the pools and vessels turned to blood.

56. Gideon captured Zebah and Zalmunna and put them to death because they had slain his brethren at Tabor.

57. Daniel's good favor with the ruler lasted from the time of his interpretation of Nebuchadnezzar's dream on through the reigns also of Belshazzar, Darius, and Cyrus.

58. The teraphim made for Aaron's wear at the order of Moses according to Jehovah's command was of blue, gold, purple, and scarlet fine thread linen intertwined with fine gold wire.

59. Succoth and Karkor were laid waste by Gideon because they refused him food when he was pursuing the fleeing Midianites.

60. The number of Israelites coming from Goshen into the wilderness in the exodus from Egypt was about 600,000 men, plus the children.

61. In Daniel's vision by the river Ulai, the he-goat was a symbol of Greece.

62. Daniel was told by the angel Gabriel that from the time of the command to rebuild Jerusalem unto the coming of Messiah should be seven and three score and two weeks.

63. The Israelites did not succeed utterly in exterminating the inhabitants of Dor.

64. Gideon was the father of at least seventy sons, the eldest of whom was Jotham.

65. Tobiah was the servant of Nehemiah.

66. The "man clothed in linen" told Daniel the interpretation of the vision of the ram and the goat.

67. Moses made sweet the bitter waters of Marah by casting therein his rod.

68. The feast of unleavened bread was appointed to be celebrated in the month Adar.

69. The ruler over the half-part of Beth-zur was Nehemiah the son of Azbuk.

70. The fear of attack by the enemies of the Jews was so urgent that, during the entire time of the rebuilding of the wall, Nehemiah and his military following from Babylon slept fully dressed.

71. The provision of manna in the wilderness was an ephah for each member of each family.

72. Joshua appointed Kedesh, Shechem, Hebron, Bezer, Ramoth,

and Golan as cities of refuge for those fleeing from blood avengers.

73. Moses brought forth water from a rock at Massah.

74. The judge succeeding Abimelech in power was Tola the son of Puah.

75. Jehovah hardened Pharaoh's heart in order that signs might be manifested which could be told of to the descendants of the Israelites as a proof of Jehovah's power.

76. The Feast of the Passover was ordained to be an exclusive Israelite feast not to be eaten by any non-Israelites except proselytes.

77. Daniel was visited while he was in the den of lions by a vision of a man with a face like lightning, eyes like lamps, arms and feet like polished brass.

78. The law as delivered to Moses provided that if a man owned an ox known to be vicious which he did not confine and serious accident ensued, the owner was to be held responsible for all damage.

79. Jephthah, who was the son of a harlot and Gilead, was thrust out by his legitimate brothers and went to the land of Tod.

80. Nehemiah stopped the extortion as practised by the nobles of Judah upon the agricultural fraction of the population.

81. The Book of Daniel records a vision which Daniel had in the seventh year of the reign of Cyrus.

82. The law as delivered to Moses in Sinai provided for only three feasts: the feast of unleavened bread, the feast of harvest, and the feast of ingathering.

83. Achan appropriated for himself a gold bar of sixty shekels' weight and 200 shekels of silver from the spoils of Jericho.

84. Samson was the son of Manoah and his wife Zorah.

85. Nehemiah made provision that, in addition to the rulers, a tithe of the people, as determined by lot, should live in Jerusalem.

86. Of the visions of Daniel record is given of two in the reign of Belshazzar, two in the reign of Darius, and two in the reign of Cyrus.

87. Shamgar the son of Anath slew 600 Ammonites with an ox-goad.

88. Forty-eight years later, Joshua performed the promise made by Moses to Caleb the spy.

89. Samson called the place where he slew a thousand Philistines with the jaw-bone of an ass Ramath-lehi.

90. Nehemiah remained in Jerusalem from the time of his appointment as governor until his death.

91. Samson told the secret of his strength to Delilah after deceiving her four times.

92. Upon two stones of onyx in the decoration of the high priests' garment made for Aaron, the names of the twelve tribes were engraved, six on each.
93. Though Zelophehad the great-great-grandson of Manasseh had daughters but no sons, they received, along with their uncles, their share in the land of their tribe as allotted by Joshua.
94. A party of 700 Danites stole from Micah his priest and his images and used them for their own religious purposes.
95. A deputation of three men from each tribe was sent by Joshua from Shiloh to visit and write a description of the unallocated land that it might be subdivided and assigned by lot to the remaining seven tribes.
96. In the intertribal war between Benjamin and the rest of Israel 25,000 Benjaminites were slain.
97. Upon the advice of Jethro, Moses chose able men as deputy rulers of tens and fifties and hundreds and thousands of the people to judge trivial cases and bring only important matters to Moses' attention.
98. Unto the descendants of Aaron twelve cities, one for each tribe, were given instead of an allotment of land, in the division of Canaan among the tribes.
99. In Jotham's parable of the trees and their king, Abimelech was symbolized by the bramble.
100. The ten curtains of the tabernacle were thirty by five cubits in size, fastened together by fives with loops and taches.

V

Completion Test on Judges

Supply words to make each sentence true and sensible. Choose words from those given below each sentence. Write one word for each row of dots.

1. And .... discomfited Sisera, and all his ...., and .... his host with the edge of the .... before Barak; and .... alighted from his .... and .... away on his feet.
    all battle carried chariot chariots Deborah ever fled horse Jehovah Joshua Joshua men plain Satan Sisera sword tower trumpets walked which
2. .... above women .... Jael be,
    The wife of .... the Kenite;
    Blessed shall .... be above .... in the ....
    all blessed cursed ever field Heber holy house

Jael Kener men Meroz shall she tent was women
you

3. And the .... said unto the trees, If in .... ye
anoint me .... over ...., then come and
.... in my shade; and if ...., let
fire come out of the ...., and devour the cedars of
....

all ape bramble bramble bring comfort Gilead
Gilgal have Israel joy king Lebanon not priest
prophet refuge rock sky to sooth spirit take
truth whole why you

4. He .... water and she .... him ....;
she brought .... in a .... dish.

asked butter cakes curd drew figs forth found
gave golden lordly milk over saw silver struck
tea upon

5. Then said .... unto him, Say now ....: and he
said ....: for he could .... to
..........it right.

come David endeavor enjoy frame hallelujah
Jonathan not pronounce rim Shibboleth Sibboleth
they try us weary work Zapat

6. And .... went and .... three hundred ....
and took firebrands and turned .... to tail and put a
..........in the midst between two ....

belly caught child firebrand found fox foxes Gilead
head heads hired Jephthah laborers lions men
Samson tail tails wolves

7. Howbeit .... may .... give them ....
of our daughters: for the .... of Israel have sworn,
saying cursed be he .... giveth a wife to ....

abundance Asher Benjamin children children con-
cubines Dan ever Israel Jehovah not often that
tribes we well will whether wives

8. Among all .... people there were seven ....
.... men left-handed; .... one could ....
stones at a .... breadth, and not miss.

all carry chosen cubit elderly every fetch Gibean
hair hand hundred Israelitish mighty no sling
this thousand young

9. "I will now .... forth a .... unto you: if
.... can certainly declare it .... within the
seven .... of the feast, and find it out, then I will
.... you thirty sheets and thirty .... of
garments."

all bring challenge changes colors come command
David days give loads me men put riddle Samson
Solomon take venture you you

10. If thou .... without fail .... the children of
    Ammon into mine ...., then it shall .... that
    whatsoever cometh forth of the doors of my .... to
    meet me, when I return in .... from the children of
    Ammon shall surely be the ...., and I will offer it up
    .... a burnt offering.

    arms ask be deliver does fail for grandeur hands his
    house into Lord's mine must net peace punish shalt
    temple tribe upon weariness wither

Appendix IV

SAMPLES OF MATERIALS USED IN EXPERIMENTS 39 AND 40

Instructions

Read these instructions carefully.

On the table there are eight sheets of things to be learned. Sheet 1 will contain 100 English words and their meanings, like *emporium* = "center of commerce," *emprise* = "enterprise." You will receive one-third cent for every word on Sheet 1 that you learn the meaning of.

Sheet 2 will contain 100 English words, each one followed by something which it does NOT mean, like *bolster,* "peanut"; *attitude,* "automobile"; *glycerine,* "truck-driver." You will receive two-thirds cent for every word on Sheet 2 for which you learn the word that it does *not* mean.

Sheet 3 will contain the names of 100 famous persons and the year of birth of each (like "John Adams, 1735"; "Alexander the Great, 356 B.C."). You will receive one-third cent for every person whose birth year you learn.

Sheet 4 will contain the names of 100 persons of no importance (like "Pedomer, 1765"; "J. Smith, 1842") and the year of birth of each. You will receive two-thirds cent for every person whose birth year you learn.

Sheet 5 will contain the dates of 100 very important events. You will receive one-third cent for every event the date of which you learn.

Sheet 6 will contain the dates of 100 events of no importance (like "Building Mr. Peters's pig-pen, 1684"; or "Mary Foster's first job, 1896"). You will receive two-thirds cent for every event the date of which you learn.

Sheet 7 will contain famous passages from famous poems. You will receive one-third cent for every line you learn.

Sheet 8 will contain passages from very inferior poetry by persons whose writings nobody cares to read or remember. You will receive two-thirds cent for every line you learn.

Choose which of the eight sheets you wish to learn. When I say "Come," come to the table and get the sheet you choose. Take it to your seat and study it for an hour. Then I will give you a test to find out how much you have learned. The words and dates will be in a different order in the test. So take care to learn them in such a way that you can give the word or date that goes with a word or name or event, no matter how much the order of the 100 is changed. A good way to learn with sheets 1 to 6 is to look at the line, cover up the second part, say what you think it is, and then look and see whether you are right.

Sheet 1. Words and Correct Meanings

adumbrate	foreshadow	benison	blessing
afflatus	inspiration	bhang	Indian hemp
agaric	mushroom	billy-cock	hard felt hat
albacore	tunny	bittern	marsh-bird
al fresco	in the open air	blatant	vulgarly noisy

[and ninety more]

Sheet 2. Words and Wrong Meanings

abigail	crafty	badinage	abnormal
ablings	flimsy	bagatelle	calculator
abscission	maroon	balderdash	hilarity
absonant	reply	baldric	message
abstergent	halibut	baleen	balustrade

[and ninety more]

Sheet 3. Birth Years of Famous Men

Statesmen		Artists		Scientists	
Kossuth	1802	Landseer	1802	Fechner	1801
Disraeli	1804	Daubigny	1817	Liebig	1803
Garibaldi	1807	Bonheur	1822	Agassiz	1807
Jefferson Davis	1808	Inness	1825	Darwin	1809

Authors		Composers	
Dumas (father)	1802	Berlioz	1803
Victor Hugo	1802	Mendelssohn	1809
Longfellow	1807	Chopin	1810
Poe	1809	Verdi	1813

[and sixteen more of each sort]

Sheet 4. Birth Years of Persons of No Importance

Cobblers		Tailors		Farmers	
Numark	1802	Ducette	1801	Gerda	1804
Vendry	1803	Nicholas Wendt	1802	Delaney	1804
Dilser	1808	Wolff	1807	Rivot	1804
Kreuger	1812	Wilson Coogan	1808	Spendesz	1806

Blacksmiths		Mechanics	
Marinelli	1806	Pariosi	1834
Oscar Reni	1814	Bovera	1806
Bruck	1818	Leonard James	1809
Fricken	1820	Benz	1811

[and sixteen more of each sort]

Sheet 5. Important Events

Music

Beethoven	*Fidelio*	1805
von Weber	*Silvana*	1810
Schubert	*Serenade*	1826
Halévy	*La Juive*	1835

Inventions

Stevens	Screw propeller	1804
Colt	Revolver (pistol)	1835
Phillips	Phosphorus friction match	1836
Goodyear	Vulcanized rubber	1839

Art

Ingres	"Madame Riveieve"	1805
Constable	"Hay Wain"	1821
Turner	"Fighting Téméraire"	1839
Turner	"Rain, Steam and Speed"	1844

Literature

Bryant	*Thanatopsis*	1811
Keats	*Endymion*	1818
Shelley	*Prometheus Unbound*	1819
Cooper	*The Spy*	1821

Events

Battle of Trafalgar	1805
First steamboat crossed the Atlantic	1819
Irish famine	1822
Slavery abolished in New York State	1827

[and eighty other similar records]

Sheet 6. Events of No Importance

Sonora, California

Katherine	got a job as an actress	1805
Bob	put on long trousers	1810
Beatrice	rode horseback	1826
Edgar	built a fire	1835

Dane County, Wisconsin

Frank	fell out of bed	1804
Sanford	went to the circus	1835
Dora	became an actress	1836
Jane	went to Paris	1839

McConnellsburg, Pennsylvania

Mr. Ames's	horse ran away	1805
John L.	broke his leg	1821
Mr. J.	bought a cow	1839
Mary	graduated	1844

Pulaski, New York

Max	found a dollar	1811
Albert	swam in the pond	1818
Daniel	had the mumps	1819
Milton	grew three inches	1821

Magnolia, Louisiana

Deborah	was drowned	1805
Virginia	went on a picnic	1819
Nathan	read Robinson Crusoe	1822
Constance	darned stockings	1827

[and eighty other similar records]

Sheet 7. Famous Passages

At ninety-six I had lived enough, that is all,
And passed to a sweet repose.
What is this I hear of sorrow and weariness,
Anger, discontent and drooping hopes?
—Masters.

There be none of Beauty's daughters
With a magic like thee;
And like music on the waters
Is thy sweet voice to me.
—Byron.

I will arise and go now for always, night and day
I hear lake-water lapping with low sounds by the shore;
While I stand on the roadway, or on the pavements gray,
I hear it in the deep heart's core.
—Yeats.

This be the verse you grave for me:
Here he lies where he longed to be;
Home is the sailor, home from the sea,
And the hunter home from the hill.

                              —Stevenson.

[and sixteen others]

Sheet 8. Inferior Poetry

No sign is made while empires pass,
The flowers and stars are still His care,
The constellations hid in grass,
The golden miracles in air.

I knew the stars, the flowers, and the birds,
The grey and wintry sides of many glens,
And did but half remember human words,
In converse with the mountains, moors and fens.

A great storm from the ocean goes shouting o'er the hill,
And there is glory in it; and terror on the wind:
But the haunted air of twilight is very strange and still,
And the little winds of twilight are dearer to my mind.

Her grieving parents cradled here
Ann Monk, a gracious child and dear.
Lord, let this epitaph suffice:
Early to Bed and Early to Rise.

[and sixteen other passages]

Appendix V

SAMPLES OF TESTIMONY CONCERNING THE INFLU-ENCE OF REWARDS AND PUNISHMENTS IN EDUCATION

We quote the testimony found concerning the influence of re-wards and punishments for a random sampling of the cases of boys from 1800 to 1899. We report the author of the book, even though the testimony may be attributed by him to some other person, since the author makes himself responsible for it.

"There were two acrid infusions . . . embittered his [Butler's] whole life. The first was the severe home discipline to which he was subjected and his revolt against it. A more stolid child might have survived having elementary education flogged into him, and a brighter child might have escaped it. The unfortunate Samuel . . . was evidently rather frail in body, sluggish in mind, and acutely sensitive in spirit. A naturally docile and affectionate dis-position was thus warped by hard and unsympathetic treatment into a defiant, vindictive retaliation."
—F. T. Russell, Introduction to *The Way of All Flesh.*

". . . his first school was Mr. Gough's at Bristol, which he began to attend as a day-boy in 1819. Of this school he said grimly in after-life: 'I was flogged every day of my life at school except one, and then I was flogged thrice.' "
—Article on J. M. Lawrence in *Dictionary of National Biography,* p. 267.

"From his boyhood's days at Eton Hawtrey . . . gained three things. . . . In the first place, the roughness . . . made a great impression on him and proved an incentive towards carrying out the refining of the school. . . . The colleges in Dr. Keate's days (his predecessor) were very roughly used and managed, 50 sleep-ing in one room. . . . The refinement which . . . was no doubt natural to him but was also in some degree an outcome of his horror of the experiences to which he was subjected as a boy. . . . Thirdly, he saw by personal experience (under Goodall) the

248

advantage of judicious and even liberal praise as a means of instigating to further exertions."

* * * * *

"The late Mr. Gladstone remembered all his life the unexpected friendliness shown him, when, a little boy of twelve, he was in the Upper Remove of the Fourth Form under Hawtrey. He was 'sent up for good' for a copy of verses, and on going to his form-master to have them looked over before taking them up, was received with such kindness and such evident interest in him *personally* as to give him 'a thrill of new hope and satisfaction'. The small boy's surprise . . . proves the novelty of the treatment he found at Hawtrey's hands, and he did not fail to acknowledge that to this he owed his first inspiration 'to learn and to do.' "

—F. D. How, *Six Great Schoolmasters,* pp. 5 f., 12.

"He [Lewis Carroll] seldom returned home without one or more prizes. . . . He conducted himself so well that he never had to enter that dreaded chamber—which is approached by a staircase that winds up a little turret. . . .

"Public school life then was not what it is now; the atrocious system of setting hundreds of lines for the most trifling offences . . . while the bad discipline which was maintained in the dormitories made even the nights intolerable—especially for the small boys, whose beds in winter were denuded of blankets that the bigger ones might not feel cold. Charles kept no diary . . . but . . . he writes in 1855: 'During my stay I suppose I made some progress in learning of various kinds, but none of it was done *con amore,* and I spent an incalculable time in writing out impositions —this last I consider one of the chief faults of Rugby School. . . . I cannot say that I look back upon my life at a Public School with any sensations of pleasure, or that any earthly consideration would induce me to go through my three years again!' . . .

"When some years afterward he visited Radley school, he was much struck by the cubicle system . . . and wrote . . . 'I can say that if I had been thus secure from annoyance at night, the hardships of the daily life would have been comparative trifles to bear.' "

—C. L. Dodgson, *Life and Letters of Lewis Carroll, passim.*

"My eldest sister was 14 years and a half older than me; she had an exquisite taste for poetry . . . and she composed easy verses herself with great facility. It is probable that her conversation and example contributed greatly to my early bent to poetry. Two versifications from Isaiah and Jeremiah which I wrote for school tasks at Xmas, 1777, my age fifteen, and which gained great applause, fixed my ambition to write verses for life."

—Sir E. Brydges, *Autobiography.*

"It is interesting to note that on this long-forgotten private stage Master Gus first played Young Norval and William Tell, and in the latter personation astonished even his elocution master by his limpid mellifluous delivery of the well-known apostrophe 'Ye crags and peaks.'

"To the praise lavished upon him in connection with these exhibitions and performances, the fostering of young Brooke's dramatic tastes has been very properly attributed. (He became a tragedian actor and acted Tell and Virginius on the stage before he was 14 years old.)"

—W. J. Lawrence, *The Life of Gustavus Vaughan Brooke*, p. 7.

"As a master he was severe, wayward, and irregular. . . . Prejudice against individual boys . . . he did not always take the trouble to conceal or disguise. . . . A very reprehensible act of indelicacy had been perpetrated in the apartment of one of the upper boys. . . . The upper boys were assembled by the master in his library . . . after a long preparatory discourse each was called upon to declare his innocence upon his honor. Why he suspected me, I never could imagine, but he from time to time cast such terror-striking looks at me that they were irresistible; I declared myself innocent upon my honor, but I was so perplexed and agitated that I must have appeared guilty to every one but the real culprit himself. It requires at this moment (50 years later) no ordinary effort of charity and forbearance entirely to forgive so great an act of cruelty and injustice. The injury done to me was incalculable. It inflicted a deep wound upon my mind; it debased and depreciated me in the eyes of my peers; it checked every ingenuous ardor, and drove me almost to despondency. Everything unseemly which occurred afterward was imputed to my agency and my situation became intolerable . . . but I had justice rendered me afterwards. My Orbilius at a subsequent period made honorable atonement."

—W. Belve, *The Sexagenarian*, p. 23.

"The only scholastic education I received was at the Town Bank School . . . Fardy Hodgson (teacher) was particularly kind to me; and being pleased one day at the manner in which I had performed my task, he took me by the hand into his shop, and spreading on the counter a great number of books for young people, he desired me to look at them and choose any one I pleased as a present. I pitched upon a small History of the Bible, with wood-cuts, which so pleased the old man, that he foretold to my parents that I should prove a treasure to them. Trifling as this was, it produced its effect, and has on many occasions recurred to my memory."

—Sir John Barrow, *An Autobiographical Memoir of*, p. 5.

"What little schooling Dwight [Dwight L. Moody] received was not greatly enjoyed, because the teacher was a quick tempered man, who used a rattan on the boy's back. Years after he (Moody) told how a happy change was effected in that school. 'After a while there was somebody who began to get up a movement in favor of controlling the school by love. I remember how we thought of the good time we should have that winter, when the rattan would be out of the school. We thought we should then have all the fun we wanted. I remember who the teacher was—a lady—and she opened the school with prayer. We hadn't seen it done before, and we were impressed, especially when she prayed that she might have grace and strength to rule the school with love. The school went on for several weeks, and we saw no rattan; but at last the rules were broken and I think I was the first boy to break them. She told me to wait after school and then she would see me. I thought the rattan was coming out sure, and stretched myself up in warlike attitude. After school, however, she sat down beside me and told me how she loved me, and how she prayed to be able to rule that school by love, and concluded by saying, 'I want to ask you one favor, that is, if you love me, try and be a good boy'; and I never gave her trouble again.

"He was very susceptible to kindness. When an old man, who had the habit of giving every new boy who came into the town a cent, put his hand on Dwight's head, and told him he had a Father in heaven, he never forgot the pressure of that old man's hand."
—Sarah K. Bolton, *Poor Boys Who Became Famous*, p. 326 f.

"Even before he could read little Phineas [P. T. Barnum] had trotted regularly to Sunday School. . . . Faithfully, every Sunday, he was there, shivering in the winter months—for stoves in village churches were then unknown—as he chattered satisfactory responses to searching inquiries as to the condition of his spiritual state here and hereafter. But it seems almost certain that more distinctly tangible rewards were partially responsible for making him so punctual. Each Sunday's attendance won a little red ticket worth one mill; thus 100 tickets meant a prize in the form of a book. 'Infinitesimal as was this recompense,' he once remarked, 'it was sufficient to spur me to intense diligence.' "
—R. F. Dibble, *Strenuous Americans*, p. 291.

"My earliest recollection of the official school was of the impatience of a Mrs. Chapman because I could not recall the letter A. She vigorously jerked my hair and told me again to look at it. I think the whole alphabet was beaten into me in this way."
—C. Ford, *The Child of Democracy*, p. 1.

[On the misrepresentation of a fellow-pupil on the first evening of his presence at school he disobeyed the rule forbidding leaving the building.] "Our absence was discovered . . . I made a clean breast of it. . . . He punished my schoolmate pretty severely on the palms of his hands with a ferule—then turned to me, said my excuse would not do, and explained, though not satisfactorily to me, why it would not; . . . I said nothing though I felt his decision was unjust as my real fault, if fault it was, consisted in believing the statement of a schoolmate whose acquaintance I had just made and whose truthfulness I had no reason to doubt. I stepped up to the Professor, held out one hand, sustained it by clasping the wrist with the other, stood erect and looked him in the face, as much as to say 'I am ready, Sir, strike away.' Something in my manner and appearance arrested his attention. . . . He looked intently . . . laid down his ferule and said 'Foot, I don't think you will violate the rules of the College again. You may take your seat.' The act and the word reached the depths of my heart and gave the Professor a controlling influence over me which he used to my great advantage. Had he punished me, my belief is that the punishment would have been a serious injury to me."

"Before going to Schenectady to school, I had no other ambition than to be conspicuous among my mates for daringness and disregard of consequences in mischievous design. In a few weeks, Prof. Thos. McAuley, by his judicious management, awakened in me a strong desire to excel in literary pursuits and make a figure in the world at some future day."

—S. A. Foot, *An Autobiography: Reminiscences and Writings*, p. 14 f.

"I went to the common or district school [now aged six; had gone earlier to another before family moved here]. My teacher was a young woman of whom I became very fond, and was never happier or prouder than when taking home to my parents her certificates of good conduct and scholarship . . . and I carefully preserved them for many years as something very precious."

[In school at same place.] "While under this teacher, I made my first attempt at writing . . . and received one of the severest punishments that was ever inflicted on me. A little girl of about my own age had been naughty and she was made to stand up in the middle of the floor before the whole school. She wriggled about in such a way as completely to upset my gravity, and I ventured to laugh, for which offence I was trotted out and placed by her side. Nor was this all. My arm and hers were tied together by a handkerchief and there we stood, she as nervous and fidgety as could be, and I covered with blushes and solemn as a funeral. But somehow I thought a good deal of that girl afterwards."

—H. Dyer, *Records of an Active Life*, p. 12 f.

"My father being a Presbyterian by principle, I was educated in all the rigor of that order, which illy suited my volatile, impatient temper of mind. . . . My thirst for amusement was insatiable, and as, in my situation, the only dependence for that gratification was entirely within myself, I sought it in pestering others, especially those who were my superiors in age. . . . My success in these undertakings was so great, that I became the terror of the people where I lived, and all were very unanimous in declaring that Stephen Burroughs was the worst boy in town; and those who could get him whipt were most worthy of esteem. Their attempts to bring on my back a flagellation were often very successful, for my heedless temper seldom studied for a retreat when I was in danger; however, the repeated application of this birchen medicine never cured my pursuit for fun."

—S. Burroughs, Memoirs of Stephen Burroughs,
p. 3.

"Being the youngest of my family . . . my time passed . . . in childish enjoyments. . . . I was much interested in the pursuit of knowledge and in the schools I attended saw none of my age before me. My advancement elicited praise from my friends and I usually gained the approbation and affection of my teachers. Penalties were not necessary to urge me on or restrain my faults. I had a pride of character which kept me aloof from boyish pranks. I could not bear the thought that my parents should suppose me capable of being a bad boy in school. Unhappily for me, about this time a teacher was employed of no great abilities . . . a ferule was placed in the hands of a lad who was directed to give it to the first he saw whisper . . . and in default of finding such, he was to be punished himself. . . . By a system of chicanery . . . he made friend of another lad . . . they conspired against me and determined, as I had never been publicly flogged, that I should escape no longer. They commenced a conversation about their lesson in my hearing. . . . The plot succeeded. I kindly attempted to set them right and for a reward of my benevolence was tendered the obnoxious ruler. I protested, wept, promised, screamed, but it was unavailing. I stated the circumstances—showed I had no evil intention in the premises—but my master was inflexible. . . . This was the first time I had been chastised in school; and oh! that some kind influence had prevented it! That punishment has been a curse to me. It laid the foundation of nearly all my folly and sin. Before, I was jealous of my reputation, was desirous to be thought the best boy in school; but now I was disgraced, shamed, mortified; and I recklessly plunged into all the wild rude excesses of childhood. I no longer sought the studious and sober for playmates, but delighted to mingle with the most rude and noisy spirits in the neighborhood; and cared little what I did, provided I could have sport and fun." *

—M. Brainerd, *Life of Rev. T. Brainerd,* p. 17.

"I was fond of school and learned rapidly; but would sometimes become very tired over the long hard words in the spelling book. I was yet in the third class when on one occasion the second class were spelling for head and a word went 'round the class.' The teacher overheard me whisper to my brother that I could spell the word, 'Thomas,' said he, 'rise and spell it.' I did so and was promoted to be head boy of the class, and felt as important as General Jackson in the presidential chair."

—T. H. Burton, *Autobiography of Thos. H. Burton,* p. 6.

"When about 7 years old I was placed at a somewhat better school. . . . [At 5 he had been under a Miss Leonard who taught him to read from primers but could go no further] taught by a Mr. May, . . . He was, however, very severe in his discipline and chastising me most unmercifully upon a time. After I had been with him several months, I fled from him in great anger and ran several miles home to my father's house without stopping."

—M. M. Henkle, *Life of Henry Bidleman Bascom, D.D., LL.D.,* p. 17.

"Notwithstanding my natural sensitiveness and susceptibility to irritation by small provocations, I was generally easily governed. . . . My mother said that she never used the rod on me but once. . . . It was before my remembrance, in my second year. I seemed to have been seized with a strange freak of destructiveness in the way of throwing things into the fire. She had chided me again and again for my misconduct, but in vain. When left to myself, article after article went rapidly into the flames. At length . . . she 'got a little tingler' and upon a repetition of the offense one day, gave me a few touches with it. I hopped about, screamed loudly, and was effectually cured."

"I think it likely that I was sent to the summer school (kept by a female, winter term by a male) earlier than I can now remember. I have a dim impression that I learned my letters of a school ma'am when about 3 years old, but I recall distinctly the first master I had. . . . I was furnished with a new spelling book which was strongly covered with sheep-skin by my mother that I might not injure it. . . . I was . . . much at loss what to do with myself or how to behave. . . . I dropped my head, stuck one corner of my book in my mouth, and unconsciously began to

* This 'recklessness' extended from age six to age twelve.

gnaw it. I had already done some mischief . . . when I was discovered by the teacher and reprimanded. But I seemed fated to round off those bookcorners. Nor was I cured of the fault for some days, though frequently threatened with something dreadful if I did not desist. At length, after much harm had been done, I was called up, ordered to take off my coat, and roll up my shirt sleeves, when the announcement was made that here was a boy with bad blood in his veins which must be taken out of him. The teacher then exhibited a fine sharp-pointed penknife as the lancet and applied it to my arm with a slight prick. By this time the terror-stricken culprit cried for mercy with such piteous penitence, that, on solemn promise of amendment, he was spared further punishment and sent to his seat. He never more treated a book disrespectfully."

—A. Ballou, *Autobiography of Adin Ballou*, pp. 9 and 15.

Appendix VI

EXPERIMENTS ON THE INFLUENCE OF CONTIGUITY VERSUS THE INFLUENCE OF OCCURRENCE AND REWARD

Experiment 45 was made with sixteen individuals. It was identical with experiment 41 with couplets reported in Chapter XIII in all respects save that the presentations with 'good' and 'bad' associates were both in the morning of one day, and the ratings twenty-four hours later. The totals after presentation with 'good' couplets were 34 LL, 104 L, 84 D, and 37 DD. The totals after presentation with 'bad' couplets were 29 LL, 93 L, 100 D, and 41 DD. The percentages of liking and disliking were 53 and 47, and 46 and 54, respectively. The average percentages of liking for both experiments are thus 55.5 after presentation with 'good' couplets and 45 after presentation with 'bad.' Using the method described in Chapter XIII, the median attitudes after presentation with 'goods' and 'bads' were +0.14 and −0.17, respectively. The average attitudes were +0.04 and −0.10.

Experiment 49 was like experiments 41 and 45 except that there was an interval of only a few minutes between the inspection along with 'good' and 'bad' couplets and the later examination and report of personal liking or disliking. There were sixty-five subjects in this experiment; the percentages of likes, indifferent and dislikes were as follows:

Couplets 1-20. After presentation with 'good' couplets: LL, 7.7; L, 34.8; Indif, 20.2; D, 30.0; DD, 7.3.
After presentation with 'bad' couplets: LL, 6.5; L, 26.5; Indif, 21.2; D, 33.3; DD, 12.3.

Couplets 21-40. After presentation with 'good' couplets: LL, 8.1; L, 39.7; Indif, 12.1; D, 31.0; DD, 9.1.
After presentation with 'bad' couplets: LL, 8.1; L, 30.8; Indif, 10.9; D, 39.9; DD, 10.4.

Averages. After presentation with 'good': 7.9, 37.2, 16.2, 30.5, and 8.2
After presentation with 'bad': 7.3, 28.7, 16.0, 36.6, and 11.4

The average percent which the likes are of the likes + the dislikes was thus 54 after association with the 'good' and 43 after association with the 'bad' couplets. The median attitudes were +0.20 and —0.38. The corresponding averages were +0.20 and —0.50.

The difference between the median attitude after inducement to like and that after inducement to dislike was 0.40 in experiment 41, 0.31 in experiment 45, and 0.58 in experiment 49. The difference between the corresponding averages was 0.32 in experiment 41, 0.14 in experiment 45, and 0.70 in experiment 49. The inducements used thus caused a difference in attitude of about 0.40.

In the case of the couplets, then, contiguity plus the inducement to take an attitude of esteem and liking (or disesteem and dislike) surely altered the response in the test later. Whatever contrary influence the contrast of the neutrals with the 'goods' (or 'bads') may have exerted was much more than overcome. The examination of a couplet in contiguity with couplets that are liked and with further inducement to take the attitude of liking and to regard it as fit and proper causes liking, and conversely for dislike.

In experiment 42 we used forty neutral lines, 120 'good' lines selected from *Bartlett's Familiar Quotations,* and 120 'bad' lines written by students in an experiment. Samples are shown below.

The instructions given before the examination of sets containing 'neutrals' and 'goods' were as follows:

"You will then receive two sheets containing twenty sets each consisting of four lines of verse or prose, mostly by famous authors. Read the four lines of set 1; mark the line you think is the best 1 and the one you think is next best 2. If you think you know who was the author of any line, write his name in the margin. Do the same for set 2, set 3, and so on. As soon as you finish, write your name on each sheet and bring the sheets to me."

The instructions given before the examination of sets containing 'neutrals' and 'bads' were as follows:

"You will then receive two sheets containing twenty sets each consisting of four lines of poetry or prose. These also were mostly written in haste by students devoid of literary gifts. Read the four lines of set 1 and mark the worst 4, and the next to the worst 3. As soon as you finish, write your name at the top of the sheets and bring the sheets to me."

Samples of Sets of One 'Neutral' with Three 'Good' Lines

1. ...A rose is sweeter in the bud than full blown.
   ...The universe begins each day anew.
   ...I would help others out of a fellow-feeling.
   ...Help thyself and God will help thee.

2. ...A rose is lovely though it fall by night.
   ...High erected thoughts seated in the heart of courtesy.
   ...Death calls ye to the crowd of common men.
   ...The starry cope of heaven.

3. ...Black is a pearl in a woman's eye.
   ...Carcasses bleed at the sight of the murderer.
   ...Beware the fury of a patient man.
   ...Are you the scourge of God or Devil's hound?

4. ...Fair words never hurt the tongue.
   ...Idleness is an appendix to nobility.
   ...The glowing fire calls phantoms from the past.
   ...Bless the hand that gave the blow.

5. ...Our wills are made by every act we will.
   ...Sacred religion! mother of form and fear.
   ...Sighed and looked and sighed again.
   ...Who loves a garden, loves a greenhouse.

Samples of Sets of One 'Neutral' with Three 'Bad' Lines

1. ...Old age should bring us thoughts almost divine.
   ...He looked upon her face and found it fair.
   ...Mad Majesty provokes with ravings wild.
   ...No lightest twitter shook the listening leaves.

2. ...The wretched man did think his soul was lost.
   ...So now we see a perfect flawless form.
   ...The tallest ladder has bottom rungs.
   ...My broken words were full of half despair.

3. ...'Tis sad to think how soon a life must end.
   ...It was a summer day all clear and bright.
   ...The good remains; the bad was let decay.
   ...Forsaken, on a shipwrecked isle they drift.

4. ...Methinks the world had never looked so fair.
   ...Wild joy prevails in maidens out of school.
   ...Hate and envy sit on the same stool.
   ...The rarest virtue known is gratitude.

5. ...His unkempt whiskers fluttered in the breeze.
    ...All saint, half scholar and half priest.
    ...What's done can't be undone, but it can be changed.
    ...No sound was heard; no moving breeze was felt.

Part of Rating Sheet for Lines

1. ...Clean and free like the air by the sea.
2. ...The universe begins each day anew.
3. ...A rose is lovely though it fall by night.
4. ...In sand and mud and slime much gold is hid.

5. ...The sea and the desert with space and peace.
6. ...Are you the scourge of God, or Devil's hound?
7. ...The glowing fire calls phantoms from the past.
8. ...A good retreat is better than defeat.

9.   ...Our wills are made by every act we will.
10. ...The bank of memory may store fine treasures.

In experiment 42, twenty 'neutral' lines were experienced by Group A with 'good' lines and by Group B with 'bad' lines. With twenty other lines, the conditions for Group A and Group B were reversed.

In the rating sheets which both Group A and Group B filled out a day or hour or a few minutes after the examination of these mixed sets, all the forty 'neutral' lines were presented.

In experiment 42, the interval was one day. The totals for LL, L, Indif, D, and DD respectively were 51, 96, 96, 53, and 24 after presentation with good lines, and 46, 94, 96, 62, and 22 after presentation with bad lines. The percent which the likes were of the likes + the dislikes were 66 and 62, respectively. The median attitudes were +0.34 and +0.29. The corresponding averages were +0.30 and +0.27.

Experiment 46 was identical in all respects with experiment 42 save that the presentations with 'good' and with 'bad' associates were in the morning of the same day and the ratings of LL, L, Indif, D, and DD were made twenty-four hours later. There were sixteen adult subjects. The totals for LL, L, Indif, D, and DD were as follows: After presentation with 'good' lines, 47, 117, 71, 60, 25; after presentation with 'bad' lines, 37, 105, 63, 73, 42. The percents which the likes were of the likes + the dislikes were 65 and 55 respectively. The median attitudes were +0.53

and $+0.21$. The corresponding averages were $+0.32$ and $+0.07$.

In experiment 50, sixty subjects (educated adults) were tested immediately after the examination of the lines and expressed their attitudes by L or D, taking one or the other by chance when they were in doubt.

The percentages of L and D after presentation with the good lines were 62 and 38. After presentation with the bad lines, they were 52.5 and 47.5. We cannot express these results as medians or averages comparable to those computed for experiments 42 and 46. But if an L is counted as $+1.25$ and a D as -1.25, there will be a rough comparability with the averages. The results are $+0.30$ after presentation with 'goods' and $+0.06$ after presentation with 'bads.'

For all three experiments, then, the difference in attitude due to the inducements to like and the inducements to dislike is about 0.18.

In experiment 54, the same sets of 'good,' 'bad,' and 'neutral' lines were used in the same way as in experiments 42, 46, and 50, except that mere contiguity was used. Nothing was said to induce a favorable attitude toward the set consisting of 'goods' and 'neutrals,' or an attitude of disfavor toward the set consisting of 'bads' and 'neutrals.' Nothing was done to the lines except to read and reread them.

After the thirty subjects had thus read twenty 'neutrals' mixed with sixty 'good' lines and twenty other 'neutrals' mixed with sixty 'bad' lines, they listened to a series of eighty lines and reported their personal liking or dislike for each and their judgment as to whether it had been among the two sets of lines previously read.

The expressions of liking and dislike were as follows *:

	LL	L	Indif	D	DD
After experience in contiguity with 'good' lines	255	121	118	61	45
After experience in contiguity with 'bad' lines	288	122	90	57	43

A comparable group of twenty-eight educated adults did the same except that the 'neutral' lines which the group of thirty had

* In cross-examination later only one subject reported any failures to express genuine personal feelings, and hers were very rare. We therefore did not exclude her record from the computations.

experienced with 'good' lines were experienced with 'bad' lines by this group of twenty-eight and the 'neutral' lines which the group of thirty had experienced with 'bad' lines were experienced with 'good' lines by the group of twenty-eight. Expressions of liking and dislike by these twenty-eight subjects were as follows:

	LL	L	Indif	D	DD
After experience in contiguity with 'good' lines	290	114	70	48	38
After experience in contiguity with 'bad' lines	260	114	83	66	37

If we multiply these results by 30/28 and combine them with those for the group of thirty, we have the following:

	LL	L	Indif	D	DD
After contiguity with 'good' lines	566	243	193	112	96
After contiguity with 'bad' lines	566	244	179	128	83

There is hardly a hair's breadth of difference. The medians are the same to the second decimal; and the averages are +0.89 and +0.90 respectively.

With the lines, as with the couplets, mere contiguity was impotent. The results of experiments 42, 46, and 50 as well as those of experiments 41, 45, and 49 were due to special conditions which caused the subjects to take certain attitudes and to feel satisfied in doing so.

Similar experiments were carried on with pictures of buildings, Christmas cards, and specimens of colored paper, each presented with three 'good' or with three 'bad' specimens and later rated as LL, L, Indif, D, or DD. In the first experiment (44) sixteen subjects chose the two best of certain sets of four on Day 1 and the two worst of certain other sets of four on Day 2 and made the ratings of LL, L, etc., forty-eight hours later. In the second experiment (48) sixteen different subjects did all the choosing on Day 1 and made the ratings twenty-four hours later. Each group of sixteen was split into two groups of eight, one of which saw certain cards with 'good' cards, the other of which saw those same cards with 'bad' cards.

In a third experiment (52) twenty-four subjects made the ratings a few minutes after they had completed the choosing.

Consider first the facts for twenty-seven pictures of buildings. Fourteen pictures (2, 3, 5, 8, 9, 10, etc.) were seen along with 'good' pictures and afterwards were liked or disliked as shown in Table 31, lines 1 and 2. Thirteen pictures (1, 4, 6, 11, 12, etc.) were seen along with 'bad' pictures and afterwards were liked or disliked as shown in Table 31, lines 4 and 5. Since the pictures were different, we must allow for any differences in their acceptability. The amount of allowance is determined by giving (in experiment 51) both sets of pictures, without any previous association with either 'good' or 'bad,' to a group of adults of the same general sort as participated in experiment 52. In this neutral condition they aroused likes and dislikes as shown in Table 31, lines 3 and 6. The two sets were closely alike in acceptability, the percentages of 'likes' being 51.1 for the former and 52.7 for the latter, the percentages of 'indifferents' being 15.0 and 13.8, and the percentages of 'dislikes' being 33.8 and 33.6. There was then a shift toward liking after association with good pictures and toward dislike after association with bad, amounting to 7.0 percent in the experiment with an interval of two days, and 15.0 percent in the experiment with a one-day interval.

Consider next the facts for thirty-eight Christmas cards, twenty of which were presented to subjects A, B, C, etc., along with 'good' cards and to subjects a, b, c, etc., along with 'bad' cards, the other eighteen being presented to A, B, C along with 'bad' cards and to a, b, c along with 'good' cards.

For these thirty-eight Christmas cards in which everything save the form of presentation was equalized, we have the results shown in Table 31, lines 7, 8, 9, and 10. The net result upon the ratings of the previous presentation along with 'good' or 'bad' pictures in experiments 44 and 48 was nil or very nearly nil. The average percentages of 'likes' and 'dislikes' were respectively 39.2 and 35.7 after 'good,' and 38.9 and 36.9 after 'bad,' associations.

In a later experiment (52) in which the ratings followed the choosings after an interval of only a few minutes, there was a strengthening of 'likes' by association with 'good' pictures and a strengthening of 'dislikes' by association with 'bad.' In experiment 52 twelve subjects saw Christmas cards 31, 32, 35, etc., first along with 'good' cards, and cards 34, 38, 39, etc., not at all until they rated them. Twelve other subjects saw cards 34, 38, 39, etc., first along with 'bad' cards, and cards 31, 32, 35, etc., not at all until they rated them. The results appear in Table 31, lines 11, 12, 13, and 14. Association with 'good' brings a shift of 6.7 toward 'likes,' and association with 'bad' a shift of 8.8 toward 'dislikes,' in comparison with the status of never having been seen before the ratings of 'likes' and 'dislikes' were made.

Consider lastly thirty-two Christmas cards and specimens of colored papers which were judged by half of the subjects in each of experiments 44, 48, and 52 along with 'good' specimens and by half along with 'bad' specimens, and later rated as to personal liking by all. The facts are given in Table 31, lines 15 to 20. Assuming that the two groups of twenty-eight subjects would have shown similar percentages if they had never seen these cards before rating them, the results show practically no influence from the associations with 'good' and 'bad.' The totals for the two groups give these percentages:

After association with 'good': LL + L, 47.8; Indif, 10.4;
D + DD, 41.9
After association with 'bad': LL + L, 46.1; Indif, 16.6;
D + DD, 37.3

Dividing the 'indifferent' attitudes equally between the L and the D, we have 53.0 and 54.4 as the percentages of LL + L after presentation with 'good' and after presentation with 'bad' respectively. On the whole, association with pictures which are liked and disliked (or at least are judged worthy of like and dislike) seems to have a slight influence toward enhancing liking and disliking respectively, in experiments 44, 48, and 52.

In order to estimate how far this difference was due to mere contiguity and how far to the provocation to take an attitude of liking (or dislike) toward the 'neutral' pictures during the examination of the groups of four, we have performed experiment 56. This is like the other experiments, except that all suggestions of liking or disliking any picture during the examination were absent. The experiment was conducted simply as one in recognition memory, the subjects examining the pictures in groups of four at a given rate with the expectation of being tested in respect of their memories of whether they had seen them. No suggestion was made that certain sets were estimable and others not. In the test they were required not only to say whether or not they had seen each picture, but also to report their liking for each (whether previously seen or not) by the LL, L, Indif, D, DD scale. In this experiment the actual occurrences of likes and dislikes during the examination in sets of four was only

TABLE 31

The influence in educated adults of experience of pictures, etc., in association with pictures judged worthy of like or dislike upon the attitude taken later toward the picture or object itself

LINE NO.	NATURE OF MATERIAL	ITEMS RATED	CONDITIONS OF RATING	EXPERIMENT	NO. OF ITEMS	NO. OF SUBJECTS	FREQUENCIES IN PERCENTS						
							LL	L	Indif	D	DD	LL+L	D+DD
1	PICTURES OF BUILDINGS	2, 3, 5, etc.	After asso. with 'good'	44	14	16	8.9	34.4	22.3	28.6	5.8	43.3	34.4
2		2, 3, 5, etc.	After asso. with 'good'	48	14	16	18.3	38.8	9.8	23.2	9.8	57.1	33.0
3		2, 3, 5, etc.	Never seen before	51	14	19	23.7	27.4	15.0	21.4	12.4	51.1	33.8
4		1, 4, 6, etc.	After asso. with 'bad'	44	13	16	13.0	29.3	17.3	32.2	8.2	42.3	40.4
5		1, 4, 6, etc.	After asso. with 'bad'	48	13	16	14.4	34.6	10.1	30.8	10.1	49.0	40.9
6		1, 4, 6, etc.	Never seen before	51	13	19	21.5	31.2	13.8	20.6	13.0	52.7	33.6
7	CHRISTMAS CARDS	31, 32, 34, etc.	After asso. with 'good'	44	38	8	6.6	27.0	31.2	24.0	11.2	33.6	35.2
8		31, 32, 34, etc.	After asso. with 'good'	48	38	8	11.5	33.2	19.1	25.7	10.5	44.7	36.2
9		31, 32, 34, etc.	After asso. with 'bad'	44	38	8	5.6	27.6	26.3	26.3	14.2	33.2	40.5
10		31, 32, 34, etc.	After asso. with 'bad'	48	38	8	11.2	33.6	22.0	24.3	8.9	44.7	33.2
11		31, 32, 35, etc.	After asso. with 'good'	52	20	12	25.5	33.3	15.4	18.8	7.1	58.8	25.8
12		31, 32, 35, etc.	Never seen before	51	20	12	19.2	37.1	14.2	17.1	12.5	56.3	29.6
13		34, 38, 39, etc.	After asso. with 'bad'	52	18	12	13.9	31.0	11.6	27.8	15.7	44.9	43.5
14		34, 38, 39, etc.	Never seen before	51	18	12	24.5	22.7	15.7	20.4	16.7	47.2	37.0
15	CARDS AND PAPERS	73...104	After asso. with 'good'	44	32	8	7.8	31.6	11.3	36.7	12.5	39.5	49.2
16		73...104	After asso. with 'good'	48	32	8	9.8	38.7	6.6	32.4	12.5	48.4	44.9
17		73...104	After asso. with 'good'	52	32	12	27.1	25.8	12.2	19.5	15.4	52.9	34.9
18		73...104	After asso. with 'bad'	44	32	8	7.4	32.0	20.3	26.6	13.7	39.5	40.2
19		73...104	After asso. with 'bad'	48	32	8	17.2	32.0	18.0	22.3	10.5	49.2	32.8
20		73...104	After asso. with 'bad'	52	32	12	18.2	30.2	13.3	23.4	14.8	48.4	38.3

such as was caused by the pictures themselves, and any tendency for likes of 'neutrals' in sets of four to be more frequent in fours containing 'goods' than in fours containing 'bads' was only such as was caused by the grouping itself.

The subjects were twenty-eight educated adults. With the thirty-eight Christmas cards (31, 32, 34, 36, etc.), the percentages of 'likes,' 'indifferents,' and 'dislikes' were as follows:

After presentation with 'goods': 'Likes,' 45.0; 'Indif,' 20.4; 'Dislikes,' 34.6

After presentation with 'bads': 'Likes,' 42.0; 'Indif,' 22.8; 'Dislikes,' 35.2

Dividing the 'indifferents' equally between the others, we have 55.2 percent 'likes' after presentation with 'goods,' and 53.4 percent 'likes' after presentation with 'bads.'

With the cards and papers (73 to 104), the percentages were:

After presentation with 'goods': 'Likes,' 39.6; 'Indif,' 22.1; 'Dislikes,' 38.3

After presentation with 'bads': 'Likes,' 42.2; 'Indif.,' 19.9; 'Dislikes,' 37.9

After dividing as before, we have 50.6 percent after presentation with 'goods' and 52.1 percent after presentation with 'bads.' Giving equal weight to the two sets of data, we have almost absolutely zero difference between the two forms of presentation.

Appendix VII

EXPERIMENTS ON THE INFLUENCE OF SATISFYING AFTER-EFFECTS UPON ATTITUDES

Experiment 64 utilized the materials of experiment 62. It was arranged, however, for group administration. Each card was mounted on a cardboard. The pre-test and post-test of experiment 62 were reversed so that cards 201-240 became the pre-test and cards 1-40 became the post-test. The cards were favored or disparaged by comments written on the back of seventy-two of the training series. The pre-test series was first passed out, then the training series and the post-test without interruption, and finally the pre-test series was repeated. The subjects had thus no indication that the post-test series was being administered as a test.

Twenty-seven undergraduates of a New York college in attendance during the summer session in 1933 were given experiment 64. The directions under which the subjects operated were as follows:

For Part I (Pre-Test). "You are to record your likes and dislikes for a series of Christmas cards. You will look at the card. If you are sure you like it, write 1 after its number on the record sheet. If there are two numbers on the card, use the one at the lower right-hand corner, or at the bottom. If you think you like it, but are not sure, write 2. If you are sure that you dislike it, write 9. If you think that you dislike it but are not sure, write 8. If you have no feeling at all, either of like or dislike, write 5 after the number. Always write some number to show that you have examined it. In every case, express your own personal feelings. We do not wish to know whether you think that the card deserves liking, but whether you do yourself like it."

For Part II (the Training Series and Post-Test Administered without Pause). "You are to record likes and dislikes just as before. The only difference is that, after you have recorded your like or dislike and put the card face down at your right, you may read what you see written on its back, if you care to know whether you agree with the general likes and dislikes of a group of artists. Do not ever turn the card over again to look at its

266

face, and, of course, do not ever look at the back of any card until after you have recorded your like or dislike. Also, do not spend time beyond one quick reading of what is written on the back. Do not stop to think about any card after you have recorded your like or dislike. Sometimes nothing is reported, either because there is no clear feeling toward the card, sentence, etc., or because the card is a new one where we have as yet no information. If the card has two or more numbers, use the pencil one at the bottom or the red one in the corner. Bear in mind that you are always to record your own personal like or dislike, not your opinion about whether the card or selection ought to be liked."

Part III (the repetition of the pre-test) was administered under the same directions as Part I.

The two test series contained two matched sets of ten cards like those favored in training, two matched sets of ten cards like those disparaged in training, and two matched sets of eleven cards like those without comment, which had been judged equivalent, card for card, in general esthetic value by the criterion group of artists. Each series was filled out to forty by the addition of nine unmatched cards.

Favorable and disparaging statements read during training act as rewards or satisfying after-effects when in agreement with the subject's like or dislike and as punishments when they are in opposition to it. The potency of the occurrences plus the rewards and punishments can be measured by calculating the difference in median ranking for each group of cards from pre-test to post-test, and from pre-test to repetition of pre-test. Below we present these and also the average rankings. These medians and averages were computed on the assumption that a rank of 5 was equivalent to the step from $+0.05$ to -0.05, that 1 was a step from $+2.5$ to $+1.5$, that 2 was a step from $+1.5$ to $+0.5$, that 8 was a step from -0.5 to -1.5, and that 9 was a step from -1.5 to -2.5. The medians are, of course, better representatives of the truth, being uninfluenced by the 1's that could not shift up and the 9's that could not shift down.

The differences and their standard errors are as follows, '$+$' meaning a change toward greater liking and '$-$' a change toward greater dislike:

Between pre-test and matched post-test:

Favored: $+0.49 \pm 0.15$, using medians; $+0.31 \pm 0.12$, using averages

Mediocre: —0.76 ± 0.11, using medians; —0.68 ± 0.09, using averages

Disparaged: —1.28 ± 0.14, using medians; —0.86 ± 0.11, using averages

Between pre-test and its repetition after training:

Favored: +0.61 ± 0.15, using medians; +0.44 ± 0.12, using averages

Mediocre: —0.58 ± 0.11, using medians; —0.54 ± 0.09, using averages

Disparaged: —1.46 ± 0.14, using medians; —0.97 ± 0.11, using averages

There is a general tendency for the subjects to like the thirty-one cards in the post-test less than their equivalents in the pre-test. This is shown by a shift down of 0.76 for the median of the mediocre group of eleven. But the influence of the rewards and punishments in the training series is sufficient to counteract this in the case of the favored cards, which show a median shift upward of 0.49, and to increase it to a shift down of 1.28 in the case of the disparaged cards. The balance of 1.77 (between 0.49 up and 1.28 down) has a probable error of 0.14. If averages are used instead of medians, the balance is 1.17 with a probable error of 0.11. If the pre-test and its repetition after training are used, this balance is 2.07 when medians are used and 1.41 when averages are used.

In order to obtain some notion of how far the shifts in likings in such experiments are due to the direct confirming action of the rewards and how far they are due to the indirect influence of the information that such and such cards are liked by experts whereas such and such others are disliked, we performed the following experiment (65):

The pre-test and matched post-test were as before, but this time the subjects, instead of examining and reporting likings for the 160 cards (41 to 200), and being rewarded (or punished) seventy-two times by finding that their attitudes were confirmed (or contradicted) by the thirty-six favorable and thirty-six unfavorable comments, examined only these seventy-two cards. They examined first the thirty-six favored cards, being told that they were highly esteemed by a jury of artists and asked only to write "No" in the case of any card which they themselves *disliked*. Then they examined the other thirty-six cards, being told that these were disliked by the jury of artists and asked only to write "No" in the case of any card which they themselves *liked*. This treatment of the seventy-two cards was repeated a day later.

In experiments 61-64 the subject expresses his feeling and then observes the feeling of the jury as expressed on the back of the card. In experiment 65 he knows beforehand the feeling of the jury and if, in spite of this knowledge, he disagrees with it, he expresses the disagreement.

In spite of having the information about the experts' feelings presented to him twice instead of once, systematically by grouping of all the 'goods' together and all the 'bads' together instead of in a mixture, and free from interference from seeing and responding to eighty-eight cards for which neither information beforehand nor after-effect was received, the change brought about in experiment 65 was only about two-fifths as great (balance of 0.72 instead of 1.77) as in experiment 64. There were thirty subjects in experiment 65, and the probable error of the balance of 0.72 is about 0.15. If averages are used, we find a balance of 0.54 (with a probable error of 0.12), compared with the 1.17 of experiment 64. The differences between 0.72 and 1.77 and between 0.54 and 1.17 are thus about five times their probable errors.

A reasonable conclusion is that the after-effect surely exerts some direct confirming influence, that indirect changes of attitude by memories in the matched post-test that such and such cards like the hitherto unseen card were esteemed (or disesteemed) by the jury of experts or that such and such qualities possessed by the new card were esteemed (or disesteemed) by the jury of experts probably were rare, and that possibly their influence was at or near zero. Possibly the shifts found in experiment 65 when the jury's attitude was presented in advance were due to the stimulation to like what one was told in advance was liked by the experts and to being satisfied by the surety that such liking was fit and proper and commendable (and similarly for the stimulation toward certain dislikes and the satisfaction of feeling them). Occurrence plus reward may possibly explain all of the modifications of attitudes by the experiences of experiment 65.

Experiment 66

The purpose of experiment 66 was to discover whether a person's likes and dislikes for words can be strengthened by the attachment of satisfying after-effects to them, in the same way that connections constituting knowledge or skill can be. Fifteen lists of about seventy-five words each were prepared, of which list 1 shown below is a sample.

The subject reported his attitude toward each of the words of List 1 in accordance with the following instructions:

"Look at each of these words as I read it. If you are sure that you like the word, write 1. If you think that you like it but are not sure, write 2. If you are sure that you dislike it, write 9. If you think that you dislike it but are not sure, write 8. If you are indifferent, write 5. You are to express your feeling toward the words, not the things or qualities which the words mean. You may like money and artichokes but dislike the words *money* and *artichoke* or be indifferent to them. You may dislike Austria, but like the word *Austria*."

List 1

acumen   almanac   anvil   bedim   belabor   celery   cessation   carboy   cm.   constancy   delinquency   daffodil   discontentment   eager   ebon   Edward   epitomization   fount   gondola   greediness   idiot   ivory   laboriousness   linen   *mélange*   summary   turpentine   wavy   *par excellence*   pledge   preachment   rectitude   result   so-so   softening   Stella   unscrupulousness   vile   zeal

alfalfa   agency   accoutrement   admiral   benison   Bertha   calm   consuetude   cobra   custom   cwt.   damage   death   diminution   dwelling   erroneousness   habitude   help   inducement   jump   lordliness   *modus vivendi*   dewy   former   harvest   *nouveau riche*   obliteration   orb   pity   ravenousness   redundancy   Robert   skunk   sully   verdant   versatile

He then reported similarly his attitude toward each of the words of Lists 2 to 14, comparable in general to List 1. After his reports of attitude toward certain of these words, he was rewarded or punished by apparently casual comments of the experimenter as follows:

(In List 2)

dawn .... almost everybody likes that word
garrulousness .... a clumsy word
murmuring .... a very attractive word
Richard .... a good strong word

ephemeral .... few people like that word, but they are of the very intelligent group
hum .... a solid word
dime .... few persons like dime, but they are highly intelligent
interrogation .... a pompous word
Katzenjammer .... a cheap-sounding word
spit .... a crisp, sharp word

(In List 3)

drink .... a good clean word
soi-disant .... a pretentious word
encirclement .... too erudite
heeler .... not needed
magnolia .... almost every one likes *magnolia*
sylph .... a mushy, sloppy word

(In List 4)

antitoxin .... a very useful word
avouch .... harsh
gate .... I like that word, I don't know why
gladsomeness .... a mushy, sloppy word
immurement .... too erudite
sailing .... I like that word, I don't know why
wrap .... a sharp, crisp word
e. g. .... indispensable
imperilment .... pompous
innocency .... silly
lilac .... almost everybody likes *lilac*
Weltgeist .... too bookish

(In List 5)

I. O. U. .... very useful
Lawrence .... I like that word, but I don't know why I do
ozone .... a very attractive word
perfidiousness .... clumsy
succor .... harsh
wordy .... few persons like that, but they are very intelligent
entrancement .... artificial
lapsus linguæ .... too pedantic
pellucid .... people of good taste dislike
plenitude .... pompous

(In List 6)

bed .... a strong solid word
blow .... a good clean word
balance .... almost everybody likes *balance*
contumeliousness ...... clumsy
tip .... I like that word, I don't know why
aspirin .... few persons like that word, but they are
very intelligent
bonne .... silly
C. O. D. .... economical and clear
fraudulency .... pompous
tryst .... a mushy, sloppy word

(In List 7)

asseveration .... pompous
job .... a solid, strong word
loud .... I like that word, I don't know why
over .... indispensable
hark .... a good clean word
enzyme .... few persons like, but they are usually intelligent
invariableness .... clumsy
minion .... too literary
disguisement .... pompous

(In List 8)

discomfit .... artificial
flame .... very attractive
incarceration .... pompous
marge .... silly
plenteousness .... weak
belabor .... people of good taste dislike that word
David .... a good clean word
dept. .... clear and handy
glow .... very attractive
inch .... the few who do like *inch* are very intelligent
pulchritude .... a cheap-sounding word

(In List 9)

barium .... rich, full sound
prolixness .... harsh-sounding
sanctification .... an oily word
tell .... a good clean word
between .... a good strong word

age .... indispensable
empyreal .... people of good taste dislike
jubilancy .... sounds weak
Dorothy .... almost everybody likes that word
solemnitude .... pompous
vowel .... I like that word

(In List 10)

bum .... cheap-sounding
A. D. .... very useful
cold .... strong word
habitation .... pompous
malignment .... not needed
augmentation .... too pedantic
grot .... silly
genera .... that word has a fine sound

(In List 11)

debasement .... clumsy
ma foi .... sounds artificial
Viola .... a very attractive word
always .... rich, full sound
drug .... indispensable
fable .... almost everybody likes *fable*
lease .... I like that word for unknown reasons
locum tenens .... too erudite
alack .... artificial

(In List 12)

inundation .... pretentious
Martha .... rich, full sound
potation .... pompous
trousers .... very useful
vigor .... good clean word
bourn .... people of good taste dislike *bourn*
gauche .... pretentious
glowing .... fine sound
plan .... a crisp, sharp word

(In List 13)

amorousness .... an oily word
enduring .... strong
lushness .... silly
opposite .... indispensable
seraph .... weak

blatancy .... cheap-sounding
cerulean .... too literary
Hercules .... a fine-sounding word
medicament .... too learned

(In List 14)

awesome .... too literary
now .... economical and clear
nuptials .... pompous
avail .... very attractive
alimentation .... pedantic
algebra .... very useful
ineptitude .... weak
passionateness .... clumsy
Nancy .... almost everybody likes *Nancy*

Assuming that the subject esteemed the experimenter's judgment, he would feel satisfied when one of these comments agreed with the attitude which he himself had felt and expressed and would feel a certain degree of discontent or lack of satisfaction when one of the comments contradicted his own feeling.

The subject then reported likes and dislikes as hitherto for the words of List 15, with no comments from the experimenter. List 15 is comparable to List 1. All the lists, as the reader probably realizes by now, were composed of:

A. Words ending in *-ation*
   Words ending in *-ment*
   Words ending in *-tude*
   Words ending in *-ness*
   Words ending in *-ncy*
   Foreign words
   Words used often by poets and literary men and rarely by others.

(Dislikes of any of the above were occasionally rewarded, and likes punished.)

B. Words ending in *-ing*
   Names of persons
   Abbreviations
   Words of one syllable

(Likes of any of these were occasionally rewarded and dislikes punished.)

C. Various words to fill out the lists

The subject then made a second report on the words of List 1, without inspection of his first report.

If likes and dislikes are strengthened by satisfying after-effects, if agreement with the experimenter's comments causes satisfaction, if this satisfaction attaches to the like or dislike which it follows, and if these attachments are made somewhat to the *-ment* or *-tude* or to 'foreignness' or 'brevity' or 'nameness' as well as to the gross total words—then there should be a rise (in list 15, and in list 1, second trial, over list 1, first trial) of dislikes for words ending in *-ation, -ment, -ness, -tude,* etc., and a rise in likes for abbreviations, names of persons, words of one syllable, etc. This rise, due to only an hour of training including only 123 comments, will naturally be small, even with all the ifs fulfilled. For it to be zero would not disprove that attitudes are learned in the same manner as ideas and skills, unless all of the last three ifs are known to have been fulfilled.

A demonstrable rise, however small, will on the other hand be a proof that attitudes are so learned, provided the subject expresses genuine attitudes. If he should replace reports of his real feelings by statements of what he thought he ought to like, or of what he thought would elevate him in the experimenter's estimation, the proof would fail. In the present experiment this possibility is not entirely eliminated.

It is also the case that the words for which a liking was approved by the experimenter's comments included some chosen because they were words often liked by people in general and that the words of which a dislike was approved by the experimenter included some chosen because they were words disliked by people in general. These inclusions were made in order to be sure that there were at least some agreements between the subjects' likings and the experimenter's comments. The slight weighting of frequency against *-ation, -ment, -tude,* etc., and for *-ing,* names of persons, etc., during an hour of experience could have only an infinitesimal influence in comparison with a score or more of years of seeing and hearing words. Later experiments can eliminate this if it seems worth while.

The subjects of experiment 66 were twenty-three educated adults. The experiment was described to them as a step in the writer's general program of obtaining the likes and dislikes of at least sixteen cultivated persons to each of 2,500 words. The second report on List 1 was said to them to be a means of determining the reliability of expressions of such likes and dislikes. Four weeks after the experiment, they answered the following questions:

1. Did the comments which the experimenter made about certain words influence you at all?....................
2. If so, how did they influence you?......................
3. In the words which you saw twice, at the beginning and at the end of the experiment, were you aware of any changes in your likes and dislikes?....................
4. If so, what were the changes?........................

In the replies to question 4, not a single person reported any increase of liking for short words, *-ing* words or any other sort commented on favorably by the experimenter, or any decrease in liking for *-ation* words, *-ment* words, foreign words, or any other sort commented on unfavorably by the experimenter. Of the replies, three could be interpreted as meaning that the subject modified his later likes and dislikes because of ideas gained concerning qualities that merit like or dislike. Of these three, the most probable case was of modification to *oppose* the ideas of the experimenter.* The others showed no indication of any influence

---

* I quote these verbatim:

L.B. 1. No—I believe not.
    2. They interested me, made me wonder about their significance.
    3. On a few occasions only.
    4. I thought that changes had occurred in those instances where I was not quite certain on a first judgment. Am not sure what caused slight changes on seeing the words a second time.

S.E.H. 1. Yes.
    2. Some words were said to be "clear-cut," "sharp," "greasy," etc., and any such indication of the instructor influenced my decision. A remark about a word such as "stupid," "silly," etc., helped me to form a decision.
    3. Yes.
    4. On seeing a word the second time, my decision was changed sometimes due to a different reaction. This might have been due to remarks of the instructor or a difference of association of ideas which did not register the first time.

M.T.M. 1. No—well I think perversely.
    2. (a) Usually I either left it blank (to get even for the attempt to influence, or an inhibition effect) or put down the opposite of what the comment would have indicated.
       (b) When my mind was already made up before the comment, then the comment produced no change of valuation of the word.
    3. No (in most cases).
    4. There was, however, sometimes a little more certainty. Again in a few instances there was a little less certainty of judgment.

from the comments beyond the intended one of providing satisfaction when the comment justified the subject's attitude and
annoyance when the two were at variance. In some cases even
this was lacking, the subjects reporting that they paid no attention whatever to the comments or that "They did not influence
me because I thought you might be trying to side-track our preference by your remark."

I report, in Table 32, the results, both inclusive and exclusive
of L.B., S.E.H., and M.T.M. I also report the results from a
control experiment in which a group of sixteen educated adults
expressed their attitude toward the words of List 1 and List 15
without any intermediate training whatsoever. Where the number
of words of a certain sort was not the same in List 15 as in List 1,
the frequencies of expressions of attitude in one list are all multi-
plied by a factor bringing the total to an equivalence with the
longer of the two.

The sorts of words favored by the experimenter's comments
are better liked in List 15 than in List 1, and those of the sort
commented on unfavorably are disliked more in List 15 than in
List 1. This occurs despite the fact that the favored sorts of
words in List 15 are a little less well liked than those in List 1 by
the control group who heard no comments. The control group
also liked the words ending in -ation, -ness, -ment, etc., in List 15
a little better than those in List 1. Excluding the three cases makes
no difference in the results, as can readily be seen by observation
of the averages in Table 32.

Using the results from the twenty-three, eight of the eleven sorts
of words showed differences from the control group in the direction of the effect intended by the comments, the amounts being, in
terms of influence per person per word, 0.41, 0.35, 0.24, 0.32, 0.50,
0.02, 0.23, and 0.04. The reverse was shown by abbreviations,
-ing words and -ment words, the amounts being 0.25, 0.15, and
0.08. The unweighted average of all eleven is 0.15.* It has a
probable error of 0.045.

I have made similar computations for the difference between
List 1 and List 1 repeated after List 15. Here we need no allowance for results in a control group. The average change per person
per word, using all twenty-three subjects, was +0.22 for words
favored by the comments, and —0.19 for words commented on

* The weighted average will be higher and somewhat more reliable.

TABLE 32

THE INFLUENCE OF REWARD AND PUNISHMENT UPON ATTITUDES

Changes in likes and dislikes consequent upon favorable and unfavorable comments and associations; experiment 66; twenty-three educated adults; Bal = the sum of the likes — the sum of the dislikes; $Infl\ per\ p$ = the change in the balance per person per word

KIND OF WORDS	NO. OF WORDS LIST	INCLUSIVE OF ALL (n=23)							EXCLUDING B., H., AND M							CONTROL (n=16)	
		1	2	Indif	8	9	Bal	Infl per p	1	2	Indif	8	9	Bal	Infl per p	Bal	Diff per p
Abbreviations	1	5	1	23	3	14	−8		5	1	23	1	10	−5		−10	
	15	8	11	9	8	10	1	+0.13	8	9	8	7	8	2	+0.12	2	+0.38
-ing words	1	30	15	20	3	1	41		27	14	18	0	1	40		22.5	
	3	28	14	11	10	6	26	−0.22	27	10	10	8	5	24	−0.27	19	−0.07
Names	4	33	16	14	13	16	20		32	12	13	11	12	21		24	
	4	48	15	12	12	5	46	+0.28	44	12	9	10	5	41	+0.25	20	−0.13
One-syllable words*	7	104	48	63	43	41	68		89	37	56	37	41	38		59.5	
	13	132	60	53	33	21	138	+0.24	120	50	38	31	21	118	+0.39	36	−0.11
Total favored	1						121							94		86	
	15						211	+0.18						185	+0.21	77	−0.03
Average for the four sorts								+0.11							+0.12		+0.02

The table below is printed sideways on the page. Each word-group occupies two data rows (upper / lower). The correlation columns carry a single value. Column headers are not printed in the source.

	1	2	3	4	5	6	7	(diff)	r	8	9	10	11	12	(diff)	r	(diff)	r
-ation words	4	1	23	23	14	20	11	15	−0.01	18	22	12	18	9	13	+0.01	3	+0.23
	4	15	27	20	11	19	14	14		26	16	9	17	11	14		18	
-ncy words	4	1	25	21	28	13	5	28	−0.57	25	17	24	9	5	28	−0.60	6	−0.25
	2	15	12	18	8	38	16	−24		12	14	8	30	16	−20		−10	
-ment words	4	1	13	22	16	28	12	−5	+0.02	12	20	15	22	11	−1	−0.00	−5	−0.06
	4	15	16	22	13	19	22	−3		15	29	11	16	19	−1		−9	
-ness words	6	1	23	17	23	43	32	−35	+0.11	22	16	18	34	30	−26	+0.04	−30	+0.61
	4	15	13	38	16	29	42	−20		13	30	11	29	37	−23		9	
-rude words	3	1	16	21	28	19	8	10	−0.24	12	20	24	16	8	8	0.00	19	−0.22
	4	15	13	12	30	18	19	−12		13	10	26	14	17	−8		5	
Foreign words	4	1	35	19	7	18	13	23	−0.34	31	16	7	15	11	21	−0.36	19	−0.11
	4	15	14	19	17	21	21	−8		13	16	14	18	19	−8		12	
Poetic words	7	1	38	34	35	36	18	18	−0.01	32	30	32	30	16	16	−0.03	30	+0.03
	7	15	46	33	20	31	31	17		39	28	18	25	30	12		32	
Total disfavored								54	−0.12						59	−0.14	42	+0.03
								−36							−34		57	
Average for the seven sorts									−0.15							−0.13		+0.03

* Excluding *orb*, *lea*, and *skunk*.

unfavorably.* Using only the twenty persons, we have +0.26 and —0.18. The three questionable records differed very little from the others. Here we can obtain interesting records for individuals. Of the twenty, fourteen showed changes in accordance with the comments, two showed no change, and four showed the reverse. The range is from 0.65 in accord to 0.28 *contra*. The average of 0.22 in accord has a probable error of 0.04.

Experiment 67 was similar to 66. The differences were that the number of comments by the experimenter were fewer,† that the lists were given in the order 15, 2, 3, 4, 5, 6, 7, 8, 9, 10, 11, 12, 13, 14, 1, and that the list given first was not repeated at the end of the experiment. The subjects were thirty-five undergraduate college students.

Table 33 is constructed in the same manner as Table 32.

If we eliminate the differences in the test words by combining the results from the twenty-three subjects of Table 31 and the thirty-five of Table 32, giving equal weight to each group, we have the following:

Favored:	Abbreviations	+0.02
	-ing words	0
	Names	+0.16
	Short words	+0.21
Disfavored:	*-ation* words	—0.33
	-ncy words	—0.23
	-ment words	—0.01
	-ness words	—0.22
	-tude words	—0.20
	Foreign words	—0.34
	Poetic words	+0.01

There is an average shift of 0.15 in accordance with the after-effects applied to the expressions of like and dislike. This is about five and a half times its probable error as computed from the shifts for the eleven varieties of words, but its real reliability as evidence that the after-effects had an influence is much greater than this.

* In computing these changes, we arbitrarily treat the differences from 9 to 8, 8 to Indif, Indif to 2, and 2 to 1 as equal, calling each 1.00.

† The comments were as follows:

Favorable: short words, 16; *-ing* words, 4; names, 6; abbreviations, 4

Unfavorable: *-ation* words, 6; *-ncy* words, 4; *-ment* words, 6; *-ness* words, 6; *-tude* words, 4; foreign words, 6; poetic words, 10

TABLE 33

THE INFLUENCE OF REWARD AND PUNISHMENT UPON ATTITUDES

Changes in likes and dislikes consequent upon favorable and unfavorable comments and associations; Experiment 67; thirty-five college students; Bal = the sum of the likes — the sum of the dislikes; $Infl$ per $person$ = the change in the balance per person per word

Kind of words	n	List	1	2	Indif	8	9	Bal	Infl per person
Abbreviations	2	15	5	17	28	17	3	2	
	2	1	2	14	34	9	11	−4	−0.09
-ing words	3	15	17	43	17	21	7	32	
	2	1	13	53	27	10	2	54	+0.21
Names	4	15	17	36	63	18	6	29	
	4	1	15	45	54	16	10	34	+0.04
One-syllable words	13	15	65	127	96	106	61	25	
	7	1	72	165	83	63	72	102	+0.17
Total favored		15						88	
		1						186	+0.13
Average for the four sorts									+0.08
-ation words	4	15	25	71	29	11	4	81	
	4	1	6	39	42	39	14	−8	−0.64
-ncy words	2	15	4	30	50	42	14	−22	
	4	1	9	43	31	39	18	−5	+0.12
-ment words	4	15	16	27	38	42	17	−16	
	4	1	3	30	49	44	14	−23	−0.05
-ness words	4	15	32	64	51	35	28	33	
	6	1	10	30	48	74	48	−82	−0.55
-tude words	4	15	18	46	44	24	8	32	
	3	1	8	44	45	31	12	9	−0.16
Foreign words	4	15	24	54	36	17	9	52	
	4	1	18	37	34	26	25	4	−0.34
Poetic words	7	15	47	80	55	50	13	64	
	7	1	36	84	77	41	7	72	+0.03
Total disfavored		15						224	
		1						−33	−0.22
Average for the seven sorts									−0.26

Appendix VIII

MISCELLANEOUS TABLES

TABLE 34

The median, upper quartile, and lower quartile of the ratings on a scale of pleasantness—unpleasantness for the situation of taking cod-liver oil; twenty-nine subjects by day and session

Day	Session	Upper quartile	Median	Lower quartile
1	1	—0.8	—8.7	—20.4
	2	—0.1	—8.0	—28.7
2*	3	+0.4	—2.5	—15.0
	4	—1.2	—7.5	—17.5
3	5	+0.4	—3.7	—14.4
	6	+0.6	—2.0	—8.7
4	7	+0.8	—1.7	—10.3
	8	+0.8	—1.7	—8.7
5	9	+0.5	—1.4	—8.7
	10	+1.0	—1.6	—10.9
6	11	+0.5	—1.7	—9.3
	12	+1.0	—1.6	—11.2
7	13	+1.3	—1.5	—6.2
	14	+1.0	—1.2	—6.2
8	15	+1.3	—1.5	—6.5

* One subject was absent on day 2.

TABLE 35

The scores of the seven individuals who rated the task *oil* highest on initial presentation and the scores of the seven individuals who rated the task *oil* lowest on the initial presentation; by sessions and by individuals

HIGHEST GROUP

INDIVIDUAL	DAY 1		DAY 2		DAY 3		DAY 4		DAY 5		DAY 6		DAY 7		DAY 8
	1	2	3	4	5	6	7	8	9	10	11	12	13	14	15
13	+25	+25	+15	+25	+10	+10	+5	+10	+5	+5	+5	+5	+5	+5	+10
19	+10	0	+15	−5	0	0	0	+10	0	+20	−20	−20	0	0	0
24	+10	−100	−80	−100	−25	+40	+40	+10	−20	+20	−20	−20	+20	+10	+10
10	0	0	0	0	0	0	0	0	0	0	0	0	0	0	0
9	0	0	0	0	0	0	0	0	0	0	0	0	0	0	0
5	0	0	0	0	0	0	0	0	0	0	0	0	0	0	0
28	0	0	−75	−75	−80	−70	−75	−75	−50	−70	−40	−10	−40	−10	−10

LOWEST GROUP

INDIVIDUAL	DAY 1		DAY 2		DAY 3		DAY 4		DAY 5		DAY 6		DAY 7		DAY 8
	1	2	3	4	5	6	7	8	9	10	11	12	13	14	15
16	−100	−100	−50	−10	−25	−25	−25	−10	0	−25	−10	−25	−25	−25	−25
12	−100	−70	−80	−70	−50	−50	−40	−40	−40	−40	−40	−40	−40	−40	−35
27	−50	−50	−10	0	0	0	0	0	0	0	0	0	0	0	0
8	−50	−20	−10	−20	−10	−10	−10	−10	−10	−15	−10	−15	−10	−15	−5
6	−45	−30	−30	−30	−25	−20	−15	−25	−10	−10	−5	−5	−5	−5	−5
3	−25	−30	−25	−20	−15	−10	−10	−10	−10	−8	−8	0	−10	−8	−10
11	−25	−10	−5	0	0	0	0	0	0	0	0	0	0	0	0

TABLE 36

The median, upper quartile, and lower quartile of the ratings on a scale of pleasantness—unpleasantness for the situation of standing on toes; twenty-nine subjects by day and session

Day	Session	Upper quartile	Median	Lower quartile
1	1	—1.2	—8.3	—12.4
	2	+0.3	—8.3	—12.4
2*	3	+1.9	—2.5	—9.2
	4	+2.0	—1.5	—8.2
3	5	+1.1	—3.7	—9.2
	6	+1.6	—0.8	—7.2
4	7	+3.8	—1.1	—5.9
	8	+7.1	+0.3	—4.0
5	9	+4.4	—0.7	—5.6
	10	+6.9	—0.2	—4.8
6	11	+6.4	+0.9	—2.4
	12	+5.4	+0.2	—2.8
7	13	+5.3	+0.5	—3.3
	14	+7.3	+1.3	—2.4
8	15	+9.4	+2.2	—1.8

* Subject 25 was absent from all sessions on day 2.

TABLE 37

The scores of the seven individuals who rated the task *toes* highest on initial presentation and the scores of the seven individuals who rated the task *toes* lowest on initial presentation; by session and by individuals

INDIVIDUAL	DAY 1		DAY 2		DAY 3		DAY 4		DAY 5		DAY 6		DAY 7		DAY 8
	1	2	3	4	5	6	7	8	9	10	11	12	13	14	15
HIGHEST GROUP															
12	60	70	80	40	50	50	50	40	40	30	20	40	30	40	50
20	50	−40	−5	−5	−5	−5	−5	−5	−5	−5	−5	−5	−3	−5	−5
24	30	20	50	80	0	25	80	90	80	90	90	90	80	80	80
17	5	−5	−5	−5	−3	0	−2	−2	0	0	5	0	0	0	5
22	0	−50	0	0	−10	−5	−1	−5	−5	−5	0	−5	0	−10	5
5	0	0	0	0	0	−1	−1	0	0	−5	5	10	0	5	5
13	5	10	20	−5	15	10	−15	10	0	−15	5	0	−5	0	15
LOWEST GROUP															
16	−100	−100	0	−10	−10	0	0	0	0	0	0	0	0	0	0
28	−60	−50	−75	−70	−75	−80	−75	−70	−25	−50	−10	−25	−25	−25	−25
4	−25	−50	−10	−10	−8	−8	−5	−4	−2	0	0	0	0	5	5
8	−20	−10	0	…	−10	−10	−10	−5	−5	−5	−10	−5	−10	−5	0
25*	−20	−10	…	…	−10	0	−10	−10	−10	−10	−10	5	−5	−10	−5
23	−20	−10	−15	−10	−20	−15	−5	0	−10	−10	−5	10	−15	15	10
19	−20	−10	−10	5	0	5	5	5	10	10	10	10	5	15	10

*Subject 25 was absent from all sessions on day 2.

TABLE 38

The median, upper quartile, and lower quartile of the ratings on a scale of pleasantness—unpleasantness for the situation of completing couplets; twenty-nine subjects, by day and session

Day	Session	Upper quartile	Median	Lower quartile
1	1	+26.3	+8.1	—6.8
	2	+12.3	0	—13.5
2*	3	+17.5	+1.8	—4.2
	4	+22.5	+5.0	—1.3
3	5	+10.0	+1.4	—1.9
	6	+10.4	0	—8.2
4	7	+11.9	+1.3	—5.9
	8	+26.3	+2.3	—1.2
5	9	+11.3	+2.3	—1.0
	10	+9.4	+1.1	—3.4
6	11	+12.1	+2.3	—0.5
	12	+16.3	+1.3	—2.4
7	13	+18.4	+2.3	—1.0
	14	+12.3	+5.0	—0.5
8	15	+16.9	+5.6	—0.5

* Subject 25 was absent from all sessions on day 2.

TABLE 39

The scores of the seven individuals who rated the task *couplets* highest on initial presentation, and the scores of the seven individuals who rated the task *couplets* lowest on initial presentation; by session and by individuals

HIGHEST GROUP

INDIVIDUAL	DAY 1		DAY 2		DAY 3		DAY 4		DAY 5		DAY 6		DAY 7		DAY 8
	1	2	3	4	5	6	7	8	9	10	11	12	13	14	15
12	100	90	90	40	50	50	40	40	30	40	40	40	20	30	30
24	100	90	100	90	50	50	90	90	90	90	90	90	90	90	90
14	90	80	80	80	80	70	50	80	70	70	50	40	50	50	50
28	65	85	75	75	60	70	25	60	65	25	25	25	25	10	25
5	65	75	65	75	75	65	65	65	75	75	65	80	65	65	75
11	40	40	10	10	10	30	20	40	10	30	20	20	20	10	20
22	30	−50	10	0	−5	−5	−10	−5	−5	−5	0	−5	0	−10	−5

LOWEST GROUP

INDIVIDUAL	1	2	3	4	5	6	7	8	9	10	11	12	13	14	15
16	−100	−75	0	0	0	0	0	0	0	0	0	0	0	0	0
3	−25	−10	−10	−20	−2	−8	−5	−3	−2	−3	−1	−3	−3	−2	−2
27	−25	−30	10	−25	−25	−30	−30	−30	−30	−30	10	10	−20	−20	−10
23	−20	−20	0	−5	10	−10	−10	0	10	−5	−10	−10	0	15	10
20	−10	−25	−5	0	−2	0	0	0	−5	0	0	0	−10	0	0
17	−10	−20	−10	−5	−2	−10	−10	−5	−10	−10	−10	−10	−10	−10	−5
6	−5	−20	−2	0	−3	−10	−7	0	−10	0	−2	0	0	−5	−5

TABLE 40

The frequency with which each subject was rewarded in experiment 62 for a rating agreeing with the composite judgment of twelve art students (1 for 'good' cards and 9 for 'poor' cards)

SUBJECT	RATING	TRIAL 1	2	3	4	TOTAL
A	1	10	19	25	27	81
	9	3	3	1	5	12
B	1	8	17	13	13	51
	9	0	0	1	4	5
C	1	12	21	22	21	76
	9	0	0	0	0	0
D	1	4	15	16	15	50
	9	4	15	16	26	61
E	1	8	7	7	8	30
	9	0	0	0	1	1
F	1	11	10	18	17	56
	9	3	3	1	2	9
G	1	11	18	19	20	68
	9	0	0	2	3	5
H	1	11	14	12	8	45
	9	3	4	2	0	9
I	1	8	16	24	21	69
	9	2	4	3	3	12
J	1	19	20	20	25	84
	9	6	4	7	11	28

SUBJECT	RATING	TRIAL 1	2	3	4	TOTAL
K	1	16	16	16	15	63
	9	0	1	0	1	2
L	1	30	29	28	28	115
	9	0	1	0	0	1
M	1	18	24	26	27	95
	9	0	0	0	0	0
N	1	23	24	30	31	108
	9	0	1	2	6	9
O	1	20	17	24	25	86
	9	13	21	25	26	85
P	1	9	13	12	11	45
	9	0	1	0	0	1
Q	1	2	0	0	0	2
	9	2	1	1	0	4
R	1	19	28	28	29	104
	9	0	0	3	5	8
S	1	14	15	19	17	65
	9	0	0	0	0	0
T	1	3	3	2	3	11
	9	1	1	0	0	2

List of References

NOTE.—Authors referred to only casually or for testimony concerning the results of rewards and punishments are not listed here, but will be found in the index.

Author	Date	Title
BALDERSTON, C. C.	'30	*Group Incentives.*
BREGMAN, E. O.		An attempt to modify the emotional attitude of infants by the conditioned-response technique, *J. Genet. Psychol.*, 1934, vol. 45, pp. 169-198.
BUNCH, M. E.	'28	The effect of electric shock as punishment for errors in human maze learning, *J. Comp. Psychol.*, vol. 8, pp. 343-359.
CLARK, J. I. C.	'18	*Japan at First Hand.*
DISERENS, C. M.: VAUGHN, J., and	'30	The relative effects of various intensities of punishment on learning and efficiency, *J. Comp. Psychol.*, vol. 10, pp. 55-66.
FORLANO, G.: THORNDIKE, E. L., and	'33	The influence of increase and decrease of the amount of reward upon the rate of learning, *J. Educ. Psychol.*, vol. 24, pp. 401-411.
GRIFFIS, W. E.	'03	*The Mikado's Empire*
GULICK, C. B.	'02	*The Life of the Ancient Greeks.*
GULICK, S. L.	'03	*The Evolution of the Japanese.*
HULL, C. L.	'33	*Hypnosis and Suggestibility.*
JONES, H. E.	'31	The conditioning of overt emotional responses, *J. Educ. Psychol.*, vol. 22, pp. 127-130.
LEUBA, C. J.	'30	A preliminary experiment to quantify an incentive and its effects, *J. Abnorm. and Soc. Psychol.*, vol. 25, pp. 275-288.
LORGE, I.	'33	The efficacy of intensified reward and of intensified punishment, *J. Exper. Psychol.*, vol. 16, pp. 177-207.

LORGE, I.   '33   The effect of the initial chances for right responses upon the efficacy of intensified reward and of intensified punishment, *J. Exper. Psychol.*, vol. 16, pp. 362-373.

LORGE, I., and THORNDIKE, E. L.   '33   The comparative strengthening of a connection by one or more occurrences of it in cases where the connection was punished and was neither punished nor rewarded, *J. Exper. Psychol.*, vol. 16, pp. 374-382.

LORGE, I., EISENSON, J., and EPSTEIN, B.   '34   Further experiments on the strengthening of connections where the connection is punished, or rewarded, or neither punished nor rewarded, *J. Exper. Psychol.*, vol. XVII, No. 3, pp. 412-423.

MARKIMO, YOSHIO   '12   *When I Was a Child.*

McTEER, W.   '31   A study of certain features of punishment in serial learning, *J. Exper. Psychol.*, vol. 14, pp. 453-476.

MEAD, M.   '30   *Growing Up in New Guinea.*

MOSS, F. A.   '24   A study of animal drives, *J. Exper. Psychol.*, vol. 7, pp. 165-185.

OGBURN, W. F.   '33   Chapter XIII of *Recent Social Trends in the United States.*

RAYNER, R.: WATSON, J. B., and   '20   Conditioned emotional reactions, *J. Exper. Psychol.*, vol. 3, pp. 1-14.

REXROAD, C. N.   '26   Administering electric shock for inaccuracy in continuous multiple-choice reactions, *J. Exper. Psychol.*, vol. 9, pp. 1-18.

ROBERTS, W. H.   '30   The effect of delayed feeding on white rats in a problem cage, *J. Genet. Psychol.*, vol. 37, pp. 35-58.

ROCK, R. T., JR.: THORNDIKE, E. L., and   '34   Learning without awareness of what is being learned or intent to learn it, *J. Exper. Psychol.*, vol. 17, pp. 1-19.

SHARP, W. H.   '06   *Educational System of Japan.*

STEPHENS, J. M.   '31   The influence of different stimuli upon preceding bonds, *Teachers College, Columbia University, Contributions to Education*, No. 493.

THORNDIKE, E. L., *et al.* '32   *The Fundamentals of Learning.*

THORNDIKE, E. L.   '32   Reward and punishment in animal learning, *Comp. Psychol. Monographs*, vol. 8, no. 4.

——————   '33a   The influence of irrelevant rewards, *J. Educ. Psychol.*, vol. 24, pp. 1-15.

——————   '33b   A proof of the law of effect, *Science*, vol. 77, p. 173 f.

THORNDIKE, E. L., *et al.* '33c   An experimental study of rewards, *Teachers College, Columbia University, Contributions to Education*, No. 580.

THORNDIKE, E. L.   '33d   The influence of use or frequency of occurrence upon the strength of connections, *Proceedings of the National Academy of Sciences*, vol. 19, pp. 734-745.

——————   '33   A theory of the action of the after-effects of a connection upon it, *Psychol. Review*, vol. 40, pp. 434-439.

THORNDIKE, E. L., and FORLANO, G.   '33   The influence of increase and decrease of the amount of reward upon the rate of learning, *J. Educ. Psychol.*, vol. 24, pp. 401-411.

THORNDIKE, E. L.: LORGE, I., and   '33   The comparative strengthening of a connection by one or more occurrences of it in cases where the connection was punished and was neither punished nor rewarded, *J. Exper. Psychol.*, vol. 16, pp. 374-382.

THORNDIKE, E. L., and ROCK, R. T., JR.   '34   Learning without awareness of what is being learned or intent to learn it, *J. Exper. Psychol.*, vol. 17, pp. 1-19.

TUCKMAN, J.   '33   The influence of varying amounts of punishment on mental connections, *Teachers College, Columbia University, Contributions to Education*, No. 590.

VALENTINE, R.   '30   The effects of punishment for errors on the maze-learning of rats, *J. Comp. Psychol.*, vol. 10, pp. 35-66.

VAUGHN, J., and DISERENS, C. M.   '30   The relative effects of various intensities of punishment on learning and efficiency, *J. Comp. Psychol.*, vol. 10, pp. 55-66.

WARDEN, C. J.   '31   *Animal Motivation.*

WATSON, J. B., and RAYNER, R.   '20   Conditioned emotional reactions, *J. Exper. Psychol.*, vol. 3, pp. 1-14.

INDEX

INDEX

$\mathcal{B}$